Themes and Conclusions

by Igor Stravinsky and Robert Craft

EXPOSITIONS AND DEVELOPMENTS

DIALOGUES AND A DIARY

Themes and Conclusions

IGOR STRAVINSKY

FABER AND FABER
3 Queen Square
London

First published in 1972
by Faber and Faber Limited
3 Queen Square London WC1
Printed in Great Britain by
W & J Mackay Limited, Chatham
All rights reserved

ISBN 0 571 08308 0

ACKNOWLEDGEMENTS

Grateful acknowledgement is made to the following publications in whose pages parts of this book have previously appeared: *Show*, *The London Magazine*, *Harper's Magazine*, the *Los Angeles Times*, *The Nation*, the *Composer*, the programme booth of the University of the State of New York at Stony Brook, *The New York Times*, *Columbia Records* (programme notes), Chicago Symphony Orchestra (programme book), The Festival of Israel (programme book), *Musical America*, *The New York Review of Books*, *Seventeen*, *The Observer*, *Esquire*, preface to *Anton von Webern* (University of Washington Press).

Photographs of Stravinsky are by the courtesy of A. Langdon Coburn, George Platt Lynes, and Bobby Klein.

PUBLISHERS' NOTE

The publishers wish to express their thanks to
Mr Robert Craft who was responsible for seeing
this book through the press.

CONTENTS

9

CONTENTS

MEMOIR

Part Two: Interviews

Part Three

PREFACES

CONTENTS

ILLUSTRATIONS

13

ILLUSTRATIONS

14

AUTHOR'S FOREWORD

This one-volume edition of *Themes and Episodes* (1966) and *Retrospectives and Conclusions* (1969) differs from the separately issued American originals in that I have revised—corrected, cut, expanded—the contents of the earlier book and added to those of the later one. Hence the present text of *Themes* supersedes that of the American edition, which will not be reprinted in its original form. And the new text of *Retrospectives* includes the increment of a year and my final work of words.

They are hardly the last words about myself or my music that I would like to have written, and in fact they say almost nothing about the latter, except tangentially, in comments on Beethoven. It is almost five years now since I have completed an original composition, a time during which I have had to transform myself from a composer to a listener. The vacuum which this left has not been filled, but I have been able to live with it, thanks, in the largest measure, to the music of Beethoven.

I could, and still did, write, speak, criticize, however, and, for what they were worth, offer my views. That they were worth a great deal to me in the most negotiable sense—but not only—will be understood by anyone acquainted with the United States Department of Internal Revenue. For I can now confess to the partly mercenary motive behind some of my prefaces, reviews, interviews. Bluntly, then—or is it an open secret?—the balance between my income and my needs has, for a decade or more, rested on the 'deductibility' of the latter; and my deductibility 'status' has depended, in turn, on the production, if not of music, then, *faute de mieux*, of words. For to write, in America, is to 'write-off'. A nuisance letter to a newspaper, now and then, a great many (ditto) autographs, and a few talks made public are about all this has come to of late. But it has been enough to certify me as at least a *monstre sacré* and not just one of the Loch Ness kind.

It is certain, now, that I will not be granted powers such as have recently enabled Señor Casals to publish a book at an age six years greater than mine. But I am thankful that I can listen to and love the music of other men in a way I could not do when I was composing my own.

I.S.
New York, March 1, 1971

PART ONE

saying "there is nothing after death, death is the end, period." I then
had the temerity ~~tried~~ to suggest that perhaps ~~nothingxafterxdeath~~ this
was also merely one point of view, but was made to feel for some time
thereafter that I should have kept my ~~piece~~ peace.

I thought I had found friends in Rimsky's sons, three young gentlemen who,
~~I thought~~ *at least* ~~in~~ provinvial St. Petersburg were beacons of enlightenment. Andrei, a man
three years my ~~senior~~ senior and a 'cellist of some ability was especially
kind to me, though this kindness lasted only while his father was alive;
when I had gone to Paris in 1910 and my name had come back to Russia he,
and in fact the entire Rimsky-Korsakov family, ~~suddenly~~ turned against me. ~~of~~
~~...~~
He reviewed Petroushka for a Russian newspaper dismissing it as "Russian
vodka with French perfumes." Vladimir, his brother, was a competent
violinist *and* I owe to him my first knowledge of violin fingering ~~problems.~~
I was not close to ~~Rimsky's~~ *daughters Sophie and Nadiejda,* Rimsky's *daughters, though*
~~Rimsky's daughters did not appeal to me at all, however, and I especially~~
~~disliked Sophie. Incidentally,~~ My last contact with the Rimsky-Korsakov
family was through her husband Maximilian Steinberg who had come to Paris
in 1924 *and heard* ~~to hear~~ me play my Piano Concerto ~~(you can~~ *that. But you can* imagine his response to
that work when I tell you that the best he could do even for my Fireworks
was to shrug his shoulders. ~~A~~fter hearing the Concerto he wanted to
lecture me on my whole mistaken career, *He* ~~and~~ returned to Russia thoroughly
annoyed when I refused to see him. ~~I was not fond of Mme. Rimsky-Korsakov~~
~~either, as I have said elsewhere. She was an avowed enemy of Diaghilev~~
~~too, but while she attacked his production of Sheherazade she was delighted~~
~~at the same time to receive very handsome royalties from it.~~

First draft of a page from *Memories and Commentaries* (Faber,
1960), with Stravinsky's deletions and one of his corrections
(line 17).

SQUIBS

Words

I expect at least nine-tenths of today's crop—an estimate from past averages—to embarrass me tomorrow, and I know that a still higher percentage will not survive my 'better judgment' for as long as a month. Whereas the relatively weatherable leftovers are largely concerned with matters of negligible consequence, moreover, the loudest howlers ('Beethoven lacks melody'; '*Falstaff* is corrupted by Wagnerism'), following the bad-penny principle, are impossible to lose.

Then why bother, when silence can keep me from being wrong and foolish? Because the mistakes and embarrassments do not count compared to even a single minor accident of truth, provisional and hypothetical as it would have to be, that could occur.

New Enemies of Art

1. Improvisers. 2. 'Indeterminists' (the inverted commas are necessary because no real parallel exists between the 'free combination' scores of 'indeterminist' composers and the sciences dealing with sub-molecular magnitudes). The least I ask of any artist is that which *he* has determined, *his* choices rather than those of his intermediary and collaborator, whose improvisatory brainstorms, if he were a member of one of the world's leading symphony orchestras, for example, would be limited to a hash of fifty-year-old ideas. But, then, we are already in the post-composer period, and sub-music and musical blindman's buff are major tourist attractions.

Art and Money

The purchase of a Renoir at Sotheby's not long ago for $170,800 is to me an example of a flagrant lack of respect for money.

The Rising Cost of Art

At a recent concert featuring one of Bell Laboratory's IBM computers, a very buxom soloist, I learned that the instrument costs more than $100 an hour to rent and a great deal more than that to operate. Hence if I were to compose even a very short work with it, the technical overhead might tally as high as a million dollars, though I could be in error, my own computing apparatus now being a rusty eighty-eight years old. The concert, by the way, persuasively demonstrated that this new means of communication has as yet nothing to communicate.

An Imperfect Science

An accident, in fact. Yet before acoustics became a branch of science owing to its importance to industry, Europe had many good concert halls. We have been told that the greater size of the new halls is one reason for acoustical disaster, and warned that the singers in the opera houses of the future will be obliged to wear microphones, while the stage frame from the crows' nests will be the equivalent of a pocket television screen. But in New York the argument of size is refuted by Carnegie Hall, which is larger than that acoustical corpse, Philharmonic Hall.

The architect of the New York State Theater, Mr. Philip Johnson, has pleaded in its defence that the acoustics should not be judged by the presentation of plays. He says that 'The theater has the perfect reverberation time for music, 1.7, which is not fitted for the human voice.' But surely 'music' sometimes includes the human voice, and the concert repertory contains a number of works, my *Perséphone* among them, with spoken texts. Is 1.7 the resonating volume of the empty hall, I wonder, and if not, what is the loss from audience absorption? Like most modern halls, in any case, the New York State Theater seems to be about .2 or .3 too short, which is to say too dry.

Acoustics, in sum, is not so much an architectural science as an occupation for repairmen, whose tools—in our day frequency filters, Helmholz resonators, electronic resonance supporters; in

Greece and Rome, the bronze resonating jars of the odeums (according to Vitruvius)—are used to recreate sound. Sometimes the re-creation is noticeable, sometimes not, but it is always good propaganda for stay-at-home listening by way of recordings. In my experience the most nearly perfect halls acoustically are the Gewandhaus, the Franz Liszt Hall in the Budapest Conservatory, the Teatro San Carlo in Naples, the Teatro Colón in Buenos Aires. All are wood-panelled and very live, more, I wager, than 1.7.[1]

Education by Automation

> Technology is the knack of so arranging the world that
> we don't have to experience it.
>
> MAX FRISCH

The knowledge explosion, the wisdom of the world on tape— made accessible by dial systems, portable units such as the Cornberg carrel, and pocket computers with plugs in the universal computer grid—is one of my visions of Purgatory. (I have also had recurrent dreams in which my bank checks became demagnetized, foiling the computer, and dreams about a berserk automaton punching new holes in my magazine subscription card[2] causing it to send me the *Journal of Musical Theory* instead of *Mad*.) It seems to me that easier access to more information, including the best that has been thought and said, is not the point. Education, at any rate in its earlier stages, is a trial-and-

---

[1] Sound waves, according to Dr. C. A. Volf of Copenhagen and his Reflex Theory of Acoustic Therapy, can be used to detect both cancer and schizophrenia. Thus the waves generated by a vibrating C-128 tuning fork held to various nodules of the body travel directly *to* a cancerous area, he says, while with schizophrenia they do not travel at all but exit instantly through the fingers and toes. One evening in Hollywood, in January 1964, Dr. Volf's resonator despatched the *1812 Overture* through my bones—it seemed—but with what, if any, therapeutic effect I never discovered. Nor is it likely that the American reader will be able to learn anything from similar experiments on himself for the method has been banned since then, not only by the American Medical Association but by the American Federation of Musicians.

[2] A government computer in Ottawa went haywire, as a result of being fed confusing data, and mailed one and a half million dollars in bonuses to students in Quebec Province.

error process necessarily supervised by beings, preferably humanid,[1] more experienced and better instructed than one's self. Then as one grows older, older stages of one's changing self must assume the supervising role.

Speaking from my own education as a composer, I know that I learned more through my mistakes and pursuits of false assumptions than from my exposures to founts of wisdom and knowledge. In the matter of the acquisition of artistic skills, furthermore, I was, and am still, a pious Aristotelian: imitation is the beginning of art. For illustration I recommend a visit to one of Balanchine's dance classes. The learning process there is a scene from Natural History, Balanchine taking flight like a mother bird while whole flocks of baby girl birds flap their wings behind and in imitation of him.

The use of automation in research is another matter, of course, and the value of the computer is beyond calculation to all serious scholars—as they like to call themselves, implying that large numbers of extremely frivolous scholars are flitting about. In fact these versatile adding machines are the salvation of those American Ph.D. candidates whose theses are counting exercises in the first place ('The Use of the Penis through the Ages'), and in the second are composed largely of footnotes tabulating agreements and disagreements with earlier statisticians. Researchers in philological textual analysis have ascertained that a computer-day is the equivalent of a year's manual labour—though progress is claimed not only in computation in this field, but in the development of speech synthesizers, or Parametric Artificial Talking devices, which provide 'resonance analogues of the human speech organs' through which mechanical translation by conversion of 'input' and 'output' languages to 'correlational structures of thought' will soon be a reality. Stylistic analyses by computer, on the other hand, as evidenced in the concordances of poets, are a depressing development. The machine finds that Shakespeare averaged 61 'ands' per two thousand words as against an average of 80 for Bacon. But what does that tell us about Shakespeare or Bacon? Which Shakespeare, moreover, and what system of differentials was devised

---

[1] In other fields, as when I think of the hands within reach of the 'hot wire,' I definitely prefer the passionless machine.

to 'co-relate' Shakespeare's poetry and Bacon's prose?

Talent and the Population Explosion

'O Divine Average' WHITMAN

Creative talent certainly seems to be spreading thinner, in any case, supporting Fourier's hypothesis that diffusion is necessarily followed by a loss of intellectual density; which is why census estimates of fifteenth-century Florence and the other fallen 'towers' seem so disparately small compared to the concentrations of creative talent. The same conclusion is supported by recent and more reliable figures for Bach's Weimar, a village of a few hundred souls. And whatever its population, the London of 1600 was hardly larger than a modern township in the matter of literacy, though a score of poets, including a few immortal ones, lived in *that* London, while the megalopolis of today (when creation hardly seems to exist, by the side of explanation) seems to contain only several thousand book reviewers. And the Art Centres? Are they not an expression of quantitative, hence primarily non-creative, ideals? It certainly seems, in any case, that the larger the Art Centre, the smaller the creative art, though this could be disproved by the advent of even one creative talent of some size (and in music we are all over-ready for him, or, more likely, her, or, if that is to ask too much, then of the advent of someone with something to say instead of merely something to exhibit).

Provincialism

Lord Clark's lecture under this title is addressed to amateurs of English painting, but his distinctions are useful in the segregation of music. The history of European art, he says, is 'the history of a series of centres from each of which radiated a style'. Thus provincialism is at first 'simply a matter of distance from a centre, where standards of skill are higher and patrons more exacting'.[1] The art of the centre fails, Lord Clark con-

[1] *Cf.* Harold Rosenberg, *The Anxious Object*: 'Only in the creative centers, if there were any, does the artist have a chance to get away from the ideas of the center. In the provinces he is swamped by the latest.'

tinues, because of the over-refinement of style, while the failure of provincial art is its lack of style; and he notes further that the provincial artist attacks the metropolitan style when he finds its sophistication and elaboration moribund and when he believes that 'human values' are being neglected for 'formal' ones. The rebellion of the tenderfoot, therefore, is launched in the name of 'common sense', 'wholesomeness', 'individual judgment', 'truth to nature'. And it follows that the ingénue genius from the perimeter is as suspicious of the foreign as he is complacent about the local. In fact Lord Clark regards this complacency as provincialism's 'worst and commonest feature', with which I dissent only in order to claim the distinction for provincial rhetoric, Livy's patavinity.

Form and Function

Building means finding shapes for the processes of our lives, the late Dr. Gropius said, and I recalled the remark many years ago in Boston during a visit to his home, which, like himself, was spare, attractive, quiet, not very cosy. But observe the absence of esthetics (*vs.* Brancusi's 'architecture is inhabited sculpture'); and of ideals, other than that the definition itself; and of symbolizing, even though the 'processes of our life' still apparently require banks and insurance companies to look solidly rectangular, and corporate images to appear reassuringly physiological, as in Fuller's breast-fixation domes, and Wright's intestinal ziggurats.[1]

How does this purely functional approach compare with the approach of the composer? I must confess a prejudice. Pure functionalism is a Protestant concept to me and therefore foreign to my natural cultural soil. But even apart from that, and in so far as exterior and interior examples can be compared, my case is the other way around. I build with what the architect seeks to avoid. In fact my processes are *determined* by esthetic

[1] The viewer is digested through the Guggenheim Museum, rather than the paintings through the viewer. But I have not visited it since 1965, being too frightened to use a wheel chair or toboggan sled; the gradient does not seem very steep, but someone has estimated that a vehicle lost control of on the highest level would be travelling 125 miles per hour at the bottom.

accidents, except that they are not really accidents, for we give the word to those that we recognize and designate—to those we catch, not to those which escape—so that in this sense they, too, are determined.[1]

Five Examples

I

Stockhausen's *Carré* never fails to interest me when I follow it with the score, but the same music strikes me as timeless in the wrong sense unless my eye is engaged along with my ear. The same is true of at least one of Stockhausen's ideogrammatic percussion scores, though there, interest is sustained primarily by the novelties of notation, and this is not the composer's intention, I think, as it is with the composers of the so-called graphic school, whose scores are avowedly designed for the eye only. I admire *Carré*, nevertheless, even if what I admire amounts to no more than a few superficialities.

Not only are the sounds attractive, but so are the *non*-sounds, meaning the blessed absence of some of those exoticisms (always excepting the *accelerando-ritardando* Kabuki drums at **39**) that now drench-perfume most fashionable music. I also like the role of the piano, both solo and in combination; and I like the *glissandi* at **67**; and among the choral effects, the whispering and muttering, which express a whole winter of discontent at one place and which, distorted electronically and distanced stereophonically, give the listener what I imagine to be the Joan-of-Arc experience of hearing 'voices'.

Stockhausen, when I first met him, at a rehearsal of his *Gruppen*,[2] introduced himself with: 'Please tell me what you *don't* like.' Very well. For my taste, *Carré* depends too heavily on pedal points, or whatever one is to call the D at **69X**, the C at **80**

[1] Theodore Lessing described history as putting accidents in order, *Die Geschichte als Sinngebung des Sinnlosen*, history as sense-giving to the senseless, or the amorphous.

[2] No. Stockhausen, with Boulez and Nono, visited Stravinsky in the Rote Kreuz Hospital in Munich in November 1956. The *Gruppen* rehearsal, which was followed by a dinner with Stockhausen, Boulez, *et al.*, at the Brenners Park Hotel in Baden-Baden, took place in October 1958. (R.C.)

(but here the instrumental combination is very good), the E flat at the beginning and at **76** (where one suspects for a time that a recording of *Das Rheingold* has been put on by mistake), and the open fifth at **74**, which lasts so long that a latecomer, entering the hall during it, might think there had been a last-minute change of programme in favour of a modish orchestration of Pérotin. The music is most interesting when it is busiest, as in the section after **82X**.

A comparison of *Carré* and *Gruppen* puts the newer work a good length ahead, in my estimation, but it also tends to identify certain lapses as characteristic: that of the $\frac{2}{4}$ march at **63X**, for instance, which repeats the not-very-successful idea in *Gruppen* where all four orchestral groups are synchronized to a ♩ = 120 Sousa beat. Another general fault that *Carré* shares with all of its kind of music is the monotony of the run, as regular as a milk train, from dense to simple, movement to stasis, loud to soft, high to low, *tutti* to *solo*—and the no less regular return trips. Berg is its originator, and it was a major formal element in his music, but Berg was too great an artist to show his hand. Enough of what I do *not* like, however, as the score contains so much of what I *do*, and the two works together may well be the most powerful of the whole post-war period.

II

The *War Requiem* is surely one of Britain's finest hours-and-a-half, yet the reception accorded the music was a phenomenon as remarkable as the music itself. In fact the Battle-of-Britten sentiment was so thick and the tide of applause, virtually packaged along with the recording, so loud, that I, for one, was not always able to hear the music. Behold *The Times*, in actual, Churchillian quotes: 'Few recordings can ever have been awaited so eagerly and by so many people . . . practically everyone who has heard it has instantly acknowledged it as a masterpiece. . . .' Farther along, after a stirring description of the 'grief-laden unison melody of the opening' and of the 'doom-laden funeral march', the same reviewer remarks that 'the grandeur and intensity of [Mme. V.'s] phrasing exorcize all conventional notions of angelic insipidness', meaning, I take it, that unconventional notions have the field. (In fact, Mme. V.'s singing is singularly harsh and out of tune.) 'Schubert, Mendelssohn, and Goetz,' G. B. Shaw writes, and one reads the third name as a misprint for 'Goethe', until going on to learn that the Symphony in F Major and the Overture to *The Taming of the Shrew* are 'masterpieces which place Goetz above all other German composers of the last hundred years save only Mozart and Beethoven.'

Kleenex at the ready, then, one goes from the critics to the music, knowing that if one should dare to disagree with 'practically everyone', one will be made to feel as if one had failed to stand up for *'God Save the Queen'*. The victim of all this, however, is the composer, for of course nothing fails like success, or hurts more than the press's ready certification of a 'masterpiece'.

III

Turangalîla, to me, is an example of *plus d'embarras que de richesses*, but the most telling criticism of it was written long in advance, by Debussy: *'Vieux chant Hindou qui sert, de nos jours encore, à apprivoiser les éléphants. Il est construit sur la gamme de "5h. du matin" et, obligatoirement, en 5/4'* (*'La boîte à joujoux'*).

I should begin, however, by confessing my disqualifications as a judge, which are that I do not know the composer's supposedly better later music[1] and hence cannot see the direction of the earlier. It seems to me, for example, that *Turangalîla* attempts to stretch small, inelastic patterns into large ones by little other means than repetition *con crescendo* and an ever-wider spread of octaves, of which there is already a plague throughout. But that the developments are disappointing at least speaks well for the promise of the first statements. Nevertheless, the main obstacle to appreciation on my part is a barrier of taste created by what seems to me like a mixture of gamelans, Lehár, and some quite superior film music. (There are no less unpalatable traces of yesteryears of oneself, including some counterfeit

---

[1] I have heard a lot of it lately, though not yet *La Transfiguration* (described by those who have as 'a huge Viennese pastry in the middle of which sits Massenet'), and I greatly admire many things in it, while still finding each piece too much like the one before. (April, 1970).

Petrushka at **9** and **17**, and in m. 6–9 of the piano cadenza beginning at **11**, to choose unornamented examples.[1] Nor is it easy to imagine music more inane than the *Joie du Sang des Etoiles*, with its stage-direction, '*dans un délire du passion*';[2] or more vapid than the melody, in *Chant d'Amour II*, for Ondes Martenot, which instrument provides the musical equivalent of a colonic irrigation. Little more can be required to write such things than a plentiful supply of ink.

IV

Ives's *Decoration Day* is genuinely felt—which does not in itself guarantee anything, much very bad music having been genuinely felt, including Ives's *The Unanswered Question* which, so far as I am concerned, can also be the unplayed. Nor, partly for the same reason, is it enough that the feeling is of a high order. And it hardly counts that the rhythmic and harmonic ingenuity (the harmony at **D**, for instance) outstrips other contemporaries, for to 'outstrip' is nothing in itself, as we know from Alkan's piano pieces in two *tempi* simultaneously, and in groupings of thirteens, fourteens, and fifteens in the time of twelves, all of which are anticipations of Ives. Nor is it completely sufficient that in *Decoration Day* hand-me-down devices are replaced by such originalities as the chord with trombones and bassoons two before **C**: the dissonant clarinet notes at **H** and three before; the string shimmy before **I** and the two-flute obbligato at **I**; the trombones (the town sports, razzing it up) 5 m. before **M**; the settings of *Taps*, *Adeste Fideles*, *Nearer, My God, to Thee*, and the *Second Regiment March*; and the surprise ending, partly prepared by the shadow violin part, as the composer describes the marginal fiddle playing in major sevenths with the others. But I have already said enough to see that I cannot say what makes a masterpiece, even though *Decoration Day* seems to me to be one.

[1] *Messiaen's Trois Petites Liturgies de la Présence Divine* include an amount of fake *Noces*.

[2] The pedigree for these annotations comes from Scriabin, whose performance instructions in *Le Poème Divin* include '*avec une joie éclatante*' and '*divin, grandiose*'.

V

Boulez's *Éclat* might have been subtitled 'music for conductor and chamber ensemble'. For the conductor's part is the essential one. He is the principal soloist, regulating all the events of the piece, its directions being subjectively verbal: *'très vif'*, *'plus modéré'*, *'très longtemps'*, etc. As every entrance depends on a cue, in fact the conductor is less dispensable than ever before; in no sense does the music 'play itself'. The cues are ordinal in most cases, but by-aleatory in some, meaning, in practice, that each player stands by, cocked and ready to discharge his bundle of notes in a turn determined by the flick of Maître Boulez's fingers. When I say that these and other time controls interest me more than the many subtleties of sonority, I do not mean to slight the latter. But the true novelty, beyond both time and colour, is that *Éclat* provides the conductor with a new role, one that, so far, Maître Boulez himself is uniquely able to fulfil.

Conspiracy of Silence

'Or, 'heard melodies are sweet, but those unheard are sweeter'   KEATS

'Why is there anything at all rather than nothing?'
                                                                            HEIDEGGER

Oimè! Weh! Miserere! Old-style modern-music festivals are doomed, and only now have we become aware of their utility, which is that thanks to them fashionable noises became unfashionable more quickly, that decorators of in-vogue ideas were more rapidly unmasked, and that 'in-the-swim' tricks were sooner sunk or more quickly dried out. These services were of special value, moreover, to those who, like myself, are inclined to believe in talented individuals rather than in movements, in Picasso and Braque and Gris, for example, rather than in Cubism.

Already one thinks nostalgically of the Mittel-Europa 12-tone fundamentalists and serial shriners; of the microtonalist sects; of the promise of new bouquets by Anis Fuleihan and Fartein Valen, both mysteriously described as 'traditional' composers; of old Bo Nilsson, who seemed to have been born at a later date each year and on an ice floe further north; of *das neue Werk*, whose enticing events were announced in sober, Bauhaus sans serifs, with no 'caps' and the letters tumbling about the page *à la* Mallarmé; of each season's crop of new Japanese and Polish geniuses, the former with half-minute pieces for several hundred percussion instruments dominated by vibes, the latter with hour-long neo-religious cinemascope epics; of the noble, never-ending Soviet symphonies in 4/4 time, honouring female cosmonauts; of Karlheinz and Iannis, tycoons of the lecture circuit then, steam-rolling old masters and mainstay BMI classics now; of the pseudo-math and technical hocus-pocus pieces composed for analysts and professional code-breakers; of the English—for who could forget the tingling anticipation of a new *Umbrage for Eleven Instruments* by Humphrey Searle, or the welling up of keen emotion at the prospect of a new *Pandemonium X* by Cornelius Cardew? And of the slogans, platforms, proclamations of the coteries, one day crying up Henze as the Fortner of the Fifties, and the next, Stockhausen as *Wirtschaftswunder* candidate for Minister of Electricity. *Etcetera, etcetera*, and sad one is to see it all pass.

Because the sixties are the Age of Aleatory. And some of the amusements that pass under that designation allow for the possibility that selected parts or even all of an opus will not be performed—one commercial benefit of which is that the impresario is able to bill every performance as a world premiere. Furthermore, in these do-it-yourself days, fewer and fewer composers actually bother to write their music out for the performer, or for that matter to compose it, which may be what Walter Lippman meant by 'masterly inactivity'. And now that Mr. Cage's delectable silent piece *4′33″* has become his most popular opus, the example will undoubtedly be followed by more and more silent pieces by other composers who, in rapid escalation, will produce their silences with more and more varied and beguiling combinations. I myself can hardly wait to hear Professor Thorkell Sigurdjörnsson's silent *Fluctuations*, and Mr. Ligeti's unwritten orchestral *Happenings*, to say nothing of Señor Kagel's toneless *Evaporations* and imaginary *Oblongs*. I hope, moreover, that they turn out to be works of Nibelungen length. Soon, though, we may settle down in an academicism of silence, with completely silent concerts and entirely silent ISCM festivals as well. 'Oh sad,' I say, 'sad.'[1]

> '. . . *(terrible nouveauté!*
> *. . . rien pour les oreilles!)*
> *Un silence d'éternité.'*
> Les Fleurs du Mal

Longevity

Recent experiments at Ann Arbor indicate that life expectancy in rats increases with an increase of ecstasy.[2] Raffish rats live as long as eight years, the tests show, while puritan rats, on love-free and grubby diets, normally succumb at five. Parallels are tempting, 'love' reputedly being a good metabolizer, and whisky sometimes being recommended for the circulation. But for me to assert that my own age has been sustained in any measure by a devotion to both would be a mere lay opinion. The facts are the rats.[3]

The Terminological Crisis

The computer prose of musical analysis is probably a necessary

[1] After the quietest phase, it may be the turn of helium atmospheres, which can extend the range of human (and other) voices by more than an octave.
[2] And decreases with too much competitiveness. See Vitus Dröscher's study of rodent society, *Mysterious Senses*.
[3] See Wynne-Edwards's *Animal Dispersion in Relation to Social Behavior*, particularly Chapter 21 on the 'glossy rat'. Professor Wynne-Edwards is concerned with animal Malthusianism, or the animals' control of their own population by a built-in social instinct that humans have lost. He distinguishes three classes of males in rodent social organization. First are the 'large, glossy-furred, unscarred individuals who roam with impunity all over the enclosure'. Second are the slightly smaller individuals with tattered fur and a tendency to slouch. Third are the small, emaciated, unaggressive, lack-lustre individuals. The glossy rat, of course, is the wheeler-dealer, company-president type, who has all the status and who gets all of the girls, while the recessive rat, the beatnik, the neurotic, the deviate and the solitary diner, does not even breed. Professor Wynne-Edwards does not indulge in facile parallels, needless to say, but the reader can hardly resist doing just that. Who, for example, are the musical melanochroi, the slick-back rats of the concert hall? Are they the masters of podium *Realpolitik*? And who are the small tattered rats? The composers?

31

tool for the new music, though it makes me feel a graybeard, left leagues behind. Nor can I see the utility of such locutions as 'pitch priorities', 'simultaneities' (yclept 'chords' in my day), and 'dyads' (the genitalia?). My vocabulary consists entirely of hangover expressions from defunct traditions, and virtually all of my words require quotation marks or the qualifier 'so-called', though these are mere warning flags for word-inflation.

By Any Other Name?

'Stravinsky' is an adjectival, not a nominative form in Russian, hence I am not Stravinsk but Stravinsky-y(an). Are any consequences of this fact discernible in my music? Certainly it has been characterized as adjectival frequently enough, in the sense of a descriptive mode, Stravinsky the adjective modifying such nouns as Gesualdo, Pergolesi, Tchaikovsky, Wolf, Bach. And no less certainly linguistic questions of this type are operative in the most active roots of culture, as in Professor Sommerfelt's argument that China could not have developed an Aristotelian logic because Chinese lacks the subject-predicate proposition. A study of 'Stravinskyan' would also have to include a differential comparative analysis with English and French of the processes of my Russian thought-language—which lacks the pluperfect tense, the definite article and the copula (for we say 'I happy', not 'I am happy')—and this interests me far more, I confess, than a catalogue of my physical and psycho-physical statistics[1] (blood group, cortisone curve, etc.).

Individuality

Some biologists maintain that the organism is not equipped at its formation with a unique label of individuality,[2] and some philosophers now denounce the doctrine of separate individuals as a myth. An end to one's mystical beliefs in one's 'self', then, and an end, as well, to 'inexplicable'. The 'I' in the tenements of

[1] Nevertheless, when psycho-physiological measurement is a part of the future state's Vocational Guidance for Economy Programme, performers of my music should be confined to very lean ectomorphs.
[2] But see P. B. Medawar's *The Uniqueness of the Individual*, London, 1957.

With C. F. Ramuz, Morges, 1915

With brother, Gury, Ustilug, 1912

Morges, winter 1915

With Sert, Misia and 'Coco' Chanel, Paris, autumn 1920

moi, Sert, Missia et
Coco Chanel 1920

my brain is formed by a chemico-electrical system, a homeostat of nerve cells.[1] And a change in my brain—in, for example, the ribonucleic acid content of my 'memory molecules' (if the experience of the senses *is* encoded in the structure of molecules) —will alter my 'thought'. What I wonder, then, is whether the increase in my blood production in recent years has affected my 'cerebration'—though whether or not my *Variations* and *Canticles* can be described as more 'sanguine' is not a matter of science but of metaphor.

O arrogant Abraham, would you be so certain now of your 'I am I', or, as Shakespeare puts it, 'Richard loves Richard', and how would you know that you knew?

Change of Life

The greatest crisis in my life as a composer was the loss of Russia, and its language not only of music but of words. The second great crisis followed *The Rake's Progress*, though I was not aware of it as such at the time, continuing as I did to move from work to work. The 'period of adjustment' was even longer, and looking back on it now I am surprised myself at how long I continued to straddle two 'styles'. Was it because at seventy unlearning is as difficult as learning? In any case, I now see the *Movements* as the turn-of-the-corner in my later music. And what of the future? I shall continue to trust my taste buds and the logic of my ear, quaint expressions which I may be able to amplify by adding that I require as much hearing at the piano as ever before. I know, too, that I will never cross the gulf from well-tempered pitches[2] to sound effects and noise, and never abdicate the rule of my ears. But predictions are dangerous. I would be wiser to say *basta*!

[1] See J. Z. Young's *A Model of the Brain*, Oxford, 1964, and W. Grey Walter's *The Mechanisms of the Mind*, Thames and Hudson, 1969.
[2] Pitch and interval relationships are the primary dimension to me, whereas to my younger colleagues they may be less important than the shape of the room or the direction of the sound; but this is understandable, if only for the reason that new people must win their spurs in new territory. What I cannot follow are the manic-depressive fluctuations from total control to no control, from the serialization of all elements to chance.

Eye Music

Balanchine's visualization of the *Movements* exposed relationships of which I had not been aware in the same way. Seeing it, therefore, was like touring a building for which I had drawn the plans but never completely explored the result. He began by identifying familiar appendages of my musical style, of which I myself became conscious only through his eyes. And as I watched him fastening on the tiniest repeated rhythmic figure, I knew that he had joined the score to my other music faster than it could ever get there by way of the concert hall. Beyond that, he discovered the lyricism of the piece; his dramatic point is a love parable—in which ballet is it not?—and his coda has a suggestion of the ending of *Apollo*.

The musical choreography is a double concerto for a solo male and a solo female dancer, each of whom is identified with the piano. The choric group is spare: no caryatids this time, but only a hexachord of those bee-like little girls—big thighs, nipped-in waists, pin-heads—who seem to be bred to the eminent choreographer's specifications. Only in the Interludes[1] does the full sextet dance as a unit, which helps to project the shape of the whole score with exceptional clarity.

I have seen the choreography only once, and then at a rehearsal, at which time I found a Japanese head movement obtrusive, a holdover from *Bugaku*, probably. I remember, however, that at one point when Balanchine asked his dancers to repeat a section without the music, they were able to count it by themselves, which is rather better than most orchestras can do. But are the *Movements* ballet music? Barbarous question to a Balanchine, who always tells me that he needs a motor impulse, not a *pas de deux*.

Envoi

And what do they come to, these scraps from the mental wastebasket? Apart from showing that away from my piano I am a consumer statistic like everyone else, do they indicate that my

---

[1] The Interludes are introductions, not codas: the conductor should pause *before* them, and I like these seams and sutures to show.

inability to adjust my mental habits to Probability has made me self-righteous and a little like a dog in a manger? The answer of the computer-Sphinx will be 'insignificant variables'. But what are the *in*variables? A natural traction attached to a mind divided by the attempt to hold *up* a shattered wall of beliefs on one side while holding *back* an encroaching scientific analysis wall on the other? A mind complicated by the tendency (of all old people?) to fall into solipsism? Not 'fall', though, for if that is where I am, I have been brought there under force (frog-marched). I have no answers. But I am grateful that I still have and am able to tend a few sprouts that still grow in my own garden—which, by the way, I must go and water.

PROGRAMME NOTES

Pribaoutki

In the spring of 1914 my sketchbooks began to fill with notations for songs, as well as for *Renard, Les Noces*, and the *Three Pieces for String Quartet*. The figure

and the cello accompaniment to the cock's aria in *Renard* were composed at this early date, and by autumn the profusion of material was so great that many bits and pieces were left over and never fashioned at all, as in the case of this little tune:

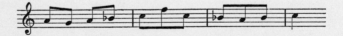

All four of the *Pribaoutki* texts come from Afanasiev's *Popular Russian Tales*, Vol. III (pp. 338, 339, 547). The melody of the second part of the first song, *Корнило* (Afanasiev's No. 543, came to my ear in London, in July 1914

(*sic*, in that octave). Next to these 2 m., in my sketchbook, are three variant notations of the bells of St. Paul, and all three, in my irregular meters, look remarkably Russian. *Корнило* was completed on August 29. The third song, *Полковник*, is Afanasiev's No. 554 (p. 338). In the original version, the last 2 m. were written this way: *Наташка*, the second song, is Afanasiev's No. 550 (p. 339), except that I changed the third word from 'сладенька' to 'сладёнка' and the last word from 'протягивать'

to 'протягать.' No. four *Старець и Заяць* is from Asenavier's p. 547, except that I omitted the к нему after прибежал. *Старець и Заяць* gave me the most trouble to compose. The original manuscript score was a minor-second lower in pitch than the published version, and the bassoon solo in the middle section was originally a solo for the clarinet, an octave higher than the bassoon; I rewrote this bassoon part in October 1964, incidentally, tampering with the rhythm, as my unsatisfactory—but not for that reason—recording shows.

Do the songs betray any homesickness for Russia? Not being a musical pathologist, I cannot be certain of the diagnosis, but what I *can* say is that I greatly regretted being unable to spend that summer of 1914 at my home in Ustilug.

The *Pribaoutki* were composed for a baritone, and should be sung by a man. If a contralto attempts them, she should have the tomcat voice required by the *Berceuses du chat*.[1]

Le Chant du Rossignol

Little has been written about the staging of this ballet, hence the following letter to me from Henri Matisse, who designed its décor, seems to me of quite unusual interest. (I hope I have transcribed it correctly; like Emily Dickinson, Matisse punctuated mainly by dashes.)

[1] No. II of *Berceuses du chat* also borrows a text from Afanasiev, No. 538, page 336, Vol. 3.

Nice, 1 Place Charles Félix
(jusqu'au 5 juin) 28 mai 25

Mon cher Ami,

Votre lettre me parvient à l'instant ici—excusez-moi de n'avoir pas répondu plus vite. Je n'ai pas pu. La reprîse du *Rossignol* me fait plaisir. Cependant j'espère que la scène ne sera pas trop petite à cause des proportions des Colonnes— qu'on pourra voir les frises—et que vous ne supprimerez pas les principaux accessoires qui font parties indispensables des murs. Quant aux costumes de la jeune danseuse—je ne vois pas grande modification à faire à celui de Karsavina— j'espère qu'il existe encore et qu'on pourra s'en inspirer— en tout cas il doit être blanc—et les plumes formées de pétales blancs en soie bordées d'un petit filet noir comme ci-contre mais probablement plus grand. J'espère que vous aurez à faire à Marie Meulle ou son père qui le feront très bien —aux chevilles et aux poignets un elastique tenant une rose blanche ainsi que sur les tempes—dans le style indou—le voile perlé attaché sur les cotés depuis le poignet jusqu'aux chevilles—ce costume avait un effet heureux de légèreté cristalline analogue du chant de l'oiseau et aussi au son de la flûte. Je ne vois pas autre chose—il est nécessaire de ne pas trop alourdir les hanches quoiqu'une fillette de 12 ans en est souvent dépourvue—

Quant au costume rossignol artificiel—celui que j'ai fait peu servir d'indication suffisante—les couleurs sont à respecter—remplacer le cartonnage par un costume souple un peu rembourré, les pieds de même couleur rose chine je crois—mais moins grands. (Cela dépend des évolutions qu'a faire l'acteur.) Enfin un costume dans le même caractère à modifier selon la mobilité du danseur—de même pour la tête j'espère qu'elle existe encore et pourra renseigner.

Je rentre à Paris vers le 5 juin et pourrai vous voir si vous le jugez utile.

A bientôt, cher ami, infatigable travailleur, tout à vous dans la mesure du possible.

HENRI MATISSE

Symphonies of Wind Instruments

The chorale which concludes the *Symphonies* was composed June 20, 1920, in Carantec, a fishing village in Finisterre. I had already leased a cottage there for the summer before discovering that no piano could be rented and that one would have to be carted in from a neighbouring village. The music was finished in abbreviated score form by July 2 (though not in full score until November 30, in Garches), but a few days later I added two adumbrative bits of chorale to the body of the piece. The earliest sketches contain notations for string quartet, and the duets for alto flute and alto clarinet were originally scored for violin and viola. Another section in one of the same duets, incidentally, was originally the waltz variation in the *Octuor*. Like my *Piano Rag Music* and *Three Pieces for Solo Clarinet*, both composed shortly before, the sketch-score is largely meterless. The phrasing of the sketch-score also differs strikingly from both of the published scores (1921 and 1947), which in turn are so different from each other in this respect (*cf.* the horns and trumpets at the return of the first motive following the first flute-clarinet duet) that the two versions will doubtless continue to be played as two different pieces, or, more likely, just as now, continue *not* to be played. On December 11, 1945, I arranged the final chorale for a wind orchestra without clarinets, to be performed with the *Symphony of Psalms*: 4 flutes, 5 oboes (1 English horn), 4 bassoons (including contra), 4 horns, 4 trumpets, 3 trombones, tuba.

Eight Instrumental Miniatures

Les Cinq Doigts, the originals of the *Miniatures*, were composed in 1921, one per day, on January 24, 26, 29, 31, and February 4, 13, 17, 18, at Garches, near Versailles, in the home of Madame Gabrielle ('Coco') Chanel. Mme. Chanel was a close friend of mine at the time, as well as one of Diaghilev's most generous supporters, for which reason alone balletomanes should always hold her name in the best odour. The Fugue in my *Octuor* was also composed at Garches at that time, incidentally, in the form of a two-piano piece, and when I began the first-movement *Allegro* (July 17, 1922), my first idea was to retain the piano as a bass to the wind group. (The Introduction to the *Allegro* was composed later, just before the recapitulation of the first movement.)

Unlike the *Easy Pieces* for piano duet, these studies were not composed for my own children, but for all piano debutants. My idea was to assign each finger of the right hand to a single note, thus limiting myself to a five-note row—in the same way as in the *Gigue* of my *Septet* I confined each *instrument* to a single row of notes. I orchestrated the *Tango* (or '*Tijuana Blues*') on December 16, 1961, for 3 trumpets, 3 trombones, 2 oboes, 2 bassoons, with which combination it was played later that month in Mexico City. I then transcribed the *Andantino* on March 21 of the following year, the *Vivace* on March 23, the *Lento* on the 25th, and the *Kosatchok Variation*, which entailed the most extensive amount of adding and rewriting, on the 26th. The *Marcialetta* was written on April 2, and I conducted the first performance of the suite of eight pieces as a complete group in Toronto, under the auspices of the Canadian Broadcasting Corporation, later that month.

Three Sacred Choruses

My *Pater Noster*, *Credo*, *Ave Maria*, and the unfinished prayer *And The Cherubim . . .* were inspired out of antipathy to the bad music and worse singing in the Russian Church at Nice, where I became a communicant in 1925, the year before composing the *Pater Noster*. I knew very little about Russian Church music at that time (or now), but I hoped to find deeper roots than those of the Russian Church composers who had merely tried to continue the Venetian (Galuppi) style from Bortniansky. Whether my choruses recapture anything of an older Russian tradition I cannot say; but perhaps some early memories of church singing survive in the simple harmonic style that was my aim. *All* traditions of Russian Church singing are in decay now, in any case, which is why I rewrote the *Credo* in June 1964 (the original was composed on August 12, 1932), spelling out the *faux bourdon*. The Latin versions of the *Pater Noster* and *Ave Maria* date from March 1949.

The *Credo* and *Pater Noster* are liturgical pieces, whereas the

Ave Maria, though it occurs in several services, is a concert piece. I composed the *Ave Maria* one Wednesday in Lent (April 4, 1934) but do not recall the first time I heard it. I *do* remember hearing the *Pater Noster*, however, sung by the Afonsky[1] Choir at the Requiem for my sister-in-law, Ludmila Beliankin, in the spring of 1937, forty days after her death, according to Russian custom.

This was in the Alexander Nevsky Church in the rue Daru, which played an important role in my life in the 1930s. Built in the period and style of Alexander II, it was an island of Russian colour in its drab Parisian quarter, and not one island only, but a whole archipelago of Russian shops, bookstores, restaurants, cafés, *bijouteries, antiquaires*. On feast days the neighbourhood would resemble an oriental fair ground both in décor and in hubbub, and I can remember gathering birch twigs myself in a forest near Paris to help deck the church at the Feast of the Trinity. I also remember the wedding there of an American heiress, Miss Hutton, and a disinherited Russian Prince, Mr. Mdivani, for which the sidewalks were strewn with flowers.

In the Paris of the twenties, the church—with the cafés and restaurants nearby—was a focus of Russian life, to believers and non-believers alike. Then in the mid-thirties a Rome *versus* Avignon split occurred, some of the congregation deciding to recognize the Metropolitan in Moscow over his opposite number in Paris. (I remained loyal to the Nevsky Church myself, which became the centre of the anti-Soviet church-in-exile.) Dissenting churches, some of them portable and pocket-sized, sprouted up all over Paris, housed in apartments and studios. I remember one, in the rue d'Odessa, that was located over a nightclub, owing to which a sum of money had to be raised to buy a half hour of quiet during the Saturday night Easter service. Then at midnight, immediately after the proclamation '*Christos Voskreseh*', business resumed below with a bam, boom, and crash.

[1] Nicolas Afonsky died in New York, aged 77, shortly after Stravinsky's death. (R.C.)

Four Etudes for Orchestra

The orchestrations of the first three *Etudes*—originally the *Three Pieces for String Quartet* (1914)[1]—were completed in 1917; the fourth, originally the *Etude for Pianola* (1917), was completed in 1928, at which time I called it *Madrid*, and added titles to the other three pieces as well. The first is a *Danse* for the woodwinds, which repeat a four-note chant—'The Four Fingers', one might call it—in varying rhythmic positions. The second, *Excentrique*, was inspired by the movements and postures of Little Tich, the clown. The third, *Cantique*, which might have been titled 'Hymne', is choral and religious in character.

I composed the string-quartet original of the *Danse* in April, 1914, in Leysin; the manuscript (fair copy) was owned by the late Ernest Ansermet. The quartet original of *Excentrique* was composed in Salvan, July 2 (1914). I began with the figure

 [sic]

and worked from it toward what was to become the beginning. My sketchbooks contain several versions of the cello motive

including the following merry tune, which would have suited a cornet à pistons:

[1] The Boston Symphony Program Book for February 7 and 8, 1969, includes a detailed account of the first American receptions of these *Pieces*, and reprints the verses by Amy Lowell reputedly 'inspired' by them. To the information collected in this Program Book I can add that I made a two-piano version of the *Three Pieces* in 1914 that has never been published, and that I revised and corrected the quartet versions in December 1918, Number 1 on December 2, and Number 2 on December 6.

The quartet original of the *Cantique* was composed in Salvan, July 25–26 (1914), by a process of much trial and error, to judge from the search recorded in my sketchbook. The first form of the melody was:

Jeu de Cartes

More than a decade before composing *Jeu de Cartes*, I was aware of an idea for a ballet with playing-card costumes and a green-baize gaming-table backdrop. I have always enjoyed card games, and almost always been interested in cartomancy. I have been a card player, moreover, ever since I learned *durachki* as a child. Poker was a favourite pastime during the composition of *Jeu de Cartes*, as Chinese checkers was during the composition of the *Rake*.

The origins of the ballet, in the sense of the attraction of the subject, go back to a childhood holiday with my parents at a German spa, and my first impressions of a casino there, the long rows of tables at which people played baccarat and bézique, roulca and faro as now, in the bowels of ocean liners, they play bingo. In fact the trombone theme with which each of the ballet's three 'Deals' begins imitates the voice of the master of ceremonies at that first casino. '*Ein neues Spiel, ein neues Glück*', he would trumpet—or, rather, trombone—and the timbre, character, and pomposity of the announcement are echoed, or caricatured, in my music.

The period and setting of *Jeu de Cartes*, if I had been obliged to fix them, would have been in a German spa such as Baden-Baden in the Romantic Age; and it is as part of that picture that the marches, and the tunes by Rossini, Messager, Johann Strauss, and from my own *Symphony in E flat* (**66** in the first movement) might be imagined drifting in from the Municipal Opera, or the concert by the Kursaal Band. The score was not designed for any particular audience, and in fact it was nearly completed before I received the commission from the new

American Ballet Company. But it has been especially popular in Germany and was performed there in all of the larger cities, and by all of the most eminent conductors, in 1937 and 1938; on February 23 of the latter year I recorded it for Telefunken in Berlin. But if spirit of place exerted any influence, the spirit of the music would have been Parisian. Only one segment, the passage from **189** to **192**, which resembles the beginning of the Limoges piece in Ravel's instrumentation of *Pictures at an Exhibition*, was written on German territory: aboard the *Kap Arcona*, on which I sailed from Boulogne to Buenos Aires in 1936; and this passage is rare in my music, too, in that it was not composed at the piano. The remainder of the score was completed in my apartment in the Faubourg St.-Honoré.

I began it on the second of December 1935 with, besides the trombone theme, some of the music in the coda of the second Deal; by the end of the month most of the first Deal had been sketched, and parts of the third. The second Deal was begun with the *Marcia*, then the *Variations*, composed in order, the second on September 8, 1936, the third on September 18. The *Waltz* in the third Deal came next and was followed by the last measures of the ballet on October 19. The intervening music of the third Deal was composed in November.

The fortunes of my music in the Third Reich are unaccountable. It was banned entirely at first, then defended for the wrong reasons, by, of all people, Richard Strauss (see the *Fränkischer Kurier*, November 28, 1934). In May 1938, I was the chief butt, along with Schoenberg, Berg, Hindemith, Weill, of the scurrilous *Entartete Musik* (Degenerate Music) exhibition in Düsseldorf. Several rooms there were devoted to a display of my 'decadent', 'Jewish', 'cultural Bolshevist' music, the visitor being confronted with viciously defamatory photographs and documents while his ears were entertained with a recording of *Pierrot lunaire*, described on a poster as '*Hexensabbat*' music. A reproduction of one of Jacques-Émile Blanche's portraits of me adorned one of the walls, with accompanying placard saying, 'Judge from this whether or not Stravinsky is a Jew'. When photographs of the exhibition and clippings from German newspapers reached me in Paris, I protested through the French Ambassador in Berlin, M. François-Ponçet, but nothing came of it. And my music was performed in Germany up to and even during the war. Charles Munch conducted a performance of *Le Sacre du printemps* at the Paris Conservatoire in 1942, in fact. But, then, Berg's *Wozzeck* was performed in the same year in Rome.

I invited Cocteau to collaborate in my card-game ballet, thinking he might devise a more interesting plot than the one I had worked out by myself—he was in his period of bicephalous eagles and bleeding bards then—but he declined. My own scheme called for a three-part division, each with a deal of poker as its argument, and with the Joker as the principal dancer. In the first deal, one of the three players is beaten and the other two remain with even straights. In the second, the Joker wins by becoming the fourth Ace, which defeats four Queens. And in the third, the Joker is beaten by three flushes. I no longer remember the details of the choreographic action I must have had in mind as I composed. But I did not provide Balanchine with an explicit programme, being confident that the character of each episode was unmistakeable in the music.

Playing-cards are ideal ballet material because of the rich possibilities in combining and grouping the four suits with the solo-dancer royalty. The latter divide into sexes, moreover, and male and female are to the ballet composer what *forte* and *piano* were to the eighteenth-century *concerto grosso* composer. The Joker is a bonus, an element of chance and an escape from these very combinations. He interrupts the music as well as the choreography, and though he wins all of the battles, he loses the war. The contest resulting in his defeat begins at **152**, where he enters at the head of a sequence of spades, and it ends at **160**. But, like Petrushka, he reappears at the end. His return is represented by the final seventh-chord, which, together with the return of the master-of-ceremonies music, signifies that the game is perpetual, as all games are.

The curtain cue is at **6**, following the orchestral introduction, which develops the master-of-ceremonies theme. A ballerina inaugurates the dancing at **7**, but I no longer remember of which suit. At **12** the lady dances a variation of **7**, until she is joined (at **16**) by her consort, at which point a new episode

45

begins. The Joker's cue is at 21, and his dance determines the action until 34, where he disappears, leaving the Queen alone for the waltz-coda which returns, *mutatis mutandis*, to the music of 7. The *March* in the Second Deal—43 and the returns—was intended as a dance for hearts and spades, interrupted by the Joker at 55. The first four variations are solo dances for the Queens, in the order hearts, diamonds, spades, clubs, while the fifth is a *pas de quatre* of their highnesses together. The Coda was conceived as a *tutti* for the whole deck, with the Joker interrupting at 92. In the Third Deal, the *corps de ballet* was much busier than in the other two, but I recall no more than that.

I did not communicate even this sketchy programme to Balanchine, and in fact hardly discussed the choreography with him. But I did send the piano score from Paris, and on my arrival in New York for a concert tour two months before the performance I rehearsed *tempi* with him. In fact, I participated in the staging only to criticize the costume designs, which were inspired by Tarot and medieval playing cards, handsome in themselves but too sumptuous for my 'brittle' and 'heartless' music. I asked the artist to copy some ordinary playing cards from the corner drugstore.

Jeu de Cartes was my first commission from Lincoln Kirstein, who has since become known as a poet as well as a learned and intelligent balletomane—though I hardly need to elaborate since Mr. Kirstein has had a whole Arts Center named for him in New York. A young giant then, Lincoln Kirstein was a bellicose champion of the beautiful and a fierce enemy of the sham. His career as patron had only begun, but too few people are aware even now that the existence of the finest ballet company and ballet school in the world today is due to him as much as to George Balanchine.

A few days after the première I received news of the death of Ludmila Beliankin, my wife's sister and my own close friend since childhood; and I returned to Europe with a heavy heart. The Paris première occurred at the time of another sad event, the death of Ravel. And it was the last work I conducted in Europe before the war, at a concert in La Scala in May 1939.

I read La Fontaine during the composition, and in him found my sermon, and a sermon for the times:

Qu'il faut faire aux méchants guerre continuelle.
La paix est fort bonne de soi,
J'en conviens; mais de quoi sert-elle
Avec des ennemis sans foi?

Dumbarton Oaks Concerto

The name is that of the District of Columbia estate of the late
Robert Woods Bliss, who commissioned the music, sponsored
its first performance there in 1938, and in April 1950 purchased the principal manuscripts for the Dumbarton Oaks
Museum. I began the composition immediately on my return
to Europe after *Jeu de Cartes*, in the Château de Montoux, near
Annemasse in the Haute Savoie, where I had moved for the
sake of my daughter Mika, who had been sent to a tuberculosis
sanitarium nearby. Not long before, Mika had married Yuri
Mandelstam, a Russian writer (no relation to Osip) who
worked for the émigré newspaper, *Sovremenniya Zapiski*, and who
was unable to leave his position there and stay with her. (Mandelstam remarried shortly after Mika's death, then soon after
the occupation of Paris he was deported to Germany and gassed
on a train in Poland.) Annemasse is near Geneva, and my good
friend Charles-Albert Cingria often came to visit me from there
during this difficult period.

I played Bach regularly in Annemasse; and I was then, and
always, greatly attracted to the Brandenburg Concertos. The
first theme of my own *Concerto* closely resembles that of the third
Brandenburg (which I have conducted), and like the Bach
concerto, too, it uses three violins and three violas, both groups
frequently *divisi a tre*, though not chordally as in the Bach. I
have been much censured for these resemblances, but I do not
think that Bach himself would have begrudged me the use of
his examples, as he frequently borrowed in this way himself.

Symphony in C

The Symphony in C was composed during the most tragic year of
my life. In fact, I accepted the commission (from the late Mrs.
Robert Woods Bliss) under the pressure of my wife's, my

daughter's, and my own medical debts, for shortly after the premiere of *Jeu de Cartes*, I, too, caught the family disease of tuberculosis. (A New York doctor had found a lesion in my left lung, and staphylococci clusters in my sputum.) On my return to France, I was ordered to the same sanitarium in which my wife and my two daughters had already been confined with the same disease.

I did not go there, however, but stayed in Paris and composed the *Dumbarton Oaks Concerto* and the Symphony in C. Most of the first movement of the Symphony was composed in the Faubourg St.-Honoré, in the autumn of 1938, though the last section was not finished until April 17, 1939. On November 22, I left for the Excelsior Hotel in Rome, and a concert in that city. On the 29th, leaving Rome for a concert in Turin, I called Paris and heard the news that Mika's condition had suddenly become grave, and the next day, calling Paris myself from the Turin railway station, learned that she had died at five o'clock that morning. It is no exaggeration to say that I survived in the weeks that followed only by working on the Symphony—which is *not* to say that the music exploits my grief.

Three months later, March 2, 1939, a hemorrhage ended my wife Catherine's fifty-year struggle with the same disease. Unable to remain in the apartment after that, and having been further warned about my own condition, I moved to the same sanitarium at Sancellemoz where Catherine and Mika had lived, and where I was an out-patient for the next five months. One of my infrequent absences was to attend the funeral of my mother, who died on June 7. For the third time in half a year I heard the Requiem service chanted for one of my own family, and for the third time walked through the fields to the cemetery of Saint-Geneviève-des-Bois, in Montlhéry, which is on the road to Orléans, and dropped a handful of dirt in an open grave. And once again I was able to go on only by composing, though no more than before do the parts of the Symphony written in these dark days represent an expression of my feelings of loss. The pastoral second movement was begun March 27, and completed July 19.

My visitors in Sancellemoz included Pierre Suvchinsky and Roland-Manuel. Suvchinsky, one of my oldest living friends,

Seville, April 1921

Stravinsky's daughter, Ludmila, her husband
Yuri Mandelstam, and granddaughter Catherine,
Paris, 1937

Vera Stravinsky in 1922 by Bakst

knew me more closely than anyone else in my later years in Paris, both in the thirties and again in the sixties. He has always fed books to me, and I remember that at Sancellemoz he brought the novel *La Nausée*, by the most discussed new writer of the moment, Jean-Paul Sartre. Having agreed to deliver the Charles Eliot Norton lectures at Harvard in the winter of 1939–40, I sought the assistance of Suvchinsky to help draft my texts in Russian, and of Roland-Manuel to revise and polish the French. Back in Paris, Suvchinsky reported that the score of Tchaikovsky's First Symphony was on my piano, and this information, together with the discovery of a similarity of first themes in my Symphony and Tchaikovsky's, was responsible for the rumour that was soon giving model status to the latter. (If Suvchinsky had reported which Haydn and Beethoven scores were on my desk, no one would have paid any attention, of course, yet both of those composers stand behind at least the first two movements of my Symphony far more profoundly than any music by my much-too-lonely compatriot.) At the same time, a rapport would naturally exist between the two works, given the Russian sentiment in the E flat minor episode in my first movement, as well as in the introduction to my last movement; but Tchaikovskyan antecedents have been discovered elsewhere as well, 'my' eighteenth century and 'Tchaikovsky's' sharing Russian family-likenesses, as numerous authorities on *The Rake's Progress* have noted.

To return to the chronicle of the later movements, the world events of 1939–40 did not bear tragically on my personal life, but they did disrupt the composition. The third movement was written in Boston (completed at the beginning of April), and the finale in California (completed August 17), where I had gone to escape New England, whose only seasons, so it seemed to a Mediterraneanized European, were winter and the Fourth of July. The American movements are said to be different in spirit and design from the European, and it has been claimed that they divide the Symphony down the middle. But I am no judge of that. Perhaps the 2 measures before **104** would not have come to my ears in Europe; and the passage beginning at **145** might not have occurred to me before I had known the neon glitter of Los Angeles's boulevards from a speeding automobile.

49

Perhaps. But I do not agree that the metrical irregularity and *tempo* changes in the third movement—the most extreme in the whole of my work, as it happens—constitute a schism, simply because they follow a second movement with a steady *ductus*, and a first movement with no variation of meter at all.

The public life of the Symphony began on November 7, 1940, in Chicago, when I conducted its first performance. But its public career has not been very conspicuous. Older conductors tend to shy away from the technical difficulties of the third movement, and younger ones avoid it because of the unfashionableness of its so-called neo-classicism. For many years virtually the only performances were my own.

Nor were the ill-fated personal associations of the Symphony at an end. I was conducting it in Berlin, October 2, 1956, when, near the end of the first movement, I felt a paralyzing pain in my right side, and an eclipsing blackness. Orchestra members said, after the concert, that I failed to beat the final measures of the movement and paused an unconscionable time before beginning the next one. I *did* continue, nevertheless, and brought the Symphony to the end, though in my dressing room I was unable to write my name and had only partial control of my speech. Two days later, in Munich, where I had flown for another concert, a doctor told me I had suffered a cerebral thrombosis, and I was sent to the Red Cross hospital there for six weeks.

But enough of autobiography. And of musical biography too, for what can one say about music that is so unmysterious, and so easy to follow at every level and in all relationships? The answer, of course, is that critics (who must earn their livelihood) will find a great deal of nothing to say—factitious comparisons to other music, profound observations on the diatonicism and the use of *fugato*, on the existence of a suite-of-dances in the third movement, on flirtations with ballet everywhere. But anyone who had failed to notice as much would require a very different sort of commentary in any case.

How do I evaluate the Symphony thirty years afterward? The answer is that I don't. It may be too episodic, the key centers may be over-emphasized, and certainly there *are* a great many *ostinati*. And these faults, if such they are, glare a little more obviously because of the ascendancy of another aesthetic, which is no more absolute than that of the Symphony, and which, in another thirty years, may look bad itself in the very directions which now seem to counter these 'weaknesses' of the *Symphony*.

The score, like that of the *Symphony of Psalms*, is inscribed '*à la gloire de Dieu*'.

Danses Concertantes

Choreographic titles notwithstanding, the *Danses Concertantes* were not composed with dance movement in mind, or intended to be staged as a ballet. The music began in the first theme of the final *Allegro* of the *Symphony in C*, and in fact I composed the tune of the *Pas d'action*, which is simply a variant of the Symphony theme, on October 19, 1939, while still sketching the third movement of the Symphony. The variation movement was completed only two years later, however, the Coda being dated October 20, 1941, and the whole score, except the reprise of the *Marche de présentation*, December 1, 1941.

Some listeners professed to hear an 'American' note in the music, even, to narrow the geography, a Broadway note, and the theme of the variations was said to sound 'like Copland'. But if this is true, I was unaware of it. The only influence that I can see, apart from the Symphony, is that of *Jeu de Cartes* in the little march at **159**; but, then, reactivated springs from past works have nourished present works all my life; which is also a reason why I think my music deserves to be considered as a whole. Finally, however, the newest music in *Danses Concertantes* occurs between **79** and **83**, and that is independent of the style of 'Broadway' or any other locale. A version of 'London Bridge is Falling Down' occurs near the end of the piece.

The instrumental ensemble resembles that of my arrangement of excerpts from the *Sleeping Beauty*, completed shortly before for a ballet orchestra greatly reduced in size by the war. About half of the music had been composed before I received the commission from Mr. Werner Janssen.

Orpheus

A new, so-called plaintiveness was detected in the *Orpheus* music, but I think that this character was already present in my *Bäsler Concerto*, in, for example, the phrase:

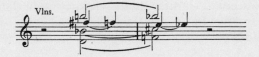

Although a composer's timing must hold for every age, how different are the time-scales of 1970 and 1947! I would not write so motionless a measure now as the one before **4**; or allow the flutes and clarinets to run to such dilatory length at **100**, and the strings *ditto* in the measure after **98**. Moreover, the whole of the *Pas d'Action* strikes me as spread out and repetitious now, even compared with the *Ebony Concerto*, which does not say the same thing quite so many times, and which comes to mind, I think, because of the similarity of their two-note motives.

Orpheus, the subject, was a Balanchine–Kirstein inspiration, communicated to me early in 1946. I began to compose on October 20 of that year, with this music from the *Prelude*:

and by July 8 of the next year I had written the 4/2 *Interlude*. The choreographer joined me in Hollywood, and with Ovid and a classical dictionary in hand we concocted a scenario that divided the action into three scenes comprising a dozen episodes. The commission stipulated a half-hour of music, and if the metronomes are observed, that is exactly the length I provided. The titles are partly mine, incidentally, partly the dictionary's; one contribution of the latter, '*L'Ange de la mort et sa danse*', might have done for Messiaen, if it had been a little less definite.

I think it was Lincoln Kirstein's idea to entrust the décor to Isamu Noguchi, who spared us Doric columns, chlamys, and the Ruins of Athens (at any rate), and whose maquettes promised some bleakly attractive landscaping. In execution, Noguchi's greatest success was the transparent curtain that fell over the scene like fog, during the Interludes. He also designed some attractive, if rather too specifically ethnographic masks, from which hair flowed like horses' manes; the vizors obstructed the dancers' sight-lines, however, and Orpheus looked like a baseball catcher in his. But the uptilting, cactus-shaped limbs projecting from the wings and suggesting hobgoblins and dildoes, are as dated now as the kicking movements of the female Furies and the cadences with added sixths, sevenths, and ninths.

The ballet was a success, nevertheless, partly because it was brilliantly danced by, among others, some of Balanchine's wives. The programme included a preview of the *Pas de Deux* in the form of a dance-duet *entr'acte* choreographed to my *Elegy* for viola *sola*.[1] But this study in slow motion of amorously intercising limbs reminded me of a pair of lobsters in a restaurant window.

The better movements in *Orpheus*, I now find, are the string music of the *Pas de Deux* and the music between **41** and **46** in the first *Interlude*, where a developing harmonic movement and an active bass line relieve the long chain of *ostinati*. As to influences, the question cannot even be broached. Monteverdi is not a presence in the end movements; nor is there any Czerny in the arpeggios before **146** and **148**, or any Ives in the tantara at **38**, which nearly spells *Taps*. Because so much of *Orpheus* is mimed song,[2] it seemed inevitable to me that my next work would be an opera.

The Rake's Progress

The Rake's Progress is cast in the mould of an eighteenth-century number-opera; the dramatic progress depends on the succession of recitatives and arias, duets and trios, choruses and instrumental interludes. These forms, moreover, are as symbolically

---

[1] Composed at the request of the violist Germain Prévost, in memory of Alphonse Onnou, founder of the Pro Arte Quartet. I arranged it for solo violin subsequently, at the suggestion of Mr. Sol Babitz, who played it *scordatura* (at F-C-G-D).

[2] The harp in the oboe aria should sound dry and choked, like a not very resonant guitar, and the violin aria should sound silky, a calculated effect (or risk) in the choice of the technically awkward key.

expressive of the dramatic content as are the more Daedalian forms in the operas of Alban Berg. In the earlier scenes the mould is pre-Gluck; it tends to crowd the story into *secco* recitatives and to reserve the arias for the reflective poetry. Later the story itself is told and enacted almost entirely in song—in contrast to Wagnerian continuous melody, which consists, in effect, of orchestral commentary enveloping continuous recitative.

Having chosen a period-piece subject, I decided to assume the conventions of the period as well, though respectable (progressive) music had pronounced them long since dead. My revival, if that is what it was, did not include modernizing or updating (which would have been self-contradictory in any case); and certainly I had no ambitions as a reformer in the line of Gluck, Wagner, Berg. In fact these great progressivists had sought to abolish many of the very clichés that, for my own ends, I was trying to re-establish. At the same time, my restitutions were not intended to supersede their, by then, conventionalized reforms— meaning, for instance, the *leitmotif* systems of Wagner and Berg.

Whether a composer can make use of the past as I did, and at the same time move in a forward direction is a question for Public Relations that concerned me not at all during the writing. Nor do I care about it now, even though now the supposed backward step of *The Rake* has taken on a radically forward-looking complexion, thanks to a plague of ill-made progressive operas. May I ask the listener to suspend these questions, as *I* did while composing, and instead try to discover the opera's own qualities? I did not compose it to fuel debates on the 'historical validity of the approach', or 'the use of pastiche'—though I will gladly allow that that is what I did if it will release people from these silly arguments and bring them to the music.

The Rake's Progress is simple to perform musically but difficult to stage. Yet the chief obstacle to the staging is the failure to accept the opera for what it is. It is true, for example, that Tom's machine-baked bread may be hard to swallow, but even *it* will go down, if the stage director does not lose sight of the opera's moral fable proposition and overplay the realism of 'the Rakewell story'. After all, as Dr. Johnson said, opera is an exotic and irrational art.

And in the matter of unrealisms, the *Rake* offers nothing quite so conspicuous as the concealed-identity scene in *Un Ballo in Maschera*, and the post-stabbing coloratura concert in *Rigoletto*, to name two other operas that, like my own, I love beyond the point where criticism makes any difference. Like the next person, I have perfect 20–20 hindsight, and I am now able to see that Shadow is a preacher as well as a Devil; that the *Epilogue* is too symmetrical; that the *ostinato* style could do with more contrasts of polyphony, the dramatic opportunities for which might have been found in another ensemble or two, in which the minor characters might have been given more connection and development. Such things matter, but are not fatal. And in any case I am not concerned with the future of the opera. I only ask for a measure of present understanding.

Hotel Berkeley, Paris
8/16/64

'LA PRIMA ASSOLUTA'
(Venice, September 11, 1951)

A Memoir by VERA STRAVINSKY

It was a night of stifling heat and the sirocco was blowing like a pair of bellows. The alleys near the theatre were roped off to keep the Fourth Estate at bay during the arrival procession, although most of those in Estates 1–3 did not arrive on foot but were deposited directly at the theatre from the redolent side canal, by gondolas and motor launches. Our own (pedestrian) party included Nadia Boulanger, who carried Igor's valise, Wystan Auden and Chester Kallman (both nervous in spite of liquid fortifications—a moat of martinis, in fact), Dr. David Protetch (for whom Auden was later to write such a moving obituary), Stephen Spender, and Louis MacNeice.

Among the immediately familiar faces in the foyer, one remotely familiar one veered toward me with an expression of great excitement. It was Zinovy Peshkov, Maxim Gorky's adopted son, last seen in the Caucasus during the Revolution. But General

55

Peshkov[1] was soon crowded out by other old friends who came to criticize and otherwise 'assist' at the performance.

The Fenice glittered that night in honour of the debut, with bouquets of roses, like debutantes' corsages, garnishing each loge. But the beauty of these stalls on the inside was even less than 'skin deep', the plush seemingly having suffered from chicken, or moth pox. (They were also greatly in need of deodorants, which may have been part of the reason for the roses.) The seats, too, were uncomfortable. And they faced each other, as they do in European railroad compartments, so that the occupants on the stage side (*i.e.*, the men, if polite) are aimed in the wrong direction—an arrangement more suited to grasshoppers, whose ears are encased in their abdomens and legs.

The audience glittered, too, all except the man from *The New York Times*, whose jobbery on the event proved to be consistent not only with his apparel but with his life-long devotion to the commonplace. (*Note*: Air travel was not yet the rule at that time, hence blue denims and Beethoven sweaters were not in evidence.)

In Italy, nothing respectable begins on time. During the long delay before the curtain my thoughts drifted back through the weeks of preparation to the first conferences with stage directors and conductors. These took place in Naples, where I spent my own mornings in the aquarium—as Paul Klee once did—drawing an old *joli laide* crustacean, a 'liquid prisoner pent in walls of glass'. I thought, too, during the wait, about some of the echoes in the opera from Igor's so-called private life; of how the card game stemmed from his own fondness for cards, of how the harpsichord arpeggios imitate Igor's way of shuffling them, and of how the *staccato* of that instrument recalls his way of snapping them on a table. Wystan Auden may have seen Igor playing solitaire; and in this case he may have heard him vent some Russian *gros mots* when the wrong card appeared, which in turn may have suggested the idea for 'the Deuce!' I thought, too, how the pointing to the audience in the *Epilogue*—'you and you'—was inspired by Walter Huston in *The Devil and Daniel Webster*, a film Igor liked.

At 21:35, a prompt thirty-five minutes late, Igor entered the

[1] See Mr. Harold Macmillan's memoirs for a view of 'Colonel Pechkoff of the Gaullist mission in North Africa.

56

pit and bowed low to the audience, which, though ultra *demi-mondaine*, seemed to applaud him with a core of genuine appreciation. He then turned to the orchestra so that only his extraordinary occipital bumps and small, vital beat were visible, and began. The singers were Robert Rounseville, who had only recently emerged, or not quite fully emerged, from a career in films, but who was aptly cast as Tom Rakewell; Elisabeth Schwarzkopf, who was a cool and perfect Anne; Hugues Cuénod, a subtle, mysterious, and precise Sellem; and Jennie Tourel, who as the diva Baba was believable to the point that she could have managed her grand exit on an elephant without risking a snigger. At first-act intermission we retired to the Campo San Fantin to drink *caffè espresso*, avoid impertinent judgments, and recover from the effects of Frl. Schwarzkopf's high-C. But one of the literary people joined us here and noted that the phrase, 'and small birds twitter' (in the reprise of the brothel chorus), occurs in Wordsworth's poems (1807).

Igor used to claim no more for the music than that it was conventional. But what beautiful *in*ventions are in it, too: the chord progressions at the end of the first half of the *Cavatina*, for instance; and the modulation to 'O wilful powers'; and the transformation of the Ballad Tune in the final scenes; and the style-embalmed representations of Tom's fear in the graveyard (the double *appoggiaturas*), and their reappearance during his madness. It seemed, however, that Igor saved his finest inspirations for the last scene: in 'Venus, mount thy throne', in the duet, 'In a foolish dream', and in 'Where art thou, Venus?' which to me is the most touching music he ever wrote.

The '*prima assoluta*' was a tentative performance in many ways, at times almost 'falling apart', in fact, and everywhere showing 'might' more as the preterite of 'may' than in the sense of power. Nevertheless it conveyed much of the opera's true feeling, and I think almost everyone except the unglittering New Yorker was moved. We went afterward to a post mortem party at the Taverna Fenice that did not break up until the bleary dawn.

V.S.

Greeting Prelude

The *Greeting Prelude* was intended as a singing telegram for the eightieth birthday of Pierre Monteux, April 4, 1955, on which date it was performed by the Boston Symphony Orchestra conducted by Charles Munch. The music is a half-minute primer of canonic art for very young kiddies and critics, and it does not require any comment. I will therefore tell the story of my acquaintance with the tune. At a rehearsal in Aspen, one morning in the summer of 1950, I gave the downbeat to Tchaikovsky's Second Symphony, when instead of the doleful C minor chord out popped this ridiculously gay little tune. I was surprised, of course, as well as piqued by the change of emotions and the substitution of arsis for thesis. It was duly explained to me that one of the orchestra players had just become a father, but I suspected that it was a practical joke on myself and was not amused. Still, I remembered the tune; and a year later when I was asked to compose a fanfare for a festival in North Carolina, I set about composing canons on it, the published version of which was composed on February 18, 1955. Now that my own birthdays are beginning to reach a frightening total, the *Greeting Prelude* is sometimes sprung on me. I hardly recognized it in Stockholm, in June 1963, and it caught me offguard during a recording session in London the year after, but it will not take me unawares again.

Abraham and Isaac

Abraham and Isaac, a sacred ballad for high baritone voice and small orchestra, was composed on the Masoretic text, *Genesis* ('*reshit*) XXII. Both as accentuation and timbre, the Hebrew syllables are a fixed element of the music, hence the work cannot be sung in translation. I did not attempt to follow Hebrew cantillation, which would have imposed crippling restrictions, but the verbal and musical accentuations *are* identical (I think), and that is a rarity in my music. Words are repeated—no rarity with me—but never accompanied by exact musical repetitions. The most often reiterated is 'Abraham', and as a special mark it is sung the first time without instruments. The vocal line is partly melismatic (*bel*-cantor), partly an interval-speech of single syllables.

The six parts of the ballad, including one purely instrumental movement, are performed without interruption; each part is distinguished by a change to a successively slower pulsation. The nineteen verses are comprised in ten musical units, but whereas the story is sometimes expressed in dialogue form in the Bible, it is entirely narrated in my setting, the change of speaker being indicated by, among more interesting devices, changes in dynamics.

I do not wish the listener any luck in discovering musical descriptions and illustrations; to my knowledge none was composed, and the notes themselves are the end of the road. Nor, whatever I may have thought about the meanings of the text, am I aware of musical symbols: in the use of canons, for example, or of 'expressive' rhythmic constructions; anyone pretending to hear such things in, say, the passage referring to Isaac and the two youths, could be making too much out of a coincidence. And as for the standard demand of the programme note for references to other music, I am not aware of any in the score; certainly not to the *Pastoral* Symphony in the flute cadenza, or to *Oedipus Rex* in the '*Vayikra Malakh Adonay*'.

A twelve-note series is employed, but hexachordal and smaller units are stressed rather than the full serial orders. Octaves are common, and fifths and doubled intervals; so, too, no doubt, gravitations of key will be found to exist. But these are merely the result of concordances—or, as I call them, serial verticals, from the several serial forms—and they do not contradict the serial basis of the composition.

Of the multiple origins of every work, the most important is the least easy to describe. The initial stimulus was in my discovery of Hebrew as sound. At the same time I do not discount a strong extra-musical motivation; which is that I wished to leave a token of my gratitude and admiration for the people of Israel, to whom the score is dedicated.

I composed the first line of the text in Venice, September 8, 1962, immediately after my first visit to Israel. On January 29, 1963, I had come as far as the '*Elohim*' (with trumpet and tuba), and two weeks later had completed the *Et-Yi-Khid-Kha Mi-Me-Ni*. The score is dated March 3.

59

Elegy for J.F.K.

New York Times: Would you tell us something about the origins of the *Elegy*, Mr. Stravinsky?

Stravinsky: The idea settled on me in mid-January 1964. I thought that the events of November were being too quickly forgotten, and I wished to protest.

Did you notice, incidentally, how some of the first reactions to the assassination resembled anthropological accounts of the Divine Kingship? They were the second such manifestation within a few months, moreover, the other being the widespread fear of occultation during the solar eclipse, reminding me of the wrath-of-god stories of tribal medicine men. After the assassination, too, one could detect vestiges of the atavistic belief in the well-being of the community deriving from the well-being of the king, hence of regicide as not only the ultimate sacrilege but the act of destruction against the tribe as well. The tribe seemed to expect punishment, too, no Theban plague, but something in its own line, such as a Bear Market. There were still other reactions, naturally, and probably some people did exploit the shock for a little sensationalism of their own: 'The President is dead, therefore I must divorce my wife' sort of thing.

But I am wandering . . .

Times: You were saying that you wished to protest . . .

I.S.: By remembering. But none of this has very much to do with the piece itself. It is a quiet little lyric.

Times: How did the collaboration with Mr. Auden come about?

I.S.: At my request. Mr. Auden knows my time-scale. Moreover, in a touchy matter like this one he could be counted on to avoid anything sticky, which I say imagining the albatrosses of epic poetry and symphonic sentiment that such events give rise to and for a time excuse. I provided him with a few hazy hints, nothing important but perhaps something to help him start. I told him that I was thinking of a choral rather than a solo piece, to confine him to the simplest language. But Auden is almost too skillful. He not only anticipates the uses of music but is so ready to subordinate himself to it that he has to be circumvented to be kept far enough upstage. In this case he devised a poem of adjustable length, by means of a movable final verse repeatable anywhere as a refrain; I composed the music for this floating stanza first. His concern for the qualities of sound, incidentally, is revealed in his request at a slightly later date to 'replace *sadness* by *sorrow*: too many s's in the former and the latter is more sonorous'.

Times: When did you start to compose?

I.S.: I had the poem in hand at the beginning of March, a few days before going to Cleveland for concerts. Melodic ideas came to me as soon as I read it through, but the first phrase I could be certain would never come unglued was written in flight between Los Angeles and the Ohio city:

the hea-vens are si-lent

I quote the two notes because they are a recurring stutter in my musical speech from as long ago as *Les Noces* to the *Concerto in D*, and earlier and later than both as well—in fact a lifelong affliction.

Times: And the subsequent stages of the composition?

I.S.: I wrote the vocal part first and only then discovered the relationships from which I was able to derive the instrumental lines. Schoenberg composed his *Phantasy* that way, incidentally, the violin part first, then the piano. I finished the opus on April 1, and it was performed in Los Angeles five days later. Later that month I arranged it for mezzo-soprano.

Times: Would you describe the music as twelve-tone?

I.S.: I wouldn't. The label carries too little information now; the twelve-tone organon no longer exists, and card-carrying twelve-toners are practically extinct. A series, or row, at one time the consistently exploited basis of a composition (I do not say it was a gravitational substitute), is seldom more than a point of departure now. And in any case a serial autopsy of the *Elegy* would hardly be worth the undertaking. If I can throw any light on my method, it would be to confess that I had already joined the various melodic fragments before finding the serial pattern inherent in them. This explains why the vocal part begins with the inverted order and the clarinet part with the reverse order: the series was discovered elsewhere in the piece. The predetermination in such a procedure is very slight.

Times: Is there a relation between the series and the verse form?

I.S.: Only in that the seventeen 'notes' of the haiku are contained in a single exposition of the series.

Times: Was the haiku your idea or Mr. Auden's?

I.S.: Mr. Auden's. In fact we had talked about a different metre; but Auden is having a haiku period now, you know, like Byron and *terza rima*. Anyway, it seems to me that the *Elegy* qualifies as a haiku only by virtue of syllable counting. The *matter* of it is closer to the parsonage and the manse than to the Mysterious East.

Times: Just one more question, Mr. Stravinsky. Were the three clarinets suggested by the *Berceuses du chat*?

I.S.: Oh no, the *Berceuses* are a different kind of masterpuss . . .

Variations

The succession of pitches and intervals on which my Variations were composed

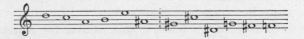

first occurred to me as a melody. The bipartite division shown here is basic, and the six-note formations are components of an importance equal to the classical twelve-note orders; the halves are units as well as fragments, moreover, and are therefore divisible in turn, and invertible, reversible, mirror-invertible, mirror-reversible.

Veränderungen—alterations or mutations—Bach's word for the 'Goldberg' Variations, describes my *Variations* as well, except that I alter or diversify a series rather than a theme or subject. In fact, I do not have a theme, in the textbook sense, whereas Bach's theme is an entire aria.

The role of rhythm seems to be larger today than ever before in music, partly because, in the absence of harmonic modulation, it must assume a larger part in the delineation of form. More than ever before, too, the composer must build rhythmic unity into his variety. In these *Variations* tempo is a variable, pulsation a constant.

So far as my own music is concerned, the twelve-part variations are the main novelty of the opus; and the one for *ponticello* violins, which sounds a little like the sprinkling of very fine broken glass, is probably the most difficult music to analyse aurally in its entirety that I have ever composed. The listener might think of these three variations as musical mobiles, whose patterns change perspective according to the different dynamic characteristics of each performance. These dense sections are set off by music of contrasting starkness and, in the first variation, by *Klangfarben* monody, which is also variation.

Length (duration) is inseparable from depth and/or height (content). But whether full, partly full, or empty, the musical statements are concise, or so I prefer to think, rather than short. Whatever anyone thinks, they are a radical contrast to the prolix speech of the music that provides the pablum of our concert life; and therein lies a difficulty, mine with you no less than yours with me.

I do not know how to guide the listener, except to urge him to listen not once but repeatedly. He should not be concerned about the boundary lines of each variation but should try instead to hear the form as a whole. The orchestra itself is a guide, though, for its contrasts of families and individuals—flutes, bassoons, trombones have the leading solo roles—are a principal projective element of the symmetries and reversibles of the form. The orchestral *dramatis personae* is unusual in that four, rather than the standard five, string parts are required (there is but one group of violins), and in that all parts must be equal in weight. No percussion instruments are used, but their function is filled by the piano and harp, which are treated as a couple. The trumpet and horn families have singularly little to do, and perhaps my economy is inconsistent in employing them at all, but I needed only a spot of 'red' and a dab of 'blue'.

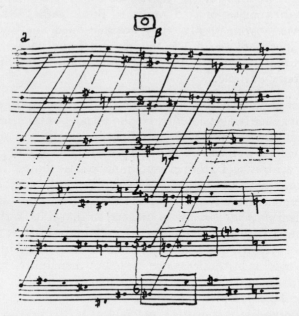

Stravinsky's first serial chart for the orchestral *Variations*.

The composition was begun at Santa Fe in July 1963, and the first twelve-part variation was completed on August 12. The *Fugato* was finished on August 13 of the following year, and the twelve-part wind variation on October 15. The whole composition was completed in Los Angeles, October 28, 1964. The first performance took place in Chicago the following April 17, since which time the music has been analysed more than it has been performed. The *Variations* are dedicated to the memory of my dear friend, the late Aldous Huxley.

Introitus: T. S. Eliot in Memoriam

In this small parting song for the great poet, the Introitus of the Latin Requiem Service is intoned by tenors and basses to an accompaniment of string and percussion instruments restricted to male-voice range. I composed the vocal line straight through, the first five words of the text coming to my ear in the twelve pitches of a series.

The only novelty in serial treatment is in chord structure—the chant is punctuated by fragments of a chordal dirge—but choice was more important than any principle of 'seriation'. The four melodic versions of the pitch orders are sung as a *cantus firmus* and in the form of a recessional, which is a small ritual the poet might have liked. When, with the fourth phrase, the trapezium shape is complete, the two choral parts unite and the last sentence is sung in counterpoint. The music of '*et lux perpetua*' is a quotation of my setting of Auden's line 'The Heavens are silent'.

The only instrumental novelty is the incidence of the complete series in timpani *coperti*. The main function of the viola and string bass is to support and clarify the tuning of these funeral drums.

The score was completed February 17, 1965, and performed in Chicago the following April 17.

66

A MEMOIR
Some Table Talk of T. S. Eliot

I first met T. S. Eliot on a December afternoon in 1956, while in London for a concert of my music in St. Martin's-in-the-Fields. I invited him for tea, but as it happened he arrived at the appointed place, the Savoy Grill Room, before me, and was waiting when I appeared. (On a later occasion he said that from seeing me on concert podiums he had expected a taller man. Conversely, I had anticipated less imposing proportions; his big, rather stolid and cumbrous frame seemed an unnecessarily large refuge even for so much shyness and modesty.) Conversation was not very easy or 'flowing', and at times you could almost hear the waiters silently polishing the silverware, as if for a wake. The Savoyard sandwiches helped, however, and so did the tea (whisky, in practice). Eliot would turn his head from speaker to speaker with a slight jerk, and from time to time emit a nervous-tic 'yes' or 'hm', which could make you feel he was registering an unfavourable impression. 'Hm, well, yes, perhaps, but not precisely in that way,' he seemed to say, and when he actually *did* say, 'Then you really think so?' the inflection left you wondering whether you would ever again be so rash as to 'think' or assert anything at all. Even the slight pause after your remarks seemed to have been timed to allow you to savour their full fatuity. This account of mine is coloured by perspective, of course, and by the need to make the subject pose to enhance a point. And I neglected to preface it by saying that I revered Eliot not only as a poet and sorcerer of words but as the very key-keeper of the language.

We managed to talk, nevertheless, and while I hardly recall the topics, I know that Wagner was one; and *Cymbeline* another, for I was on my way to see it that night at the Old Vic; and

Rudolph Kassner, whose 'On Vanity' Eliot had published in an early *Criterion*; and ballet. Eliot was an able critic of dance technique, and, in fact, a critic of more varied and versatile interests than is generally known.

Eliot has drawn his own portraits—Sweeney, Tiresias, the church warden, Old Possum—and the truest of them will remain these creations by himself. But why should we look for another, or ask what he was 'like'? (That the creations *are* the man is proven by a parody of *Prufrock* I have just fallen into in an attempt to describe him: 'deferential but a bit severe, and somewhat restless, somewhat weary, somewhat grave.') He may also have been a great actor, with a secret life behind his words, but I do not think so, and for me, in any case, his prepared faces, as he called them, are enough.

My recollections of our last two meetings are more distinct. The earlier occasion is associated with a fiftieth-anniversary performance of *Le Sacre du printemps* in, of all changes of venue from the Théâtre des Champs-Élysées, Albert Hall. The Eliots, who lived near by, had invited me for a drink after these, as they turned out, depressing revels. And Eliot applauded me as I crossed the threshold of his apartment. He had heard the concert 'on the wireless'—he was fond of horsedrawn phrases—and he compared the 'ovation' after it with 'the shaky reception in 1921, when the audience refrained from demonstrations but was in a violent mood'.

A Homburg was on the hat-stand in the vestibule, and, more optimistically, a straw Stetson for next winter's Bahama beach. The walls here were graced with drawings of cats by Eliot's father, and an autograph letter by Coleridge framed together with a *précis* of his life and work written by Eliot for a BBC programme during the war, and retrieved from his waste-basket by Mrs. Eliot, then her future husband's secretary. The art displayed in the other rooms included a water colour by Henry Moore; a water colour by Ruskin in the manner of Turner, which Eliot aptly described as 'gradely'; an Edward Lear landscape; some Wyndham Lewis drawings; Jacob Epstein's head of Eliot; and several towers of books standing on the end tables like modern sculptures.

Conversation centered for a time around the Derby, which I had watched on television at Oxford in the afternoon and on which I had lost a bet. Eliot remarked that he 'used to wager in the Calcutta Sweepstakes but never drew a horse. During a visit to Stockholm in 1948 I put some money on a long shot called "Queen Mary"—out of loyalty, of course; it was not a hunch—but we came in last.' He asked about my impressions of the Soviet Union on my trip there some months before, and he was particularly keen to hear whether I had noted any very striking changes in pronunciation. (I hadn't.) Then he said he had received the poet Yevtushenko a short time ago, but that 'the young man's eyes were frightened, and he was too careful of what he was saying and of what I would think, though I am quite unable to speak through a translator myself unless I know him'. He also said that one of my Russian 'r's reminded him of the variety of 'r' sounds in Sanskrit, 'which Indians do not recognize as differentiations, although they pronounce them'.

Switching to his own work, Eliot said that a re-reading of his doctoral thesis on F. H. Bradley had shown him that Bradley was a primary influence on his own prose style. He then remarked that the best parts of his new essay on George Herbert were the quotations, but he had not had a sense of his audience while writing it, he added (as if he did not know that his audiences were the English departments of several thousand American universities). 'Herbert is a great poet,' he continued, 'and one of the very few I can still read and read again. Mallarmé is another, incidentally, and, hm, so is Edward Lear.' And with this he boasted of not having read any serious prose fiction since 1927. 'I think the last novel was *Middlemarch* . . . no, I am forgetting *The Heart of Midlothian*, which I enjoyed in hospital a few years ago. I confess I never finished *War and Peace*. But one shouldn't say so, I suppose. Remarks like that cut the critics' cake in half.'

As I was due to go to Dublin for a concert in a few days, he offered some comments about the city. 'When I lectured there, almost every Irishman to whom I was introduced told me that almost every other Irishman was not to be trusted.' He said, too, that the account of his meeting with Joyce in Wyndham Lewis's *Blasting and Bombardiering* was accurate. The thought of lecturing reminded him of a tour in Germany, shortly after the war, during which he read his Goethe essay; but my own memory is ajar now, and I recall only that he complained about 'official receptions at which totally humourless people tried to shout ultimate philosophy back and forth with me'. Then he asked if I had noticed, on the other hand, 'how English people laugh when they are confronted with something serious that they do not understand, because they wish to be polite'.

I described my visit to Hampton Court, the day before, remarking that Giulio Romano's portrait of Isabella d'Este there is remarkable only for the snarling effect produced by the everted lower lip, whereas, for comparison, Titian's portrait reveals the woman's intelligence. This got us on to the subject of Ferrara and the emanations from the Romagnol hemp that supposedly addle the natives but do not account for the oddity of such characters as Pirro Ligorio, and Gesualdo, and Biagio Rossetti. Eliot said that he was bitten once by Ferrarese fleas, and though details were not forthcoming, I assumed the incident must have occurred in a 'one-night cheap hotel'. I remember that he used the word 'transpadane' in this description, and though it may have had to be dredged up and artificially resuscitated, it was, like all of Eliot's words, both exact and beautiful.

I was very touched that night by Mrs. Eliot's devotion to her husband, by her gentleness with him when he rested his head on her shoulder for a moment or squeezed her hand. His marriage to her was undoubtedly the happiest event of his life.

What was destined to be our last meeting came about seven months later (December 12), in New York. While T.S.E., when I called for him at the River Club, on East Fifty-Second Street, was swathed in mufflers, pullover, heavy blue cashmere overcoat, Mrs. Eliot entered the limousine complaining about overheated American hotels and wearing not only no coat or wrap, but a silk frock. As we drove away from the Club, Eliot said he was especially fond of East Fifty-Second Street because 'it is a dead end, which makes it so convenient'. Then as we caught sight of the United Nations building, he said he suspected 'an anti-European conspiracy' was afoot there.

But all was not well. His walk faltered, and the restaurant's revolving door had to be held back to enable him to pass through. And there were other tokens of his progressing illness. His complexion was cinereous, and his throat-clearings were frequent and somewhat convulsive. He bent over his plate, drinking a little but hardly eating at all. Two or three times he raised himself bolt upright and fixed us in those clear hazel eyes, the force of whose intelligence was undiminished. But his voice had dwindled to a scrannel murmur. And owing to his low resonance, other speakers tended to jam him with their louder equipment, myself included, for I always talk too much when I find my neighbours difficult to understand.

The conversation began with some exchanges on Joseph Conrad, in whom I have a special interest both because his Polish-Ruthenian background was partly the same as my own (he had lived as a small child in Chernigov, which is near my father's birthplace), and because, like myself, he moved in maturity from a Slav culture with French inlay to an English-speaking culture. Eliot described Conrad as 'a Grand Seigneur, the grandest I have ever met, but it was a terrible shock after reading him to hear him talk. He had a very guttural accent.' 'Was it like mine?' I asked. And Eliot replied that mine was easier to understand, which did not quite answer the question. He was re-reading *Nostromo* at the moment, he said, and he declared *Youth* and *The End of the Tether* to be 'the finest stories of their kind that I know'.

Lamenting the untimely death of Louis MacNeice, Eliot said that he had had 'a very warm feeling for him, but he was a disappointing person to meet'. Of St.-John Perse, Eliot remarked that what he most admired about him was 'his handwriting and his intelligence', which both raised and forbade one to ask the question whether he meant he did *not* like the poems. Mention of Apollinaire provoked the opinion that *Alcools* was greatly overrated. As always with Eliot, some of the talk was about language, and Eliot told me (no, Eliot never 'told', he imparted) that his Italian had been fluent during his period at Lloyds Bank. 'But it was Dante's Italian, not the most suitable instrument for modern business phraseology. I had a smattering of Romanian and modern Greek, too, and this for some reason convinced the manager of the bank that I also knew Polish; in fact he was incredulous when I said I did not, as if it were downright illogical not to know Polish when one knew Romanian and Greek.'

We drank gin martinis (except for Eliot who took a daiquiri); a Pouilly-Fumé; a Cheval Blanc; Armagnac (but Eliot took a Drambuie). In the Armagnac–Drambuie stage he suddenly sat straight up and, using my first name for the first time ever, proposed a toast to 'another ten years for both of us'. But perdurability on that scale seemed so improbable that the clink of our glasses rang hollow, and the words sounded more like a farewell; obviously he felt closer to me than ever before. Then, too, warmed by the wines, he decided to shed his pullover, exposing flamboyant flannel braces in the process, as a ringside of Le Pavillon patrons (*luxe, calme,* and fat bank accounts) gazed on aghast.

The assassination of the President was mentioned, and Eliot said that during the past winter in Nassau he had had two telephone calls from the White House inviting him respectively to a dinner for Nobel Prize winners and to another, general gathering. 'And of all horrible coincidences,' he continued, 'can you believe that I was once made an honourary deputy sheriff of Dallas?' And though I didn't say it, no, in fact I could not see Eliot in boots and spurs, badge and ten-gallon hat.

At every meeting with the poet the conversation was eventually drawn to the Mississippi, but as much on my account as on his, the lure of the river having been instilled in me as in many Russian children by reading Mark Twain; when I first came to America and regularly travelled from coast to coast by train, the crossing of the 'strong, brown god'—though the god of the poem, as Eliot once corrected me, is 'the muddy "Mo" '—was always a thrill. That night Eliot described how on cold mornings in the Missouri of his youth the housekeeper came to his room 'to light the fire under a kettle of water and pull a tub from under the bed'. And he added that when he gave the Yeats memorial lecture at Trinity College, Dublin, during the war, 'an old charwoman came in the morning, lighting a fire in my room and pulling the same kind of tub from under my bed, which made me feel as though I were a boy again, and back in Missouri'.

Eliot was a touching figure that night. Stopping for our coats on our way out of the restaurant, we could not help overhearing the *maître d'hotel* say to the *vestiaire* that 'there you see the greatest living poet and the greatest living composer together'. But my wife saved the day by saying in just the right tone, 'Well, they do their best.'

PART TWO
Interviews

TRANSCRIPT
OF BBC TELEVISION INTERVIEW

Hollywood, November 5, 1965

I invited Wystan Auden to write the *Rake's Progress* libretto because I was attracted by his talents as a versifier. I have never been able to compose music to prose, even or especially to poetic prose, and what I needed was a versifier with whom I could collaborate in writing songs. This may seem an unusual starting point for an opera, most other composers having sought qualities of dramatic imagination in their librettists, or powers of invention in theatrical situations. But I gave all priority to verse, trusting that we would be able to evolve a dramatic form together, and that it would inspire him to dramatic poetry.

He *was* inspired, and he inspired me. In fact I wonder whether any poet since the Elizabethans has made a composer such a beautiful gift of words for music as the 'Lanterloo' dance in our opera. He had a genius for operatic wording, moreover, his lines being the right length for singing, and his words the right ones to sustain musical emphasis. Their character and succession always suggested musical speeds, too, but without imposing them. No less convenient, the rhythmic values of his verse could be altered through singing without destroying the verse; or perhaps I had better say that at least the author has never complained.

At a different level, I discovered when we began to work together that we shared the same beliefs not only about the opera, but also about the nature of the Beautiful and the Good. Thus the opera is a collaboration in the highest sense.

Wystan has lived in Austria too long now. I wish you could convince him to come back. We cannot afford to lend our greatest poet to the Germans.

77

IN THE NAME OF JEAN-JACQUES!

New York, January 1964

Show Magazine: What did you think of *The Last Savage*, Mr. Stravinsky?

Stravinsky: I did very little thinking, I assure you.

Show: But did you enjoy it?

I.S.: Not really. One sees everything miles away but has to wait eons while a largely anonymous and never good-enough composer slowly and without ever confounding any expectation brings it near. And that first scene! Well, what *is* the opposite of a flying start! A diving start?

Show: How would you characterize the work generally?

I.S.: As unconscious slapstick. In musical tendency it is 'farther out' than anything in a decade, but in the wrong direction.

Show: Is it really so humourless? By all accounts the Metropolitan audience . . .

I.S.: Exactly.

Show: A Met audience *is* rather special, you know.

I.S.: Yes. Many of them would have come to the late Mr. Blitzstein's *Sacco and Vanzetti* expecting a contemporary *Romeo and Juliet*.

Show: But are audiences entirely responsible for their ignorance?

I.S.: Hardly. They may 'like what they know', but before they can 'know what they like', they must be given an opportunity to choose. If instead of *Cav* and *Pag*, *Adrianna Lecouvreur*, *Manon*, *Samson*, *Andrea Chénier* and so on through the last few seasons, the Met audience had been offered good productions of a few contemporary masterpieces, could it be served with such an ear of corn as *The Last Savage*? Naturally the Met audience is palateless, and naturally it does not know how to receive anything new.

Show: But what *are* the masterpieces of contemporary opera?

78

I.S.: *Wozzeck, Lulu, Erwartung, Moses und Aron*, even perhaps my *Rake* and my *Rex*; even possibly something by Janáček, though the only example of which I have had any experience was the thinnest, longest, and least succulent noodle I have ever tried to swallow. Admittedly none of these is very new, but none except *Wozzeck* and the *Rake* has ever been staged by the Met. A contemporary masterpiece needs the support of a whole community of contemporary operas, however, masterpieces or not, and certainly *The Last Savage* should be one of them. But to bring it forth alone suggests the Machiavellian possibility that the Met is using it as an alibi to prove that contemporary operas are not worth doing.

Show: Did you find no merit in the music at all?

I.S.: I enjoyed the 'dodecaphonic' string quartet. The composer should try an entire dodecaphonic scene in his next opera. Otherwise the last nine-tenths of the music might have been composed by feeding the first tenth to a machine. Of course I appreciate that it was intended as parody, and even partly sympathize with the composer's desire that the twelve-tone system should 'drop dead'. But parody is effective only as an excursus from a home style, which is what *The Savage* lacks. Pastiche, too, requires a certain talent. Thus when the composer tries to launch an ensemble with the rhythm of '*Zitti, zitti*,' he invites and receives devastating comparison. To ridicule 'modern life' with pseudo-Mascagni is not easy, moreover—leaving aside the question of whether an assault on the kingdoms of this world is the proper business of a composer who has made it all on this side. It is somewhat later, as the saying goes, than the composer of *The Savage* thinks.

Show: Do you concede no personality at all to the music? Aren't such devices as the 'Oh Mother, Oh Mother' in *Amahl*, and the 'Oh Father, Oh Father' in *The Savage*—aren't they marks of a *persona*?

I.S.: They are the composer's bread and butter, at any rate.

Show: In short?

I.S.: In short.

A TALK WITH STRAVINSKY

> There was money in the air, ever so much money—that
> was, grossly expressed, the sense of the whole intimation.
> And the money was to be for all the most exquisite things
> —all the most exquisite things except creation . . .
>
> HENRY JAMES: *The American Scene*

New York, January 1965

New York Review: We hope you are enjoying your stay in New
York, Mr. Stravinsky. Have you been to any interesting concerts or other performances?

I.S.: No concerts. But I attended a good enough performance
of *Falstaff* at the Metropolitan. And, oh yes, there was a television programme about Pablo Casals. The cellist and Zoltán
Kodály were talking at some length (a half-hour, in fact, in the
unreleased portion of the film) about the trouble with me, which
is that I must always be doing the latest thing—*they* say, who
have been doing exactly the same old thing for the last hundred
years. After attacking me, Señor Casals offered extracts of his
philosophy. He is against Franco, in favour of peace and of
playing Bach in the style of Brahms. But never mind. You
wished to talk about music-reviewing.

N.Y.R.: We wanted to ask you why you bother to complain
about it, since it is so inconsequential in the long run.

I.S.: The short run is what concerns me. And what I protest is
the right to say it—Voltaire in reverse. The right must be earned
by knowledge and skill. But few of the present, or yesterday's,
or in fact the perennial crop of reviewers, ever do earn it. It
was said to me recently in a certain reviewer's defense that
though he may often be wrong, at least he is honest. I find this
both illogical and, as an indication of the state of ethics, alarm-
ing. It is not the *honesty* of the opinion that matters but its worth.
And has honesty become so exceptional that it deserves citation?

N.Y.R.: What is your main complaint against the present system of reviewing?

I.S.: When the time limit is very short, the review of a new composition (performance is another matter) should be confined to reporting rather than to snap-judging. Undoubtedly the reviewer should possess some qualifications, too, such as a good audiogram report. At the moment the only requirement is the knack of delivering the five hundred more or less readable words in the allotted hour and a half. In New York, this capacity to deliver the pulp, whether the daily dose or the Sunday causerie, can capture thrones of authority in each of several formerly quite specialized fields. *The Times* has demonstrated its promiscuous hospitality in this regard by successively transferring a sportswriter to the desks of chief music critic and chief drama critic.

N.Y.R.: But does that matter? After all, critical organs *do* exist, of a different calibre from the dailies and weeklies.

I.S.: Again, I am talking about the short run. Delayed and deliberated reactions exercise far less effect on the immediate, popular-minded commercial processes by which musicians live. A bad, meaning unfavourable, newspaper notice may have disastrous consequences for the gifted unknown whose work, if it were in any way truly new, probably could not be evaluated on a single hearing anyway.

N.Y.R.: What kind of consequences? Do such matters differ substantially today from other times?

I.S.: The answer to the first is that further performances and publication are very definitely affected by the reviews. To the second, I can say that the position of the composer has changed radically, but whether it is more parlous commercially today I do not know. The performance outlets available to him are few, and the circuits heavily overloaded. This is why he has had to become an entrepreneur, and form performing organizations that can be used to swap performances with other composer–entrepreneurs. His artistic position, meanwhile, is composed mainly of dilemmas. 'As luck will have it', he hears on one side, and on another, 'Long live combinatoriality', yet he has probably not even been informed of the existence of these concepts at his conservatory, which instead has grounded him in techniques that are about as useful to him now as spare parts for machinery last manufactured some seventy-five years ago. His subsequent teachers, moreover, have undoubtedly bewildered him all the more by their own ever more cynical departures on the seasonal bandwagons. Though in fairness to the teacher it must be admitted that at no other period in the art has notation itself fallen into such abuse that notational gimmicks and musical invention could be confounded. In sum, contemporary music is a complex affair at every level and it should be ruled over at none by amateur critics.

N.Y.R.: But composers *are* published and performed, some good ones included, if only by laws of averages.

I.S.: Yes. But the whole cannot be absolved by a few happy accidents. The argument of the whole, of course, is the argument of quantity, which is specious and grossly misrepresentative. Some recent hoopla on the nation's culture in *Time* Magazine included the claim that our symphony orchestras have grown in number 'from 800 to 1300' since 1950, and that 'eighteen million classical records' were sold in the United States last year. Now whatever the slant of truth in these figures, it and they are as dangerously misleading as any outright falsehood. The statements are outrageously incomplete, of course, and as such, not harmless nonsense but culpable distortion. *Which* classical records? 17.9 million Tchaikovsky retreads? (And why are they called *high* fidelity records? Isn't fidelity enough?) The count of symphony orchestras, moreover, must be about ninety-eight per cent inflated. Of those deserving the name, we have more likely grown from eight to thirteen, though I doubt that as many as thirteen offer full-time livelihood to their entire personnel, and I am certain that far fewer than thirteen are capable of preparing first-rate performances of the new scores of our leading contemporary composers. In fact, I know of *no* combination of a major orchestra with its *resident* conductor—the failure of the New York Philharmonic to play the complete Wolpe Symphony last year is a case in point—to which such a composer as Elliott Carter might entrust a major new work (Magna Carter). But the lack of alignment between composers and performers is another large question, one that is reflected by the absence, even in the *title*, of the word 'Creative', in those proliferating Centers for Performing Arts. For the moment it is enough of a point to expose the disservice in a type of cultural publicity and to arouse the suspicions of gulled readers of statistical fictions.

N.Y.R.: Would you comment on any other aspect of that culture cover story?

I.S.: As I said, it showed the need of redefining the object, for the object of a Music Center is not by any means music *tout court*. Los Angeles, for example, chose to baptize its Center with Strauss's *Fanfare* and Respighi's *Feste Romane*, two culture products of what used to be called the Axis. Now at the risk of being called a chauvinist, I will go so far as to suggest that music by Los Angeles composers might have been a more apt choice, even possibly music by a refugee *from* the Axis—Schoenberg, for instance, the fact of whose residence in the movie village would be acknowledged in less remote parts of the world as the choicest flower it could have worn in its musical buttonhole at such an event. To play Respighi rather than Schoenberg at the debut of a Los Angeles Music Center is like unveiling a bust of Lysenko instead of Einstein at the opening of a museum of science at Princeton; or dedicating a museum of art in Cannes with an exposition of Buffet rather than Picasso. In the dark of antics such as these the celebration of our cultural coming of age seems more than a little ludicrous. In fact, our culture politics are about as competent as our world politics, except that the former is ruled by an inferiority, the latter by a superiority complex. America was eminently 'of age' with C. S. Peirce, Henry Adams, Ives, of course, and in fact it sometimes looks—the view from the eastern side of the bridge, anyway—to be growing the other way.

N.Y.R.: To return to our question about reviewers, Mr. Stravinsky? Are they alone responsible, or are they victims of the system as well?

I.S.: They are both, sometimes. But I have tried to impute to them no more than their share; and certainly I do not hold them responsible every time. In fact only yesterday I found myself defending them. This remarkable occurrence was provoked by a tape of the new Covent Garden *Wozzeck*, and a chance reading afterward of a file of the reviews. The failure of the latter to mention that the singing was at least half of the time very wide of the mark in respect to pitch was unanimous. But are the reviewers entirely to blame? The vocal parts in the denser passages are difficult to follow even now, after all, and in the case of a 50-year-old classic such as *Wozzeck*, is the reviewer not justified in assuming that at some point in the preparation the conductor would have discovered and arrested the wholesale tendency to sing wrong notes?

But to restore the picture to *status quo*, I will conclude with another instance, fresh from my own experience, in which I think the reviewer is at fault. The New York newspaper which knows what is 'fit to print' recently described my *Abraham and Isaac* as 'monotonous' and 'minor'. Now, both epithets may very well be 'true' (I have no doubt that they represent the writer's 'honest opinion'); but they have to be explained, the impression has to be justified. The reader deserves the dignity of argument, and if the reviewer cannot supply it, he should stick to the facts of reporting. The two words, by themselves and thrown like mud, are nothing.

N.Y.R.: Do you have any observations to offer concerning the approach to criticism?

I.S.: You must be able to *hear* (have some conception of) what you are listening to. And you must find a point of balance between past and present. The new cannot be isolated from the old, yet must not be judged entirely in terms of it either. The question then turns to the measurement of the individuating newness. Of how, for example, to describe whatever in my new *Variations* is new? And whatever it may be, it came to me naturally, yet cannot seem natural to a critic, even to one who knows me in the form of my entire past, for the simple reason that he is not me. The usual approach to the new, however, depends on the identification of 'influences', which in my case has resulted of late in some jejune comparisons with isorhythmic motets. To such critics the Variations will no doubt reveal that I have received a transfusion from Messiaen or been sideswiped by Stockhausen.

N.Y.R.: Do you expect the practices you deplore to be corrected on the accession of a new generation?

I.S.: For what reason, by what training and what example now in operation? No. In fact I am tempted to fly to the other extreme of '*plus ça change . . .*' except that it is an even less likeable complacency. Let us suppose for a moment that it was *not* complacency, though, but a matter of biology. Suppose that a kind of Bertillon measurement was discovered for reviewers? After all, cockroaches have not changed in these 150,000,000 years.

A PERFECT TOTAL

. . . I would rejoice in it more
If I knew more clearly what
We wanted the knowledge for . . .
>> AUDEN: *After Reading A Child's Guide*
>> *to Modern Physics*

Seventeen: Mr. Stravinsky, what are some of the general problems facing young people who wish to pursue careers in the arts—not the timeless problems of art, but those peculiar to our age of science?

I.S.: Generality itself is one of the largest. But before I go on, let me say that I consider it a mistake to think of making in art, as distinguished from selling in art—giving interviews, newspaper reviewing, teaching, lecturing to women's clubs, conducting orchestras—in terms of a career. Making is its own end; there is no other. As to generality, the problem is that whereas in past cultures the arts interpreted, symbolized, adorned general ideas—religious beliefs, 'ends', etc.—the general no less than the particular ideas of science are incomprehensible to artists and are likely to remain so. How, then, is an artist who aspires to associate with science to make his arrangements with (how interpret, symbolize, adorn?) ideas that he is able to apprehend only through the paraphrases of an intermediate and inexact language of words? How, in fact, is he even to make his representations *against* them in the event that, like myself, he objects to being taken for a ride to an unannounced destination as a strap-hanger to concepts he does not understand? Speaking for myself, I can say that *my* generalities, apart from my work, are those of a remote and comparatively primitive past. But this is no help to young people whose work is yet to be fashioned. Thank heaven, or some other generality, that you only ask me to name the difficulties, not to try to solve them.

Another large one is the increasing domination by technical

processes, or 'means'. And closely related to it, a chief consequence of it, in fact, is the problem of the increasingly rapid
turnover of conventions. And here I should stop—having some
views of my own on these two points—and try to disentangle
myself from the wool of my own generalities. Except that one
further problem on my list is the only one on which I am *really*
qualified to speak: old age, that nightmare even to a few near-
nonegenarian newsworthies such as myself who have escaped
the neglect which, thanks partly to the news-drugged public's
obsession with novelty, is the fate of the elderly.

Seventeen: Would you explain what you mean by encroaching
technical processes and the consequences thereof?

I.S.: Consider the effect of recording both as industry and as art.
For one thing, the distribution of printed music, which in any
case can no longer be imagined by *reading*, has little or no
influence any more compared with the distribution of recordings.
Thanks to the latter, the latest product to come on the market
can go directly from the launching pad in the European and
American fashion center to Djakarta, Stanleyville, Des Moines.
But if world standardization is a dismaying prospect, it is a
lesser one, to me, than that of the technical domination of the
performance itself. Recording technique has been determined
by wasteful competition. It is now at the stage where the
manufactured performance supplants the true one, and where,
moreover, most of us, on choice, would reject the true, being so
accustomed to the refinements of technical processing that we
find the natural to be less and less acceptable. Natural balance,
natural dynamics, natural echo, natural colour, natural human
error: these have been replaced by added echo and reverberation, by a neutralizing dynamic range, by filtered sound, by an
engineered balance. (In fact, it has seemed to me at orchestra
concerts of late that the players are lost without the sound
engineer to tell them what to do, and that the conductors, for
the same reason, hardly bother about dynamic relationships.)
The resulting record is a super-glossy, chem-fab music-substi-
ture never heard on sea or land, or even in Philadelphia.
Obviously, recording requires improvements—such as the
editing out of gross and distracting errors—so long as the vital
cohesion of the performance is not intercepted. But sound

engineers and tape-splicers have exceeded minor surgery of this kind by so much that they deserve equal billing with the conductor.

Seventeen: What do you mean by convention?

I.S.: Something quite comprehensive. But the impinging notions are numerous and I cannot offer a definition. I could say that I am a conventional composer myself, but that would shed no light as I am unable to imagine any other kind. And I could turn to some of the labels conventionally cast in opposition to 'conventional', such as 'revolutionary' and 'spontaneous', but the attitudes evoked thereunder would prove to have their conventions, too, however different the emphasis put on the word. Or I could try definition *per differentiam*, and discard meanings that are definitely *not* mine, such as the equating of the conventional with the old-fashioned. But this is meaningless to me because a fashion is a smaller word for a lesser phenomenon. Thus the fashions of the fifties included automobile tail-fins, jazzy glasses, and snoods, but the principle governing the incidence of such things is a convention, partly of economics. The word is applied also to a kind of art that carries over with little change from its immediate legacy; Rachmaninoff is an example, and so, I think, is most commercially successful art. And the word is used in still another sense by cartographers, as I have lately learned from *The Vinland Map*, a 'conventional' outline meaning a copy of an existing one, as distinguished from a 'realistic' outline, which is one that has actually been explored.

But these are *not* my meanings, as I said. To me, conventions are codes of agreement and, as such, agencies of tradition and genre. They differ from traditions in that they are modified rather than developed. And in that they are tied to a time: traditions, being major lines of descent, are timeless. Perhaps tradition might be thought of as a universal fact of art, and convention as a local fact.

Doubtless you recall the discussion in the *Cratylus*, Socrates refereeing at first, then refuting Hermogenes' argument that names are not attached to things by nature but are conventions of the users? Well, so far as my *art* is concerned I am on the side of Hermogenes, even though he is opposed by modern philology, which holds that names possess 'echoic' value and that word conventions are anything but arbitrary; and by modern physics, too, if I understand Dr. Oppenheimer's 'prejudices of nature'. But in art, the agreements of the users, the mutual understanding of the parties to the artistic transaction, are enough. Derivations in nature are not the artist's affair, nature being only another convention to him.

Seventeen: Then why does the accelerating speed with which conventions are modified nowadays so disturb you?

I.S.: Because the community of criteria that has always existed somewhere in the background has crumbled. But does it matter, you say, won't posterity sort the sheep from the goats? Well, I am not very confident of time's justice, and it is to me complacent to think that though what *is* may be wrong, time will right it. (Was Solon the first to claim that time will tell the truth, and Mill to claim the contrary, that 'Truth has [no] inherent power denied to error, of prevailing'? But time can consecrate the wrong. All histories are deterministic, offering not 'what was', but the determinations of 'what was', conscious and unconscious, of the choosers. I have lived long enough to have watched 'history' in operation on my own music, to have seen the complexion put upon the same pieces turn from Red red to Establishment grey. What actually occurred was that the music recorded the conditions of its own environment, provoked reaction and was reacted upon in turn, according to laws of social biology the historians did not take into account.

Seventeen: Are conventions modified in a similar manner? Does a biological transforming process of some kind take place until at some point the succession of modifications produces a new species? Thus electronically fabricated sound might be described as a mutation.

I.S.: But that is picture language, no more, and only a further contribution to the semantic mess.

Seventeen: Are the semantic obstacles greater between yourself and your audience, Mr. Stravinsky, or between yourself and your colleagues?

I.S.: I imagine that they are about equal. I feel about equally estranged, at any rate.

Seventeen: And how do you envisage your audience today?

I.S.: It has no visage for me. I do not have any audience in mind when I compose. Audiences exist for my past works, but they have yet to be developed for my present ones. I deplore the breach, but, unlike some of my more socially active colleagues, I do not believe that a *rapprochement* in a musically backward direction can close it. The attempt to return to past safeties is as futile, it seems to me, as the proposal to return to conventional (another meaning!)—pre-H- or A-bomb—weapons. We can neither put back the clock nor slow down our speed, and as we are already flying pilotless, on instrument controls, it is probably even too late to ask where we are going.

Seventeen: A final question concerning the last of the problems you mentioned: age. How do you see yourself in relation to the youth of today?

I.S.: As a discarded automobile in one of those roadside grave-yards is seen by speeding motorists. But I do not mind the relegation. Nor has my long experience watching each year's crop of youths arrive and unpack suitcases full of bright new ideas made me unduly cynical. These young people and myself are a necessary equation. So are the two of *us*, your seventeen and my eighty-three. Together we make a perfect total.

A DECADE LATER

When sounds are smooth and clear, and have a single pure tone, then they are not relatively but absolutely beautiful. *Philebus*, 51

Music unites the contrary attributes of being both intelligible and untranslatable.
LEVI-STRAUSS, *The Raw and the Cooked*

University of Washington Interviewer: You were complaining about Antonolatry, Mr. Stravinsky, saying that it is time to replace cultism with criticism.

I.S.: Still, we should not altogether despise cults, and as prime movers they are more useful than critics; our knowledge of Webern is almost entirely due to them. But they tend to become dome-shaped, and domes tend to exclude the light. The Webern cult, moreover, made the mistake of switching from the music to the musician, always a barren devotion, but especially so in this instance because of the unexploitable nature of the mahatma-to-be. Now the pendulum has started back. Tastes and discriminations are beginning to emerge. Soon we will have to listen from a new angle. But poor Webern!

U.W.I.: What do you mean by that?

I.S.: I was musing on the destiny of artists, to be subject to the depredations of amateur appraisers, with their cycles of inflation and deflation. Webern suffers from the latter at present, mainly because of the over-supply of simulacra produced by cheap, or, more precisely—for Foundation wages are generous— superficial labour. Even the thought of such commerce would have been comprehensible to the composer, and the heliocentricity accorded him—above Schoenberg!—by, for example, the Domaine Musical (with its anti-Brahms deaf spot, and hence the Brahmsian heredity in Schoenberg,) would have shocked him.

Nothing in the appraisals of a decade ago was more absurd than the Schoenberg-Webern syzygy. Over to you, U.W.I.

U.W.I.: But is the state of the market the only reason for the *de*flation, or was there some real, meaning artistic, *in*flation?

I.S.: A bit of the latter, surely, but errors of inflation on a first encounter with the radically new should not surprise us. What *does* amaze is the attempt to multiply originality. One would have thought that the more original and individual, so, obviously, the more unrepeatable and inimitable. Yet multiplication became the rule, and not only of 'abstract structural devices' (as if there were any other kind) but of the tone of voice. The manufacture of pseudo-Webern has been discontinued now, however, and in fact the group that sprang from him into prominence in the fifties now tends to see him as a 'precursor', a sort of tugboat which, having brought to shore such liners as themselves, can be sent to rest in shallow waters (where for companionship it will find another old skiff in myself). At times, too, one has the impression that Webern's precursory miniatures are programmed along with grander confections from the newer establishments only to show how his music has been 'turned to wider account' and 'given more scope'. That the newer establishments are meant to supersede is clear, too, for they have recognized the futility of the serial techniques Webern was so obsessed with and consigned the method to completed history (between-the-wars Vienna, according to the dates on the tombstone). In short, today's progressive has formed a coalition with yesterday's non-starter, meaning anyone who opposed the substitution of an 'arbitrary order' (those Draconian twelve-tone laws!) for a 'natural gravitational system', as if both the arbitrary and the natural were not equally artificial and composed. Like all debates of the *ars nova* and *ars antiqua* type, however, this one is of little use to practicing composers, nor is it likely that the music to come will be determined by the rules of the rule-makers.

U.W.I.: To go back to the question of scope, Mr. Stravinsky, do you consider Webern's to be too narrow?

I.S.: Not for Webern—which is no answer, I know, but I cannot understand the word in musical terms. Webern's time-scale is tiny, his quantity minute, his variety limited; but are these the measurements of scope? If scope were concerned with depth, for example, and not merely with width and expanse, then Webern's can be very great; and it is in any case perfectly circumscribed, which I say because we can judge only what the composer has done, not what he did not set out to do. Admittedly Webern seems to put a low premium on the listener's sense of involvement. Not only is the music wholly unrhetorical but it does not invite participation in the argument of its own creation as, say, Beethoven's does, with its second subjects, fugal episodes, developments of subsidiary parts, its schematic elaboration and integration. Instead, each opus offers itself only as a whole, a unity to be contemplated. It is essentially static, therefore, and thus the cost in subjectivity is high. But if one feels constricted listening to a succession of Webern's very short pieces, and attributes the feeling to 'lack of scope', let me say that the attempt to follow a chain of unities is a quantitative misunderstanding in the first place. Let me add that some years ago, in Venice, I heard the Parennin Quartet follow a half-hour or so of Boulez's *Livre pour quatuor* with the three and a half minutes of Webern's *Bagatelles*, and scope, I assure you, did not seem to be a matter of duration.

U.W.I.: What are your present criticisms of the music, Mr. Stravinsky?

I.S.: They are mere differences of palate, doubtless more revealing of myself than of Webern. But those dying-away, *molto ritenuto e molto espressivo* phrase endings have become a little tiresome; and the touch of cuteness in some of the vocal music: the too-frisky piano figure introducing '*Wie bin ich froh!*', for instance; the '*Glück*' at the end of the Chinese choruses (in which the *chinoiserie* is also less subtle than in the early Li-Tai-Po song); and that wretched '*Bienchen*' in *Gleich und Gleich* (did Webern know Hugo Wolf's setting of this poem?), which should have been a large wasp with a good sting. But these are minor objections, arising from simple conflicts of temperament. Perhaps you will understand them better if I add that I prefer unhappiness to happiness, misery to gaiety, in a great deal of German music besides Webern.

U.W.I.: But do you have other, larger criticisms of specific pieces, that you had not felt a decade ago?

I.S.: The String Quartet left me with a sense of aridity when I

93

heard it recently but my impression of the music might have been different if the performance had been better. The saxophone quartet, too, when I heard it conducted by Kagel in Paris a few seasons ago, sounded rather scatty in the second movement. But it seems to me that the hammering impression in the succession of downbeats there is the fault of the notation. The note-values are too large, the measures too small. Webern seems to have been obsessed with the device of the silent or 'suspended' beat, with the note on the anacrusis. He employs it most successfully, to my mind, near the end of the Concerto, and most controversially in the last dozen measures of the piano Variations, where, because of attenuating changes of *tempo*, the effect seems to belong to the category of *Papiermusik*. The metrical accent obtains only if the listener is watching a score or a conductor, the ear otherwise perceiving the notes not in relation to silent beats but as beats themselves.

Webern's choral harmony disconcerts me, too, for example at the words '*Im Dunkel*', near the end of the First Cantata, and again in the parallel-interval passages in the fifth movement of the Second Cantata. I can see the interval logic and the purity in these constructions. And I am willing to believe that they derive from a teleological conception of form, though some might call it a mania for total serial identification. But it *is* harmony, after all, and in the case of the '*Im Dunkel*' passage, banal harmony.

U.W.I.: You agree that the quality of performance is vital. How have performance standards changed in the last decade?

I.S.: But there are far too few performances even now, apart from the String Quartet pieces and that conductors' Bucephalus, the *Six Pieces for Orchestra*, to speak of 'standards'. And performance *can* make the hundred percent difference between nonsense and comprehension, as it cannot do with a popular classic. Even in the case of so simple and accessible a piece as my own *Symphonies of Wind Instruments*, I ought not to have blamed the listeners who took it for an ugly duckling at its London debut (though I have launched an unsuitable metaphor; the work is no swan even when perfectly played): it was unintelligibly performed. Recently, leafing through the concert programmes of Jean Wiéner and others in Paris in the early twenties, I was surprised to discover that songs and chamber music by Webern had been performed together with my own music. But I have no recollection of it, not even of a circumstantial nature, such as whether the few twitches and squeaks the music was then reputed to consist of provoked any derision;[1] and I can account for this blank only by doubting the quality of the performances. A notion of what they may have been like can perhaps be gleaned from the Dial recording, a quarter of a century later (1950), of the *Bagatelles*. The performers are authorities, from the very *sanctum sanctorum* of the composer. Yet their reading fails even on the level of accuracy. And I do not intend this as criticism of the players, who were a long way ahead in mastering the music. I mean it rather as a contribution to the history of performance, just as, at less remote dates, the Domaine Musical recordings of Webern, and Columbia's 'Complete' Webern, maps to undiscovered treasure in their day, are of interest now only to students of performance limitations of the time.

I was a witness at every stage of the Columbia project, incidentally, and can only sum it up by saying that ten years now seem very long ago indeed. Even the scores and parts were unobtainable then and had to be extracted from poor photostats of the composer's autographs; the publishers were actually obliged to issue the music because of the demand created by the recordings. And though the chamber music could be—and was—recorded in conjunction with concerts, the orchestral music had to be recorded without any rehearsal at all, as, for financial reasons, there *were* no concerts, and the Musicians Union forbade free, even if volunteered, rehearsals. The only recourse was to coach each player individually until each had learned his part like a cipher. And this is actually what happened in the case of the *Variations*, the three cantatas, the *Six Pieces*, the *Passacaglia*, the *Ricercar*, and the *Symphony*, all eight works taped

---

[1] This non-awareness is especially painful to me now when I read Webern's letter to Berg dated June 9, 1919. 'Strawinsky war herrlich. Wunderbar sind diese Lieder. Mir geht dieser Musik ganz unglaublich nähe. Ich liebe die ganz besonders. Etwas so unsäglich Ruhrendes wie diese Wiegenlieder. Wie diese drei Klarinetten klingen! Und *'Pribaoutki'*. Ah, mein lieber, etwas ganz herrlich! Diese Wörtlichkeit (realismus) führt ins Metaphysische. Strawinsky-Lieder waren ausserordentlich gelungen.'

in two three-hour periods, and with no assistance from Columbia
in the form of musical or engineering supervisors—none, that
is, besides my own.

Yet recording companies can hardly be expected to support
such ventures. Columbia, in this instance, is less to blame than
the conductors who *had* orchestras, could have found the money
to purchase the time, but lacked foresight and imagination.
In the context of this account it strikes me as quite beside the
point to complain that notes were not always played as nodes.
Yet I have never again heard such perfect distinctions of pitch
as those of Miss Marni Nixon. Not from Miss Nixon herself, to
be sure, for she has graduated from Webern to Liza Doolittle!

U.W.I.: What, to you, are Webern's high points?

I.S.: The *Five Movements* and *Six Pieces* are the first peaks, then
come the Trakl songs, the *Canons*, the *Volkstexte*. The *Symphony*
is a higher eminence still, and the tallest of all is the orchestra
Variations.

U.W.I.: Has your estimate of Webern's position changed
appreciably in the last decade?

I.S.: Not mine. But those composers whose own early music was
largely a *catalogue raisonné* of derivations from his generally
concede that it has changed. All of us owe something to him,
nevertheless—in the vocabulary of rhythm, in the measurement
of time, in sensibility. Webern has raised everyone's sense of
refinement in these regards. (Well, *nearly* everyone's.) He brings
a new and intensely individual voice to music, and he *has* a power
to move; contemporary music contains no more eloquent
moment than the *Coda* of the *Symphony*. In spite of what I said at
first, therefore, if you are 'seeking strange gods' you might do
worse than continue to revere Anton Webern.

Hollywood, November 5, 1965

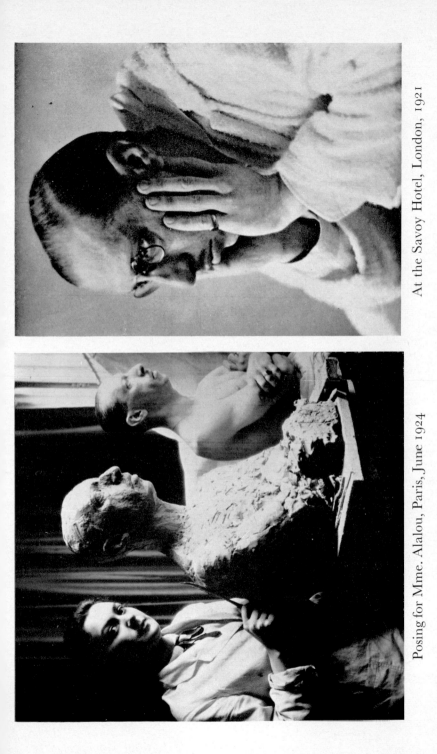

At the Savoy Hotel, London, 1921

Posing for Mme. Alalou, Paris, June 1924

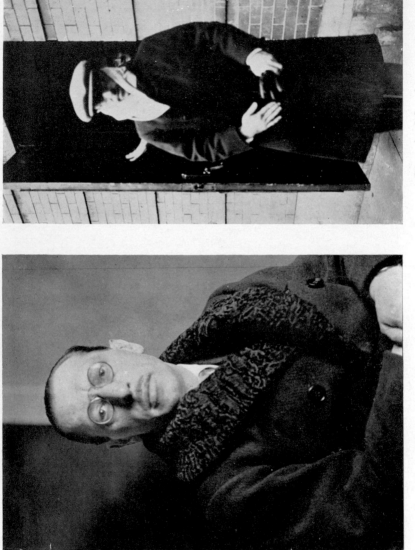

Detroit, March 2, 1925

Boston, 1925

INTERVIEW

Q.: What did you think of the recent CBS television portrait of yourself, Mr. Stravinsky?

I.S.: It made me seem like a kind of musical Rolls-Royce, the best and most expensive composer running. But it is morally embarrassing to see oneself in a film—and chastening to read one's talk, in spite of which I seem to be in a perpetual state of interview of late.

Q.: Do you agree with Duchamp that an object can be transformed simply by being chosen and invested with a new context?

I.S.: Duchamp's objects can be, at any rate, because of the quality of his choices. But as a mode of art-making, choosing seems to depend as much on literary as on visual transactions. And even in Duchamp's case I value some of his other achievements more highly: his demonstration that the machine-made can be better made than the handmade, for instance, and still be 'aesthetic'.

My own views, though hardly in need of airing, are diametrically different. I have never looked on art as an amusement or drug, as he once did, or held with him, in his sense, that 'life' is more interesting. And though we may well have come to the end of the masterpiece era, as he believes, a masterpiece, to me, is all that counts.

Q.: Would you comment on the charge of aestheticism in your own work, Mr. Stravinsky?

I.S.: I still think of music in terms of 'the beautiful', in any case, though of course I do not work with any formulations as to what it is, and certainly my musical ear does not consciously follow the options of any aesthetic code. But 'aestheticism' implies an ingrowing, and the word is probably aimed at the self-sufficiency, or, as it may be, the selfishness, of an artist who refuses to come out and play. Whether or not the description fits me, I suspect

97

that its use against me derives from very different terms: my indifference to the new progressivism (call it the Fibonacci numbers game), for example, and my lack of sympathy with music as an advertisement for extra-musical causes. As I see it, even the greatest symphony is able to do very little about Hiroshima.

Q.: The classifiers also agree in claiming you as a humanist, Mr. Stravinsky.

I.S.: And who is not? The word is too slippery to handle. Besides, I dislike its norm-loving, middle-of-the-road associations. I might add that it had a bad name with me already in my Russian youth, when it was used to describe a type of liberal whose unique course of action was the sympathy strike—dressing in peasants' *rubashkis* and sleeping on the floor, as if that could be profitable for anyone except chiropractors.

Q.: What were the origins of the *Requiem Canticles*?

I.S.: Intervallic designs which I expanded into contrapuntal forms and from which, in turn, I conceived the larger shape of the work. The twofold series was also discovered early on, in fact while I was completing the first musical sentence. And so was the work's instrumental bias an early idea; my original title was *Sinfonia da Requiem*, and I did not use it only because I seem to have shared too many titles and subjects with Mr. Britten already. The idea of the triangulate instrumental frame—string prelude, wind-instrument interlude, percussion postlude—came quickly after, and I then began to compose the interlude, which is the formal lament. The prelude puzzled the audience. Some thought it too 'light', while others said it was 'like Bartók'; still others compared it with the beginning of Mozart's *Dissonant* Quartet. I think, myself, that its preluding manner is exactly suited to the musical matter to be expounded.

Q.: May we ask if the music sounded exactly as you expected it to sound?

I.S.: You may, and it did, instrumental changes implemented during rehearsals notwithstanding: two passages for trumpets were rescored for trombones, the mallet parts were adjusted slightly, and a harmonium part was eliminated, its music being distributed at different times to horns, a string bass, bassoons. What I did not expect, as I said, were the echoes other people professed to hear in it: *Oedipus Rex* in the *Tuba Mirum*, *Svadebka* in the *Postlude*, the noises of the inmates in *Marat/Sade* in the mumbled congregational prayer at the background of *Libera Me*. Still, most listeners seemed to find it the easiest to take home of my last-period—or last-ditch-period—music, and though I know of no universal decision as to whether it is to be thought of as compressed or merely brief, I think the opus may safely be called the first mini-*Requiem*.

Q.: And the origins of *The Owl and the Pussy-Cat*?

I.S.: It is a musical sigh of relief, composed so rapidly after the *Requiem Canticles*—a *Requiem* at my age rubs close to home—that I must have been gestating it at the same time. The origins were in the trimeter rhythms of the title. Rhythm first, in this instance, therefore, and in contrast to the *Requiem*. The rhythmic cell suggested a group of pitches, which I expanded into a twelve-note series in correspondence to the stanzaic shape of the poem. The piano octaves form a syncopated canonic voice as well as a double mirror, the vocal movement being reflected between both the upper and lower notes. Octaves are peculiarly pianistic. No other instrument produces them so well.

Q.: Having composed with series for so many years now, are you aware of any compulsiveness in certain combinations of numbers?

I.S.: All composers become obsessed with numbers, I suspect, the rapport expressed between numbers being so much greater than most expressions of rapport in other forms of reality. I cannot explain this to non-musicians, and the point is not transferable to another medium. Still, some parallel sense of what I mean may be found in photography, where certain kinds of rapport—of distance and balance, say—are seen more clearly in a black-and-white than in a colour print, although the colour print is more real. (The circumstance that newsreels, in the past, were in black-and-white, is partly responsible for the reflex that has conditioned us to think the contrary.) So, too, certain musical relationships are clearly expressed as numbers. But to return to your question, it may well be that my love of combining twos, threes, fours, and sixes is compulsive, and that I am behaving in music like the man who locks his door three times or steps on all of the cracks in the sidewalk. But if this is true, and musical composition involves nervous disorders, I do not want to be cured.

Q.: What will be the chief cultural consequences to a society in which more than half of the population is under twenty, and to what do you attribute your own rapport with the younger majority?

I.S.: One early consequence will be a large crop of sad, the-bloom-is-off, ex-youth, and another, the overthrowing of the biblical tradition of 'the wisdom of the elders' by 'youth culture'. But the repudiation of the past in favour of the newest and latest is hardly a new disease in the body politic (*'cupidus rerum novarum'*), nor is the rejection by young people of an unacceptable reality. I attribute my own rapport with them, a better one that I had with their parents and grandparents at that same age (*everyone* is younger than I am!), to a natural desire to cling to an old man in hopes that he can point the road to the future. What is needed, of course, is simply *any* road that offers enough mileage and a reasonably good safety record. And my road satisfies these requirements, although the direction in which it extends to such length is not the future but the past. It will soon become a detour, I realize, as newer pavements, newly surfaced and custom-built for new vehicles, are laid down. But I do not mind that. Detours sometimes afford more pleasant driving than those super-turnpikes on which the traffic has yet to discover that the race is not always to the swift.

Drake Hotel, Chicago, December 26, 1966

STRAVINSKY AT EIGHTY-FIVE

I turned the tuneful art
From sounds to things . . .
An Essay on Man

N.Y.R.: We read that you had cancelled your European tour, Mr. Stravinsky. I hope not because of illness?

I.S.: Not illness, thank you, though if I sneeze nowadays you may count on the newspapers reporting it. In fact I have just returned from a concert tour, a Via Dolorosa further darkened by some unscheduled glimpses of the Culture Explosion (the violent arts), in so far as this phenomenon may be said to have reached Miami, Beverly Hills, Seattle, and Honolulu.

N.Y.R.: What were the local detonations like?

I.S.: Pfft. Miami might at least be expected to possess a first-rate orchestra. But nothing in the city seems to be propitious to the arts, apart from the hotel I stayed in, which had a Venus de Milo with the arms restored. Certainly the sun-worshipping life —the entire population looks as if it had been fried in butter— is against it, and so, apparently, are the musicians themselves, a description that in some cases appeared to mean anyone aware that a violin is more or less held under the chin.

Nor did a sampling of the state of culture in Beverly Hills force the imagination to travel as far as Florence or Athens in search of adequate comparisons. It did, however, make me change one of my own tunes. Heretofore I have belaboured the policy of building more and bigger halls for bad and worse performances. Now I say at least halls. The boudoir-pink ballroom of the Beverly Hilton was an absurd setting for *The Rite of Spring*, and the switching off of the lights while I conducted—it did not help that the music we fizzled through during the blackout was the *Fireworks*—made a concentrated performance impossible.

The management must have thought that the long overdue air raid had finally begun.

In Seattle, my *Histoire du Soldat* was embellished with panel backdrops by Saul Steinberg. But they were undecipherable, without telescopes, beyond the first row. I had to squint even on stage to make out the pagoda-like first scene (Vietnam?), while the Soldier—who may have had weak eyes (he was surprisingly ready to weep, a degree of fortitude being expected in his profession)—seemed baffled by the 'Royal Palace' at a distance of only a few feet. (A penthouse? Condominium? Space-needle?)

N.Y.R.: And Honolulu?

I.S.: I enjoyed it more than my last visit there, which was in 1959, shortly before the islands became a state. There were annoying airport formalities then, including a health inspection for which I tried to look sober and refrain from blowing my nose, but the standards must have been extremely low; the inspector strode by so quickly that he could have noticed no more than whether anyone was actually dead or unusually green. The new state is easier to enter, in spite of the strangulation and asphyxiation threats from the *leis* of the hula welcoming committees. And once it is entered, the only perils, that I was aware of at least, were those of the deep. I watched a 'native' fisherman haul in a net of crustaceans at the very place where I had been dipping my toes an hour before. But in Hilton's Honolulu even the crabs could be smarmy. Besides, the scene was too picturesque: the catch was probably planted.

There is a pineapple problem, too. It is practically impossible to obtain any form of food unmixed with *ananas* (the French sounds like a biblical sin). Nine days passed before I found an unpatriotic waiter to whom I could risk saying: 'Now take this ten-dollar bribe and please try, this once, to smuggle the spaghetti in without any pineapple.' The day I visited Pearl Harbor, incidentally, the tourists were mostly Japanese, which made me wonder about the monuments our descendants will be visiting in Hanoi in another twenty-five years. 'Ah, so, Perarber, Perarber', they were saying, wistfully it seemed to me, though I doubt we can expect a film *Pearl Harbor, Mon Amour*.

N.Y.R.: What do you think of the 'mod' *Rake's Progress* in Boston last month?

I.S.: I didn't see it, but I gather that the opera was able to sustain the 'mod' apparatus, and I have even heard that the staging and the music managed to turn each other a few compliments. I also noted a change in the press: no more rallying behind the idiotic prejudice that the conventional must be the feelingless, and the experimental the expressive. It is obvious of course that leather jackets and motorcycles, psychedelic and strobe lighting, Stravinsky sweatshirts and discothèque dancing, pin-ups of Allen Ginsberg and Tim Leary in the *Rake's* pad (is *he* queer?), have no connection with the opera, although mutability *is* one of its themes. But I would have objected to them only if they destroyed the intimacy of the music. (I suppose the argument *for* them is that as the music parodies and time-travels, why not the décors as well?) The staging was said to offer a novel solution to the problem of Baba the Turk, and for that I regret not having seen it, for Baba opens the opera's largest credibility gap. The motivation for the Rake's marriage to this 'freak of nature', namely freedom from 'the twin tyrants of appetite and conscience', can seem a little makeshift, and the absence at this point of any thought of his betrothed may appear a little unlikely. 'Do you desire her [Baba]?' asks Shadow. 'Like the falling sickness,' answers the Rake. 'Then marry her,' Shadow rejoins and his words provoked a scream from a woman in the audience, an effect that might be written into the score. After being sold as an object in an auction, Baba reappeared, like a *dea ex machina*, on closed-circuit TV. Her revelation in Act Two was staged in rain, moreover, which justifies the brevity of the scene, and allows for the display of some pretty brollies.

N.Y.R.: Your basso profundo has been rather noticeably absent from the cheering section of the culture boom, Mr. Stravinsky.

I.S.: That is because the cultural prosperity, like the missile-rattling economic prosperity, seems to me inflated, naïvely quantitative, misdirected in emphasis. The inescapable illustration is the re-opening, in flashier quarters, of the very old Met. Here, one would have supposed, was yet another platinum opportunity to overrate the growth of the arts in America. This time, too, the cover stories could be devoted to a real, live, local artist, instead of the usual paeans for tax-deducting patrons, and budget figures for the gross national product. Mr. Barber *had* been entrusted with the baptismal score, after all, and he was the *maker* in the musical community, which includes the operatic community, no matter how low the present musical standards of opera. What Mr. Bing and the anonymous middle-opinion glossies knew, and were not saying, was that Mr. Barber had been chosen for a sacrificial role by the same people (namely themselves) who had pampered him in the days when his brand of music had not yet become bad news. The Great Society being short of great composers, he alone satisfied the indispensable requirements of being at the same time home-grown, well-known, efficient and reliable, and unnoticeable in musical tendency; in short, he could be counted on not to divert publicity from the house, the staff, and the social event, or otherwise detract from the occasion.

What I find more difficult to explain is the installation of Mr. Bing as a culture hero, not *how* it came about, of course—he has virtually no competition—but *why*. Why mythologize an artistic director who denies the possibility of new opera, as his com-missions for the new house show; who supports the now generally discredited star system, which in effect contradicts the idea, at last gaining circulation elsewhere, that opera is drama; and who keeps the tiniest inventory of operas of any company of its class in the world? Mr. Bing disingenuously justifies his repertory as box-office taste, knowing full well that taste must be created, and, anyway, that a good salesman should be able to sell good merchandise as well as bad. With the advent of new interest in Wagner, wouldn't a new *Tristan* better have befitted the celebra-tions of the new house than the revival of a moth-eaten comedy like *La Gioconda*? Or a progressive novelty, for example a double bill of *Curlew River* and *Suor Angelica*? But in spite of *Gioconda* and *Cleopatra* and *Adrianna Lecouvreur* and *Cav* and *Pag*, Mr. Bing is one of New York's top swingers. No doubt he will be made into a musical, which is a cultural achievement of a sort.

N.Y.R.: You were courted by the Musical Establishment your-self, not long ago, Mr. Stravinsky. What, may we ask, were your morning-after reactions to the New York Philharmonic's Stra-vinsky Festival?

I.S.: No hangover. Nor did I feel scathed, whatever I looked like. Perhaps I was spared by the circumstance that all of the concerts except my own were group shows. Would-be assassins were not lacking, of course, but all except the one dispatched by that society of failed newspapers, the *Trib Sun Telegram Post News Mirror*, seemed to have lost heart; and he backfired; a collection is now going around to put up a small public lavatory to his memory in some plumbing-poor neighbourhood of his native city.

N.Y.R.: Do you think that the audiences in general were attracted more by what was being played, or by who was playing it?

I.S.: The latter. But the ad-men can give you factual answers, and also to the metrics-of-taste question (Bentham's idea). Lincoln Center audiences are probably exceptional in that some percentage of the people might still come as much to see the buildings as to watch Mr. Bernstein, as was once the case with the Music Hall and the Rockettes. It seemed to me, at any rate, that of the 2,000 customers who attended the Festival's chamber-music concert, not more than a tenth could have come with foreknowledge in kind expressly to hear what they heard. This was apparent from the initial giggles of the captive majority, who, however, when the dynamics were conducive, tried to settle down and make the best of it. (I have never seen so many eyelids at half-mast.) As for the programme, it was an error to relegate Milton Babbitt's electronic composition to the lobby during intermission. At a time when noise pollution is reaching saturation point, a time of pocket transistors, processed classics, and round-the-clock mood music (music for mealtimes, music for meditation, music for everything in fact except undivided listening), resistance to intermission sub-concerts, at least on *my* indifference curve, is very strong.

N.Y.R.: And what did you think of the programmes, Mr. Stravinsky?

I.S.: Some g., some n.g., but my lips are sealed. Besides, I am no judge of programmes; I go to concerts myself to hear only one work. My early music was favoured, but not my audience lollipop, *The Firebird*. And my neo-classicism—in which the slump seems to be lifting—was well represented. *Apollo*, the

U-turn itself, was missing, but *Oedipus* and *Perséphone* were there, as well as *Pulcinella*, the first of my purported raids on the past. As for my later music, which is no less neo-classical, the only considerable example was *The Flood*. The trouble it gave the orchestra partly explains why. The title episode itself was so un-weatherable to them (what did they expect, sea chanties?) that I was tempted to cut it to only a few measures—a flash-flood, in fact. Music sociologists might note that for whatever reasons of rehearsal time and morale, it was the orchestra, not the audience, which required larger diets of familiar music.

N.Y.R.: And the other performances?

I.S.: Well, frugging is apparently *de rigueur* for Philharmonic conductors. Even Kondrashin did it. (Where did he learn *that* in the USSR? Do conductors study films there, like secret agents?) But Mr. Bernstein is unflappable in competition, and so glittering a performer[1] that he could get a dozen curtain calls out of the National Anthem. (Not, however, out of *my* version, which needed a more tightly cranked-up performance.) The character of articulation in my music eluded most of the conductors, even in so simple a point as that the metrical lines are constituent to the rhythm, not mute, inglorious markers which the conductor is invited to ignore for the sake of something he calls the phrase. But the performance standards, both bad—*Oedipus Rex*—and good—*Histoire du Soldat*, the high point of the summer's revels thanks to John Cage's *opéra-bouffe* Devil—were determined by extra-musical antics. As for the standards of the music itself, July was too hot even for a soft look. I did notice, however, that whereas the Ragtime in the *Histoire* is as smoothly integrated as a minuet in Mozart, the one for eleven instruments is as dated as a coonskin coat.

The curtain-raiser concert of *Le Sacre* and its American beneficiaries was a fine gesture of homage to Mr. Bernstein's youth. Even the peculiarities of *tempi* and *rubati* in the *Sacre*—a more handwringing reading than I am accustomed to—were derived, as he told me, from Stokowski's performances in the

[1] He was much less effective on TV a few days ago giving his endorsement of Rock 'n' Roll (which seemed not to have the remotest need of it), and expressing the sophisticated musician's wonder at such prodigies of invention as The Beatles' use of a three-beat measure in a four-beat song.

thirties. Of the other pieces, Copland's *Dance Symphony*, a very precocious opus for a composer of twenty-three, would have been equally serviceable in a festival of Ravel, while Revueltas's *Sensemaya* offers several composers for the price of one and would do as an influenced piece in any number of surveys of the sort.

N.Y.R.: But do you think Revueltas would have developed if, like yourself, he had been given another thirty-five years of working life?

I.S.: I have no opinion. I can answer only in the other direction, telling you about people who might better have disappeared thirty-five years sooner.

N.Y.R.: Have you any late-hour prescriptions for a young composer, Mr. Stravinsky?

I.S.: If he can turn an honest million outside music he might seriously consider neglecting his talents for a time and turn it. Otherwise, and untempted by all lesser sums, he should go directly underground and do nothing but compose; that is, not strive for Foundation awards, academic prizes, college presidencies, foreign fellowships; not attend culture congresses, not give interviews, not prattle on the radio about music appreciation, not review new scores (except his own, pseudonymously); and not push, promote, manoeuver, advertise, finagle, operate.

N.Y.R.: Some composers borrow structural patterns from the sciences. Xenakis, for instance, uses Bernouilli's Limit Theorem, and his *Metastasis* was derived from the same blueprint as the architecture for the Philips Pavilion at the Brussels Fair.

I.S.: I admire the economy. And I look forward to the days when Mr. Xenakis's successors are writing music that can at the same time compute taxes and regulate urban renewal. Meanwhile, I confess that I would be frightened to enter some of the compositions I have heard of late, in their forms as buildings.

N.Y.R.: Now that computer programming is our fastest-growing profession, do you foresee a larger role for computers in the service of the creative arts?

I.S.: When the computer has become the electronic culture's universal knowledge distillery, artistic creation, if there is any, obviously will have been technically, theoretically, and teleologically overhauled. But I am undergoing a Luddite reaction myself, and foresee very little. Like everyone else, I welcome the benefits of, say, the computerizing of medical information (which no physician could keep up with anyway), but unlike most other people, I am frightened by the prospects of, say, the IBM project for the direct conversion of information to speech; the very thought of millions of electronic voices indistinguishable from live ones (to say nothing of the noise) almost makes me jump the tracks. 'Till human voices wake us and we drown.'

N.Y.R.: Nowadays, Mr. Stravinsky, how is an upper-average (middle to high) Playbrow to know 'what is art'? I mean, when is a crushed car sculpture, when are 'ditties of no tone' music—that sort of thing?

I.S.: It is still generally thought of as art if it is shown in a gallery, and as music if it takes place in premises traditionally associated with concerts. Another way of knowing is by way of the dealers who are obliged to keep the racket going. Their formula, and it seems to be working very well, is 'Buy now on the likelihood that it may later turn out to *be* Art.' Speaking for myself, I could not begin to distinguish music and non-music in some of the concert-hall activity I have observed of late. Nor would I be at all confident of recognizing a new musical genius. If I were asked to fill Schumann's role today and hail a new Chopin, I would probably have to modify his dictum to: 'Keep your hats on, gentlemen, for all I know he may be a charlatan.'

N.Y.R.: As the term avant-garde implies direction, in what direction do you think today's avant-garde is going?

I.S.: Not knowing what kind of music is looking ahead, or even what ahead means, I have no idea. If, for example, the *Diabelli* Variations seem to forecast so much, it is retrospective prophecy that enables us to say so. Compared with science, many of whose future conquests are known goals, even the areas in which musical developments might be expected to take place are not generally predictable. And whereas progress in science is measurable and even absolute, agreement rarely exists in music as to what progress is. Musical languages seem to develop by new infusions of emotion, or new emphases and combinations of emotion, in correspondence with shifts and changes—losses as well as additions—in vocabulary. But a new linguistic mode can also be more crude than the one it supersedes.

As to the actual avant-garde, I have had little contact with it in the last few seasons, and this in a field where six weeks can count as an era, and ownership of an idea, at the present rate of 'dynamic obsolescence', lasts about six minutes. It seems, however, that the trend is still to mixed media, corporate expression, the instant *Gesamtkunstwerk*, and therefore away from music by and in itself; and this is understandable, too, if only for the reason 'The lyf so short, the craft so long to lerne.' It is also a trend away from composition, for, in my fuddy-duddy view, effects plotlessly stumbled on are very different from those that occur in the course and frame of an unfolding order. What I found of some, but less than inexhaustible, interest in the avant-garde of a few years ago was the exploration of minutiae of sensibility in a man alone and immobile. This was not entirely new (think of Gulliver, swarming with a '*Fourmillante cité* . . .'), but it did not become an all-out movement, I think, until Beckett. For a parallel in music we have to thank Mr. Cage for making us aware of our breathing and swallowing, amplified (this sounds like Niagara Falls), and the crinkle of a single hair.

N.Y.R.: Are those changes of vocabulary and new infusions of emotion strictly interior musical developments or is there a relationship of a metaphorical kind with the real world?

I.S.: As I see it, the metaphorical alignments, symbolizations, reflected thoughts and feelings are purely the listener's, without any 'real' basis in the music; or, in other words, the investing of the musical object with the listener's subjective responses is actually nothing more than a form of the pathetic fallacy. I doubt, furthermore, that the subjective regions of most metaphorically inclined listeners are as rich and varied as they suppose, most 'free' association really being a comparatively narrow and patterned habit association. But this begs further questions which would eventually lead back to the postulate (it appears in Marx's *Contribution to the Critique of Political Economy*, I think, but I am not an answering service) that reality is not determined by our consciousness but the other way around.

N.Y.R.: Surely pieces of music can have valid meanings beyond themselves?

I.S.: Certainly: your own. And you may look to them for whatever you like: comments on the times, for example, as embodied in formal, substantive, and structural characteristics (the method of the 'contextual interpretation' industry); or exercises in analogy—I could get up a Platonic dialogue myself on the proposition that good music expresses high truths and bad music platitudes and lies. It is all up to—since it also begins and ends in—you.

N.Y.R.: But in your own mind, Mr. Stravinsky?

I.S.: My 'mind' does not count. I am not mirror-struck by my mental functions. My interest passes entirely to the object, the thing made; it follows that I am more concerned with the concrete than the other thing, in which, as you see, I am easily muddled. And in the first place I do not regard composition as more of a mental function than a sensual pleasure. 'Lascivious pleasing' is a famous description of the performance of a—very chaste, it would seem to us—lute song, and performances are but pale memories of creative acts. In music as in love, pleasure is the waste product of creation.

N.Y.R.: Would you comment on Leopardi's claim that old age deprives us of every pleasure while leaving every appetite, but that men fear death and desire old age?

I.S.: Prefer, not desire, and the logical symmetry is also untrue: there are pleasures still, and in parity with appetites. But if old age is hardly more appealing today than it was in the time of Leopardi, who died too young to know anything about it, we treat it cosmetically now and it may at least look better. Under the slogan of senior citizenry, in any case, it is being sold as a vocation, its salesmen likening senility to a late, more effulgent phase of the moon, and pretending that our loss of momentum, when too evident to be denied, is the price of a compensatory larger wisdom. They even find substitute love affairs for us with our own illnesses, whose progresses they teach us to follow as if 'we' were hardly involved.

Reality is different and it *could* be like a mental deep-freeze. A doctor recently prescribed a new tranquilizer for me on the recommendation that it had worked wonders for his grand-mother, meaning that it had probably kept her in a semi-coma and out of his way. But did the venerable lady also write music? I asked, and the shocked answer implied that if *I* did, I should stop immediately for the sake of my own tranquility—which, I now know, is no longer a place where emotion is recollected but a near-vegetable state.

N.Y.R.: May we inquire about age in your own thoughts, Mr. Stravinsky?

I.S.: If you mean the knowledge that in a half-decade at the most, but probably sooner, I will be dead, that has little effect on me: the possibility of death is always present, always in the cards, after all, and it is only the likelihood that has increased. If, on the other hand, you are inquiring about changes of mind and character, then I will have to admit that I am aware of some of them only from other people. They tell me when I am being too suspicious and refractory, for example. But surely faults of this kind, life being what it is, are independent of questions of age. One change that is apparent to me with no outside help is my tendency to magnify my smallest bruises. No doubt a simple bio-chemical explanation exists, but I cannot control my bile count. In the past I constrained myself against the complacency of all judgments with exemplary charity ('They have ears but hear not'), and the thought that while death *is* there is hope. But now I know that where there is death there is succession.

Like childhood—my childhood—old age is a time of humiliations. For me the most disagreeable is that I cannot work long at sustained high pressure and with no leaks in concentration. But there are others. My slips in writing are frequent now, and my manuscripts have to be vetted. This is 'understandable in a man of his age', people say, but it disturbs me, understandable or not. So is my hide-and-seek memory, now in hiding more often than not. I have orchestrated the same page twice, greeted perfect strangers in Russian, and performed other equally scatterbrained acts. Coué would have said that Nature is protecting me, in reducing my power to retain the nugatory. But I prefer not to need the shelter.

One night last week I dreamed a new episode of my work-in-progress, but realized, when I awoke, that I could not walk to my desk to write it down and that it would be gone by morning; in that instant I wondered for the first time how much longer it will be before I shall have to close down as a composer altogether.

N.Y.R.: Have eighty-five years strengthened your belief in the continuity of life and art, Mr. Stravinsky?

I.S.: It seems to me, on the contrary, that discontinuity must be only a short way ahead. Certainly in another four-score-and-five the 'clones' bred by genetic engineers to the specifications of Bureaus of Human Uses will differ from me far more than I differ from, say, the astronomers of Fowlis Wester and Stonehenge (who, it now appears, must have known a lunar movement later 'discovered' by Tycho Brahe). I lack confidence in genetic and other Utopias, as you see, and am tired of analogies based on successful demonstrations in frogs. But, then, the present has already begun to make me giddy—that discovery at Cambridge, for instance, showing that in certain insects the sense of time itself is encoded in two or three cells. (So, then, time *is* ontological?) But do not misunderstand me. Though I would refuse any Faustian bargain, I am far from content with myself. I simply want to go from here on out trying to do better what I have always done, and in spite of statistical tallies telling me that it must be getting worse. And I want to do it in this same battered but long-lived-in Identikit. 'Myself I must remake', Yeats's poem says. And so must we all.

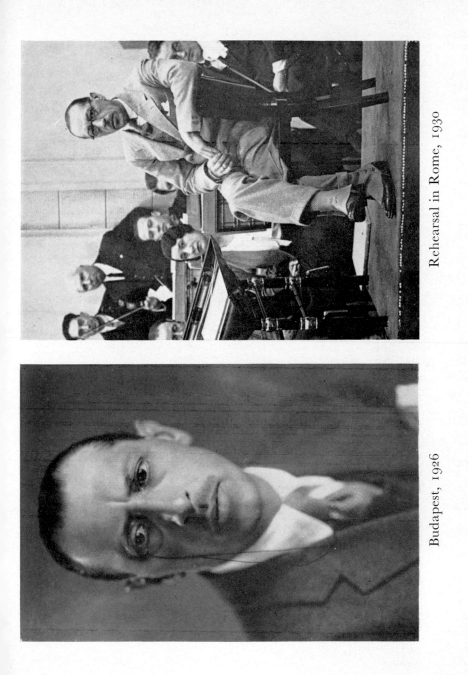

Rehearsal in Rome, 1930

Budapest, 1926

Düsseldorf an der
probe am 5 Febr 1930

Rehearsal in Dusseldorf, February 5, 1930

SIDE EFFECTS I

I

To avenge the wrongs of our time . . . the wounds of
Igor.

The Song of Igor's Campaign (Nabokov translation)

Harper's: Your New York appearances have become rare, Mr.
Stravinsky. The cancellation of the recent Carnegie Hall
concerts was a great disappointment to us.[1]

I.S.: The city itself is hazardous for me now. I started on a walk
one afternoon during my last visit, but the wind was so strong
I had to lean against walls and hold on to 'No Parking' signs. A
Meter Maid was soon watching me censoriously, no doubt
thinking I was drunk. Then a young man approached, not to
offer help, as I expected, but to ask for an autograph. To oblige
him I inched my way like a mountain climber out of the Sixty-
First Street wind-tunnel and back into the hotel lobby, where I
duly signed my name. But the absence of any sense of the absurd
in this collector, or dealer in disguise, left me so out of spirits I
did not try to resume my wind-blown promenade.

Harper's: Newspaper accounts of the cancellation said you had
been in the hospital.

I.S.: True. I was confined for two weeks because of a gastric
ulcer—a 'benign' one in medicalese, but if it isn't 'benign' you
are as good as dead. The doctors attributed the lesion to too
much alcoholic vasodilation, but of course their report mentioned only the alcohol part and omitted the virtuous intentions.
I was not greatly worried at first, and my presentiments that the
real trouble might lie further upstream, that in fact I might be
headed for the rapids, were aroused only by the sudden bedside

---

[1] Stravinsky was to have conducted the French National Orchestra. (R.C.)

113

manner of certain music critics. But it *was* only an ulcer. And I recovered more quickly from it than from the hospital for ailing philanthropists to which I was sent, and whose bill might still have to be paid by a charity ball.

But seriously, penitential orders, Desert Fathers and such, seeking to update their mortifications could hardly find more ingenious examplars than those in a modern hospital. My day began at 5 AM with an urgent and for some reason unpostponable mopping of my cell. (Once it began even earlier, when the television started by itself.) From then until 'lights out', when I was regularly awakened and told it was time to sleep, I remained constantly, even ulceratingly vigilant to avoid being injected with someone else's medicines, nearly having been fatally so injected during another hospital siege some years before. As it was, not many fakirs can have been so often stuck, jabbed, poked, punctured, perforated; and considering that loss of blood was the reason for my incarceration in the first place, the further withdrawals seemed remarkably copious and frequent. I also swallowed, was pumped with, breathed, absorbed through the pores, an impressive variety and volume of medications; and was between times tourniquetted for blood-pressure, radiologically sensitized, laxitized, squeezed, thumped, and subjected to much 'laying on of hands'.

The hospital was partly audio-tactile, the patient being obliged to address his pleas to wall-tubes sieve-ended like the speaking grilles in confessional boxes, and then to wait for the answers to boom back at him from the ceiling like flight announcements. This ceiling voice reminding me to drink my milk was a torture worse than the milk itself, I might add, my tongue becoming ermine-coated at the first crackle of the sound system. And some of the humans were as automated as the automata. One of them brought jello three times a day and another yogurt, but so far as I could discover, neither did anything else. At first I assumed that this arrangement had been devised to safeguard easily overtaxed brains, but now I suspect that there weren't any (brains), that all cerebral zones except those controlling jello and yogurt deliveries had been surgically removed. I now wonder, too, as these automatons had been programmed to clear away empty but not unconsumed dishes, how long it took to discover a certain forty or so uneaten jars of jello in my closet.

My own nurses were not yet automated, and in fact one of them was so old-fashioned that she drew a curtain around my bed before giving me B-12 shots *in the arm*! Her sense of delicacy in keeping me informed on the new diseases caused by the new medicines was less acute, but she *did* teach me an effective sleep-inducing formula: gamma globulin, hemoglobin, balneotherapy, the threshold of pain, the front door of pain, pain itself . . . ZZZZZZ.

My love of pain-killers has now been confirmed, incidentally, and if I had been a 'terminal' patient I would not have supported the anti-drug lobbyists who claim to be 'entitled' to their deaths. A mere three doses of morphine were enough to 'hook' me, and to increase my allowance of Demerol I began to 'put' the doctors 'on'. Finally I have been able to overcome the colchicine habit—shared by gophers, incidentally—only through the irrelevant but disquieting knowledge that it splits chromosomes in plant cells; but Darvon is still prescribed, and I am therefore, temporarily, a legal addict.

My recovery has now been certified, but I still feel like Amfortas and suffer giddiness at moments as if I had stepped from a ferris wheel. I have become a milk dipsomaniac, too, but worst of all, the retreating ulcer left a booby-trap of digital gout. The pains are difficult to accustom to, being both erratic and pedantic, as well as so strong at times (I do not believe Aubrey's account of Milton singing in his 'gout fits': he was more likely howling) that I am no longer certain of being 'an artist to my fingertips'. It is almost impossible to hatch any new music for the moment, as you see, and absolutely impossible to do so at the piano, the gout having robbed me of my dexterity.

Harper's: Only 'almost', Mr. Stravinsky?

I.S.: I am composing, or thinking about continuing to compose, a set of pieces provisionally titled *Etudes, Inventions, and a Sonata*. Only two sections, both ante-ulcer, are completed. I hope the plural does not prove to have been over-optimistic.

II

Of Paradys ne can I not speken propurly for I was not there.

MANDEVILLE

. . . for months together, vast, wet, melancholy fogs arise and come shoreward from the ocean . . . it is always sad.

R. L. STEVENSON ON CALIFORNIA (1880)

Harper's: Why do you live in Los Angeles, Mr. Stravinsky?

I.S.: I migrated there for my health, originally, or in other words for the same reason I am now advised to leave. The effects of smog are currently estimated as the equivalent damage of two packs of cigarettes a day; the poet's 'Fear death?—to feel the fog in my throat' takes on a literal meaning here. I had been considering La Paz as the next step. Gastric ulcers are unknown there, owing to what is thought to be the 'benign' influence of altitude on the gastric enzymes.

Harper's: But is Los Angeles really so different, or is it merely that certain forms of social behaviour are developing there ahead of the rest of the world?

I.S.: The latter; unless by ahead you mean in the *real* sense, *i.e.* retrogressing faster. Los Angeles is well ahead (meaning behind) in, for example, such relatively minor developments as the cinematizing of politics. And it leads in all fads, currently in decal tattooing and silicon rejuvenating. But the city is also ahead in such fairly important developments as the change-over, men to women, women to men, and in the elimination of death.

Dying in Los Angeles seems to be only remotely, if at all, connected with death. To judge by the notices of burial bargains all over the city, in any case, the only question involved is that of tidying up a few problems (including your remains) which, thanks to certain altruistic business services, can be arranged by a telephone call and then put out of mind. In the past, these advertisements had struck me as merely ribald, except in the centre pages of Philharmonic programme-books where they were often quite fitting; and on bus-stop benches where, buses being the transportation of elderly poor people, they seemed cruel. But I see them now as the logical end of the local philosophy of life (meaning death). By taking the funereal out of funerals, and with it the nonsense about bereavement (as well as the sense of a 'supreme irony' and lingering superstitions about a 'victory over the grave'); by substituting the movie-style fade-out for the baroque-style celebration with trumpets, elegies, and marble tombs; in short, by connecting the trans-action to negotiables, and reducing it to a supermarket service, we make death in some measure less unknowable. And this, I think, is why the moribund take such a lively interest in ascer-taining the relative advantages of cremation (no 'putrescence' and no 'worms') *versus* Pharaonic preservation ('keeping up appearances'); and in securing the most favourable installment ('pay now, go later') terms.

A late lamented friend of mine, shortly before her own final collapse, told me that a salesman in the mortuary 'studio' she first visited had tried to persuade her that satin was the most becoming material for her casket lining; which so annoyed my friend that she had to remind him who was dying, that it was *her* funeral and not *his*. She also said that this atelier's musical resources included, in addition to the usual assortment of Japanese electronic canaries, a choice of 'cremation blues', one of which really did make her flesh creep. Next year's advertise-ments will undoubtedly be offering to present the corpse not only in its daily habiliments (Polaroid glasses being *de rigeur* in Los Angeles) but in 'not quite living colour' as well.

The trans-sexual trend, the switching of sexual roles, is hardly less interesting, but more difficult to follow because sociology is switching as well. At first the new *Nacktkultur* was classified, presumably by unvested interests, as merely the latest manifesta-tion of the visual-tactile revolution, but now, probably under pressure from the Garment Industry, the same experts tend to see it as a reactive phenomenon. The nude waitress is a sexual suffragette, the argument now runs, a die-hard demonstrator in the cause of the old-style binary design of the sexes.

However her issue is decided, the sexual acculturation of the rest of the world sags farthest behind Los Angeles in the free exposure of the American former-male's mammary fixations. And by this I mean not only the topless restaurant, but the ice cream parlour; for at the time of day when the French-

man downs his *marc* or his Pernod, the adult Angeleno male, a
parent, it may be, of consenting daughters majoring in sun-
tanning at UCLA, is himself ensconced in a milk pub sucking an
ice cream soda. (Let me remind you that my own present in-
continence in the matter of milk does not stem from the same
cause, which is that of not being properly 'fed-up' as an infant.)
But what of the mammalogical future? What, after a few
centuries of natural selection, will the Supergirl foldout of A.D.
2500 look like, taking as outside measurements of progress the
Eves of Cranach or Clouet and *Playboy*?

(I sometimes wonder whether *au nature* restaurant service can
be beneficial to digestion. For instance, do lower-area exposures
exert any effect on the course of digestive juices? And does anyone ever inadvertently order a tomato or a figleaf? Music appears
to have entered the bottomless era, too, incidentally, not in the
sense of profundity, but in the actual use of the anatomical
surfaces for musical notations, as in the film *Night Games*.)

III

. . . a few are riding but the rest have been run over.
                                                    THOREAU

A personal God . . . who loves us dearly with some
exceptions for reasons unknown.
                                        Waiting for Godot

Is it possible that Shakespeare should be forced to
accuse himself of ignorance of the 'ism'?
Is it possible that Stravinsky should be dragged through
screaming streets with a pail of garbage on his white hair?
                                    VOZNESENSKY, March 1967

Harper's: Are you aware of a 'gap' between yourself and the
young, Mr. Stravinsky?
I.S.: Judging from a news programme that I happened to watch
for a moment last night, an Arizona-size canyon divides me from
practically *everyone* else. The telecast began with an announcement about overpopulation. It employed statistics like '7.2
people' and concluded that by the end of the century the expression 'joined the majority' will mean born rather than died.
This was followed by a revelation about Mrs. Alliluyeva, whose

appeal, of course, is an exiled princess, a kind of Communist Anastasia. Next came the day's tally in Vietnam followed by a reassurance that the families of non-Communists killed by mistake are to be reimbursed at the going price of $34 *per* non-Communist corpse, which is like paying hunters for pelts but which was made to sound like a matter for handshakes all around.

Now the 'gap' between myself and the protesting young, to return to your question, is only as deep as my furrows compared to the chasm separating me from anyone who can be so mendaciously mouthed to. In fact, as the Sunset Strip, that dry Ganges for hippie holies (immersions in water not being in their line), is only a few steps from me, I shall probably apply for membership among the young Hindus myself. As for their elders, it hardly seems to be worth asking whether they know what became of humanity.

(*P.S.*: Voznesensky must have been thinking of Stokowski. I am bald.)

IV

Claudio Monteverdi, in moving the affections . . . becomes the most pleasant tyrant of human minds.
AQUILINO COPPINI (1608)

Harper's: A picture of Monteverdi is conspicuous among the photographs in your workroom, Mr. Stravinsky. What are your thoughts about him in this quater-centenary?

I.S.: I keep the portrait of him by my piano because I feel very close to him. But isn't he the first musician to whom we *can* feel very close? The scope of his music, both as emotion and as architecture (parts of the same thing) is a new dimension compared to which the grandest conceptions and the most profound ardours and dolours of his predecessors shrink to the status of miniatures. The man himself, in for instance Goretti's description of his habits of composing and conversation while at Parma, as well as in his own letters, with their moodiness, anxieties about shortage of time, complaints of migraines, sounds not only strikingly contemporary to me, but even, if I may so so, rather *like* me.

Speaking for myself, the progressivist sense in the labelling of the great composer's 'First and Second Practices' has been re-versed, as the forward-looking and backward-looking have some-times done. What I mean is that the older polyphonic style, with its explorations of rhythm and contrapuntal tensions (such as the suspending seconds in the 'Gloria' of the *Magnificat à 7*), sounds even newer now than the harmonic novelties of the declamatory style. But I concede, through a recent discovery of my own, that the most modern effect of all did undoubtedly occur in the 'Second Practice'. A newly published [1966] letter indicates that Monteverdi must have had something very like *Sprechstimme* in mind for a scene in a lost dramatic work. At any rate that is how *I* read his phrase '*a parlar nel modo come se l'avesse a cantare*'.

If I marvel at Monteverdi's rhythmic inventions first, it is partly because I have worked all my life in the same directions (at least), and they are part of my psychometrics as a composer. I know of no music before or since the *Sonata sopra Sancta Maria* which so felicitously exploits accentual and metrical variation and irregularity, and no more subtle rhythmic construction of any kind than that which is set in motion at the beginning of the '*Laudate Pueri*', if, that is, the music is sung according to the verbal accents instead of the *tactus* or the editor's bar-lines. On the other hand, a listener gratified primarily by rich harmonies would naturally find the almost purely rhythmic interest of the '*Dixit Dominus*' monotonous. I relish that canonic monotony myself, and to me the simple drop to G minor at the '*Gloria Patri*', after the long A minor, is a musical earthquake as powerful as the three unmodulated plunges in tonality of the first theme of the *Eroica*.

One of the greatest honours of my life was the invitation to introduce two of my own works in rooms hallowed by *il divino Claudio*, the *Canticum Sacrum* in the Basilica di San Marco, and *Threni* (*I Treni*, *The New York Times* called the opus, as if it had come from the same track as *Pacific 231*) in the Scuola di San Rocco. But in Mantua, Monteverdi's stature is diminished some-what by Isabella d'Este's music room, that monument to the high condition of music in the Gonzaga court both of an earlier time and as a whole: miracle that the occurrence of Monteverdi was, a highly developed language awaited him. But then, no

musical association of that most romantic palace in the world
is as haunting as the Gonzagas themselves, at least in Mantegna's
frescoes where they all seem to be on a poppy mandragora
'trip'—Lodovico apparently being unable to retract more than
half of his eyelids for sheer drugged drowsiness.

V

2nd Mus.: I say, 'silver sound', because musicians sound
for silver.

Romeo and Juliet

The third, doubtless a serving-man, Carries a musical
instrument.

Yeats: *Lapis Lazuli*

Harper's: What can we learn or borrow from art patronage
systems of other times, Mr. Stravinsky?
I.S.: Little, except to try to improve the taste of individuals, for
example by teaching the piper-payers some of the tunes.
Patronage systems are inseparable from social systems and
belief systems as wholes. Nevertheless, one rather consequential
difference between the ruling-class culture of our own and, say,
Monteverdi's time, is that art was important, in fact very near
the centre of life, to the heads of church and state who were
Monteverdi's patrons, and who were able as a class to exercise
trained judgment on the qualities of architects, sculptors,
painters, poets, composers. Now certainly no one would dare to
accuse any high officeholder in our L. B. Johnsonian Golden Age
of even the slightest interest in art, at least not without incurring
the risk of libel action. Art, to our middle-class millionaire
politicians, is something to be collected and dowered, which is
part of the reason why our yachting millionaires and racehorse
millionaires include so many French Impressionist millionaires
but so few musical millionaires: the tangible, resaleable musical
artifacts are comparatively insignificant.

Nor are the cultural economics of other societies more
instructive, except for drawing still more invidious comparisons.
We can learn from them that musicians have not always been
starvelings, and in such undemanded supply as they are now. In
Sophocles' Greece, for example, musicians' salaries were fixed

by law (*cf.* Sifakis's *Studies in the History of Hellenistic Drama*). And in Greece, as well as at Mantua, Esterházy, and Monticello (Virginia), they seem to have been regulated by merit. To recur to the trained-judgment question, if Haydn was hired help, at least his employers did him the honour of knowing something of and about his work. Jefferson was musically cultivated, by the way, and though he appears to have been a difficult source of income to his orchestra-players (demanding that they should also be gardeners, *etc.*), he spent a far greater share of his money on music than the 'eleven cents out of every hundred dollars of disposable income' (according to the Twentieth Century Fund survey) that his fellow countrymen are now squandering on the 'performing arts'.

Harper's: What *are* musical artifacts?

I.S.: The marketable commodities. Publicity is the largest, but the manuscript trade is brisk, and letters and 'associated objects' (soap from hotels where the artist has stayed, *etc.*) are coming along. This switching of the price tags from the functioning talent to souvenirs of its penmanship (my own manuscripts have always fetched far more than I received for writing the *music* in them), from the actual delectation of a piece of music to a collector's association with its author through an autograph album, accounts for a large part of art commerce. And composers *are* valued now less for their composing function than as committee-sitters, meeting-attenders, and teachers. In fact many of them, including one great one, have been, and still are, too poor to afford the time from teaching to compose. The great one illustrates another aspect of my argument, incidentally, in that a university has recently put up a museum to exhibit his pocket-knife, underwear, and last cigar, no doubt having paid more for the least of these relics than the composer received for all of his music. When you consider what a thousand dollars won't buy nowadays, think about that thousand-dollar commission on which a good composer must work for a year or two.

As for 'associational objects', not long ago I tried to give away a fur coat which I had worn for a number of years but which was still in good condition. I failed to find anyone chilly enough, however, and even the Salvation Army turned it down. At this point a Foundation scout heard about my garment of no *useful* value, the issue of which was that my old *shuba* is now enshrined at the Paris Conservatory (its conveyance there doubtless having incurred some substantial entries on a number of expense accounts). And it is the same with my music as with my overcoat. My new composition will serve musical commerce less for its real value of musical content than for its consumer value as publicity, meaning its use as a première. But then, publicity has become almost the only value for the artist now, and he must be a publicist before all else.

Harper's: And Foundation patronage, Mr. Stravinsky?

I.S.: Foundations are tax-escape systems and as such their money has been diverted from society as a whole; certainly more pressing social needs exist than some so-called art activity. It seems unreasonable to complain about that, however, in view of other wastes compared with which all expenditures for art are insignificant. And, anyway, money is not the only ingredient; to have subsidised a Bach or Fulbrighted a Beethoven would have done no good at all. Money may kindle but it cannot by itself, for very long, burn. (Conscience money may smoulder for a while though.)

Harper's: Do you think that society undervalues artists?

I.S.: For their art, yes. Otherwise, it is the contrary, which is why their opinions about matters beyond their competence are publicised (*viz.* this interview). But intelligence and virtue do not occur together in natural incidence with artistic gifts, as popularly supposed, and *good* artists do not have the time to know very much about anything except their work. The political wisdom of painters, actors, cellists, composers continues to be propagated, nevertheless, though these people can be as foolish and dangerous as professional politicians, and so far from being morally superior to them, are often, owing to their exceptional vanity and egotism, a shade worse.

VI

To occupy the sense of hearing . . . with many noises.
The Imperfections of Modern Music (1600)

Harper's: Is there a talent famine, Mr. Stravinsky?

I.S.: Not of small talent, if sheer volume means anything. But I must hold my tongue. I am a drop-out myself, no longer being able to attend the picnics of those small, ingrown, and not always saturnalian new-music groups through whose offices, nevertheless, a talent of any size would most likely *have* to appear. My opinions are now formed entirely from the tapes and scores I receive in the mail. (The scores, by the way, are for the most part verbal descriptions and diagrams, some of which I suspect of being fashion-market research charts in the literal as well as graphic sense.) This method has yielded nothing enticing, though I may have learned something from it about aleatory. In short, my discovery about aleatory is not so much that it doesn't make any difference but that in not making any difference it still sounds very much the same. In other words, the infinite range of possibilities between those *à la mode* landslides of noise which neither man nor beast can unscramble (I say nothing about machines), and those equally *à la mode* silences, is in practice a small and patented area of cliché. And I say this not forgetting that the harvest of my mailbox is also an aleatory. But do I hear this way merely because I am less permissive than my youngers, and still require music, not just sounds; and because 'open-ended' art does nothing for me, or 'minimal' art (already leaning indistinguishably flatly on 'no' art), or that glare of publicity and high commerce which calls itself the 'Underground'?

What, may I ask, has become even of the *idea* of universality —of a character of expression not necessarily popular but compelling to the highest imaginations of at least a decade beyond its own time—and which artist in any medium born in the last fifty years has come within a moon-shot of it?

Harper's: But do you find nothing to applaud in the young art, Mr. Stravinsky?

I.S.: Apart from some slow hand-claps for aleatory I hail the invisible sculpture movement (Takis's *Radar*, for instance, which the 'viewer' is supposed to 'energize' in an 'environment'). All forms of throwaway art and self-exploding art are also surefire with me.

Harper's: May we ask why you have tended to disparage the 'expanding possibilities'—quarter-tones, synthesizers, multiple sound-systems, and so forth—of the young composer's arsenal?

I.S.: But I haven't. I only ask whether they are related to art, for they seem to kill even the possibility of it: *parvo in multum*, to reverse the slogan. The use of the new scientific hardware naturally appears to the new musician as 'historically imperative'; and my warnings that music is made out of musical imperatives only, and that the awareness of historical process is better left to future and different kinds of wage earners, are weightless to him. But who can doubt that mathematical machines will soon be making something that will be called art? (How will art be defined, anyway? What, for example, was Holbach's idea of '*le bonheur*', in his *Traité mathématique sur le bonheur*?) In any case, whether *I* think that the composer's new hardware has landed him in an impasse cannot count, for I have no title to an opinion; even the exact nature of the problem is as remote from me as the Gluck-Piccinni debate. (I examined the latest models of musical typewriters not long ago and found *that* musical hardware to be marvellously suited to the needs of . . . Bach.)

Harper's: You have named Messiaen as the dominating influence of the decade, Mr. Stravinsky, and at the same time criticized important elements of his music. How do you appraise his music generally?

I.S.: High. In fact, one of those great hymns of his might be the wisest choice of all our music for the deck-band concert on the *Titanic* of our sinking civilization. Rescuing vessels—other planets—would have a good chance of hearing it, among other advantages. I unrashly predict, as well, that his more recent works will last as long as any music of the decade. But I still can't take *Turangalîla*.

So far as criticisms are mere likings and dislikings, they define the critic more than the target. Even the larger antinomical definition I attempted to draw between myself and Messiaen said more about my brand of convention, my way of holding the mirror up to nature, than about his. (I would accept the *shang* in the pentatonic scale as an autumn symbol, for example, but not the description of the note itself as autumnal.) But my main reservation was founded in a personal, even perhaps a neurological, disability. Our ever more noise-energized environment, which includes highly dangerous inaudible noise, has made me ever more nervous. I have had nightmare visions of new

Jerichos lately, and dreams of being trapped with a hearing aid
that I cannot turn down. Acoustic wattage of a certain intensity
can be lethal, after all.

Harper's: In connection with your remark concerning universality, Mr. Stravinsky, do you believe that all of the great
emotions have already appeared in music?

I.S.: Until new ones appear and prove that they haven't.

VII

Everything must be learned, from talking to dying.

FLAUBERT

Harper's: What, apart from your new composition, has most
occupied your thoughts, Mr. Stravinsky?

I.S.: The ultimate *force majeure*, naturally. In spite of all those
little capsules ('mood raisers') to shoo away the truth, a hospital
bed provides an abundance of both time and 'motivation'. The
blackest thoughts have been dispelled since then, and I feel as
if I had been reprieved from, say, one minute before twelve to
eleven-thirty (I hope it is no later than that!). But I look and
feel like the Seventh Age of Man. Stiff, creaky, slow, I am hardly
certain at times of being 'in possession of all my facilities'.

The chief mental problem in being eighty-five, though
intelligent people are afflicted with it already at thirty-five or
even twenty-five, is the realization that one may be powerless to
change the *quality* of one's work. The quantity can be increased,
of course, even at eighty-five, but can one change the whole? I,
at any rate, am absolutely certain that my *Variations* and *Requiem
Canticles* have altered the picture of my whole life, and I seek the
strength now to change that 'completed' picture just one
more time.

By some unlucky circumstance I happened to re-read *The
Death of Ivan Ilych* a few months ago, and, as every reader of the
story must, I have been seeing myself in it ever since. (For
similar reasons Groddeck's *Das Buch vom Es* is to be avoided
by anyone with an over-active auto-suggestivity.) But even when
identifying with Ivan Ilych, I admired the skill with which
Tolstoy projects his hero's consciousness of growing separate-
ness and of the irrelevance of himself and his condition in the

lives of younger people. As for Ivan Ilych's awareness of the transparency of doctors' professionalism, of the diplomatic dishonesty of his family, as well as of such subtleties as the feeling that a good-night kiss must be underexpressed to avoid a collision of unsaid thoughts: of these things my recent experience has equipped me to be an ideal literary critic. No less brilliant, as my experience has also taught me, is Tolstoy's delineation of the awareness of transitional stages, of the alternation of struggle and acceptance; of the need for sympathy and the rejection of sympathy; of the onslaughts of childhood memories and the attacks of philosophy in endless interior dialogues about the meaning of life; and above all of the sick man's acute sense both of the nature of his destiny and of the terrifying accidental aspect of life (and how much of it *is* accident if, as Rank claims, our birth history—instrument landings and so forth—is the all-important-event in it).

But thank Heavens it is Ivan Ilych I am talking about! As for myself, let me say, 'to be continued, I hope'.

September–October, 1967

SIDE EFFECTS II

I

One of the difficulties in assessing the skill of the medical practitioners of the time is the almost complete absence of any records of the patients who had come for treatment.
From a review of *Medicine in Medieval England*,
T.L.S., 11/1/68

N.Y.R.: We were sorry to hear you had to go to the hospital a second time, Mr. Stravinsky.
I.S.: I appreciate the sympathy. And I need it, too. It has seemed to me lately that the greater the medical advances, the narrower the patient's chances of surviving doctors and hospitals. Until this last adventure I was unaware of the extent to which medicine men, like generals and politicians, enjoy the right to be wrong; and unaware of the breach between medical science for its own disinterested sake—'operation a success, patient dead'—and medical practice for the sake of interested people. Some of the publicity concerning the late Mr. Washkansky's new heart helped to obviate the distinction by too blatantly showing that the man's life was less important than the symbiotic experiment for which it provided the opportunity. Freshly primed by my own experience, I worried not only about Mr. Washkansky but about his news-unworthy fellow patients as well. While the nurses were posing for *Life*, and the doctors talking to the cover-story team of *Time*, who was distributing the digitalis?

My second confinement was twice as long as the first and, the so-called maharajah care notwithstanding, a hundred times more harrowing. I was too drugged, luckily, to have been aware of all of it, but clear enough to realize that a great deal was going wrong quite apart from what was wrong with me. My confidence in doctors had begun to dwindle, too, though the preoccupation with status in their profession—the AMA must harbour many a '*médecin malgré lui*'—had already disaffected me, even more than the surgical *Schadenfreude* and the pill-pushing indifference (equanimity, if you prefer, but I am smarting from my experience). Nor was my confidence in routine hospital functions on the upswing. I was fed the wrong X-ray dye on one occasion, and on another nearly perfused with the wrong intravenous fluid; when the right bottle was found, moreover—about to be piped into a visitor—and finally attached to my arm, the needle slipped out and inflated the skin like a balloon. I 'blew my stack', as one of the nurses used to say, with less reason, but this protest had little effect. The spigot on the next bottle was too loose, and I was soon so over-irrigated that I began to wonder how much of the deleted me was the erstwhile me and how much the synthetic.

Identity problems of this type will become increasingly common as more and more brains are washed, and as—overcoming complications of histology and apartheid—spare-part banks and surgical mergers ('grafts' and 'transplants' in the horticulturalized, antivivisectionist terminology) become more efficient. Another eventuality to allow for is the accidental transference of the soul and the id. This could lead to a revival of Eleatic divisibility/indivisibility arguments (the One and the Many); to theological tangles concerning prevenient grace; and to forensic medical arguments in personal property suits (*very* personal property) as to the exact contents of a 'me' or a 'you', the settlements of which could end by hyphenating the donors' and the donees' names. Ever since molecular biologists activated the laboratory-made DNA, after all, former definitions of 'life' itself have become obsolete. But I am straying.

N.Y.R.: You were talking about the harassments of the hospital.
I.S.: Most of the other incidents were excusable. In any event it would be difficult to fix responsibility for the invasion of my floor by an escapee from the neuropathic ward on the neuro-warpath, or for the replacing of my broken windowshade one night by a black screen so that I was uncertain in the morning whether I *had* awakened or had gone over. Nor is it reasonable to blame the staff for a mis-aimed 'pain-killing' injection. The psychology of the staff in dealing with pain, incidentally, was to

coax the victim into classifying its intensities himself, according to a scale of euphemisms ranging from 'very slight' to 'somewhat severe'. But no headway was made with this martyrizing appeal in my case. I am insusceptible to masochistic enticements, and I recognized long ago that the arrows in most of those Sebastians are really Cupid's *flèches d'amour*. ('With Phoebus' amorous pinches blacke,' as Cleopatra says.) To me all pain is extreme, and the question is not how much but how long.

It also could not be helped that my dose of radioactive phosphorus had to be consigned by the Atomic Energy Commission and transported, like money, in an armoured van. But guilt feelings at the thought of burdening the War Effort were less unnerving than the jitters of the administering technician who seemed to regard me as a one-man test site, or human atomic atoll. Perhaps I shall find consolation in the knowledge that I am magnetic to fireflies and glow-worms, if not to mine-detectors, but this has not happened yet.

The worst of the hospital, nevertheless, was the musical frustration. My pilot-light may not be very gem-like or hard any more, but it is still burning even when the stove is not in use. Musical ideas stalked me, but I could compose them mentally only, being unable to write at the time and unable to remember now. And the mind needs its daily work at such times, not the contemplation of its temporality. To be deprived of art and left alone with philosophy is to be close to Hell.

N.Y.R.: And your convalescence, Mr. Stravinsky?

I.S.: My nurses and 'physiatrists' are flourishing, I assure you, and if my rehabilitation continues at the present rate for long, I will soon be obliged to apply to the Rolling Stones for a loan. But *I* don't flourish. And in spite of protestations by the medical moguls that I have recovered (what else, for those prices, *could* they say?), I feel like a centenarian, am as thin as Kafka's Hunger Artist, and as pale—in spite of being kept in the garden, apparently for photosynthesis—as the afternoon moon.

But I complain too much, and too splenetically (which is reasonable, trouble having been found in that department as well); if my caducity were as bad as I make it sound, some College of Fine Arts would have rushed in by now with a last-minute doctorate. Besides, positive cause for elation has been found in my encephalogram, which seems more important now than ever, for the reason that I am not permitted to sit for long at the piano and must compose most of whatever I *can* compose, in my head. This is hampering because the instrument helps to push my imagination into position; and ironic because I am writing my first solo-piano piece since 1925. Yesterday I worked at the piano for the first time in five months (the feel of dust on the keys was unpleasant), beginning with a C- to B-flat trill, very slow, like the vibrato of a prima donna on a farewell tour. The trilling impulse came, I think, from exposure to a Christmas-present canary (someone had overestimated my fondness for *The Pines of Rome*) whose finest *fioriture* seem to be mating responses to our electric juice-squeezer.

II

Neue Kraft fühlend

N.Y.R.: Have you noted any fresh developments in the musical world, Mr. Stravinsky?
I.S.: The Ivesian vogue of 'simultaneous strands', the musical equivalent to multiple projection films, is at high tide. So is pop, to the extent that the record companies spend most of their resources panning, like old-time prospectors, for pop hits. Certainly there has been no 'breakthrough' in the classical establishment. Conductors are still the lapdogs of musical life, and the laps are still not much like 'the gods'. The most dazzling instrumental virtuosity hardly counts in comparison. It may be true that an infant phenomenon playing *Turangalîla* in an arrangement for the left hand could make a certain *bruit d'estime*, but the histrionic range of infant phenomena playing instruments is naturally more constricting than that of men playing themselves. Furthermore, instrumental mastery is acquired at an expense of time and work, whereas the *musical* training of conductors—who before all else must be experts in aeroplane schedules, international tax laws, hair-styling (the expression 'the silver-haired Karajan' having attained a myth-like status comparable to 'the rosy-fingered dawn' in Homer)— is briefer with each season's increasingly rapid turnover in the *stupor-mundi* market.

But I have already 'made my representations' against the visual standards of an activity that is contiguous to music without always being of it. It may even be time now to redress the criticism slightly, pointing out that while amateurism is deplorable, so is too much professionalism. In the sense of technique, the most admired conductor in the country—by me too, though I often wish his *tempi* were a heartbeat slower—is the ombudsman-elect of the New York Philharmonic.[1] But what about that goal toward which conducting is hardly more than a necessary evil? Is it not possible that a *chef* with lesser technical powers but a wider and deeper scope might make better music? A musician such as Von Mehta, for instance, who can give humid and intensely suffered performances of Dvořák symphonies, and ingenuously felt and at times even searing ones of Rumanian, Hungarian, and other rhapsodies, including some with different titles by composers who did not actually intend that sort of thing.

Part of what I mean by scope is simply a larger stretch of sympathies. But in the first place I fail to see how a musician based almost exclusively in last-century repertory can ombudsmanize the affairs of the fast-getting-on present one. Imagine my pleasure therefore in the discovery that at least this sort of limitation no longer impedes the swell of progress in the Quaker City, the conductor there having proclaimed the new state of enlightenment (see my italics below) while lifting the veil from the long-cherished secret of his acquaintance with Alban Berg. 'At that time I was not as well versed in the twelve-tone school of music *as I am now*,' he says, and goes on to compliment Berg for giving 'logical, intelligent, and understandable' answers to his questions. I like that 'understandable'. As for the Philharmonic, I think it might do better in the Yellow Pages.

N.Y.R.: Have any new developments on the critical front caught your attention, Mr. Stravinsky?

I.S.: I am in arrears, but the new thing seems to be the critic as hero. A recent advertisement in *The New York Times* for a new Broadway play featured a photograph not of the author, or director, or set, or leading lady or animal, but of *The New York Times* reviewer who had given it a rave. This should help to restore a sense of importance to a function heavily inroaded

[1] George Szell. (R.C.)

by the pre-reviewing of producers' and publishers' blurbs.

Largely, however, reviewing is the unabated *old* thing, music, dance, drama still being treated primarily as means of easing unemployment among roving all-purpose journalists rather than as fairly specialized assignments. I used to blame the 'intellectual community' for the failure to demand better, and in fact have only lately realized that no such community exists, nor even much respect for the individual voices who might have formed it. An appeal on behalf of an American Jean Genet (unthinkable as the equivalents may be, not only to Genet but to his entreaters, Gide, Claudel, and Sartre) would receive no acknowledgement, let alone result in effective action. And the press would most likely deride the petitioners, as *Time* derided Mr. Lowell for declining a certain invitation to dinner. But if the 'intellectual community' has no representation in public affairs, it cannot claim a great deal more in the public arts. One wonders whether any student, or artist, or writer has ever ventured among the tiers of bankers, stockbrokers, and board-chairmen who comprise the 'public' of New York's ghetto of the performing arts, granting, of course, that *Martha* and *Hänsel* are deterrents as formidable as the ticket prices.

As for my own PR, I have seen no sign of a suspension of normal uncouthness for the sake of defunct traditions about courtesy to older people. But *I* have no intention of calling a moratorium either, or abiding by rules of games I neither made up nor agreed to play.

N.Y.R.: Debussy predicted that you would 'tolerate no music whatever as an old man', Mr. Stravinsky.

I.S.: But I love more music than ever before; if I seem to stint unduly on the Smetana tone poems, Mendelssohn oratorios, and the type of concerto employed at pianists' Olympic Games, the reason is simply to have more time for the Beethoven quartets. I have revisited a great deal of music lately, some of it after a seventy-year interim, the revisiting therefore heavily buffeted by past involvements and discoveries of radical differences between remembered and renewed experiences. Certain songs and piano pieces by Schumann, for instance, have jolted me sharply. Schumann is *the* composer of childhood (first child-hood; I will not say who I think is the composer of second childhood), both because he created a children's imaginative world and because children learn some of their first music in his marvellous piano albums. In fact I have just realized that the reason I dislike *Carnaval* is not, as I had supposed, that my musical personality lacks identities corresponding to the Florestan and Eusebius archetypes of all of Schumann's music, but simply that I was told to like it as a child; and the force of these childhood atavisms is such that I am not old enough to dislike it independently even now.

I must have been insufferably proscribing when Debussy projected that estimate of me. He also referred to me, I think in the same letter, as a 'primitive' and 'instinctual', rather than a 'schooled' composer. And he was right. Like Ramanujan, who did his mathematics without formal mathematical education, I have had to depend on 'natural' insight and instinct for all the learning I would have acquired if I had taken a Ph.D. in composition, except that I would have flunked the finals and never taken it.

N.Y.R.: What is the outlook for the Ph.D. composer at the moment, Mr. Stravinsky?

I.S.: I don't know. He used to plead allegiance to either of two totalitarian banners, the one pro-science, the other anti-, to the extent that the scientific pieties of the data-processed society were its main target. But now the lines of these affiliations have crossed, 'infighting' has ceased, and the bitterest factions have linked up, perhaps under the influence of the Maharishi, for the one commodity everybody is willing to buy comes from the Royal Liverpudlian Academy of Music. Well, not *quite* everybody. At least a few of the tougher-minded scientists have resisted the general wash away into mixed-media pastimes, as I learn from their announcements of new reductions in encoding time, and of the development of new systems able to accept both digital and analog input. In short, the final goal, computer facilities for all, is getting closer.

But I am no bellwether myself. I am losing patience with music that does not sing or dance (the day has long gone by since we have had very much of that) and that makes no other gesture I can understand except to reflect mechanical processes that quickly set me adrift. Nor am I satisfied by the promise of 'consequentiality' in these processes; I am only interested in, at my age I can only afford to be interested in, content. A further, personal, handicap is that I am more of a craftsman than a computer or an engineer, and I find no common ground of craftsmanship in most new machine-made art products; which may be similar to the way an easel painter of my epoch feels about the latest creations in liquid fibreglass.

I also admit to a need to go from a beginning to an end through related parts. Perhaps in sympathy with the body's diminished mobility, the mind no longer seems to be willing or able to jump from isolated 'present' moments to other isolated 'present' moments. I have been listening this week to the recorded piano music of a composer now widely esteemed for his ability to stay an hour or so ahead of his time. But I find the alternation of note-clumps and silences of which it consists impossibly monotonous, and I long for the leverage of Beethoven's timing, to say nothing of harmonic and other leverages. The *matter* of the music is so limited in effect, too, and so solemn, that I was sustained only by the hope, during each longer silence, that finally the pianist might have 'had it' too and shot himself.

N.Y.R.: Would you amplify your remark about 'consequential processes'?

I.S.: It is progressivist jargon. Of course it *sounds* better to be consequential than not to be, the promise of higher development in forthcoming stages implying superiority. But I do not believe in linear historicism, except as a means of opening more Midwestern territories of the mind to Ph.D. candidates.

The most consequential is often simply the better sited, the more easily seen or heard, and the inconsequential (historical sense) simply the less accessible, often owing to internal and external innovations of thought and communication. Works of the highest value of all, the Beethoven quartets for instance, are historically inconsequential, though incalculable in these terms anyway, because a value-history would move cyclically at times and wholly out of chronology at other times, skipping generations and even centuries in both directions. One might conclude that fashion plays the largest role, apart from the biological law that beginnings are naturally consequential and endings the other thing. But such speculations only lead to more historicity, whereas

135

what I believe in is the unpredictability, rising above period, style, school, context, historical circumstance, of Beethoven.

N.Y.R.: An essential quality of your own work is the balance in it between past and present, and the continual discovery of the one in the other.

I.S.: Thank you. But it is precisely that debate of yesterday and today that is now relegating *me* to the past, to an annex of the nineteenth century, as I have been told, among less flattering rulings. 'Nothing happened before us,' the post-contemporary composer proclaims, and he is perfectly right. The non-existence of the past is a necessary hypothesis to anyone proposing to start from scratch, and protection from annihilating comparisons is no less necessary to a *modus vivendi*; amusements that wither along with the giggles they provoke should not have to suffer exposure next to music that is without a wrinkle after a century and a half.

Post-contemporary composers are modest or hermetic concerning their materials and origins. I have been able to discover little about either, apart from 'no content', a backward limit of three years, and an explanation that all school-taught traditions are out, though it is some time since there *was* any school worth flouting. But the youngsters' own platform, the 'celebration of "now"', presumably by spontaneously combustible means, seems a little lacking in sustenance; before it is too late they should apply to the science musicians for instruction in *im*-probability theory. The next three years and the three years after that will soon be over, just as telephone booth-packing, panty-raids, hamsters, and Batmania were soon over. In short, the 'no-past' will soon be a part of the 'non-past', except that, to begin with, the past is difficult to deny, the *tabula*, however looked at, being a long way from *rasa*. I have a growing suspicion, in fact, that the pot at the end of this particular rainbow contains only pot.

N.Y.R.: Have you ever tried any drug yourself, Mr. Stravinsky, perhaps during your association with Cocteau?

I.S.: I use a very ordinary drug, procured chiefly from Scotland and France in the forms I favour. Cocteau's opium-taking, at least when I knew him, was of a kind with Mr. Plimpton's percussion- and football-playing, in other words book-making.

The late Max Reinkel of M.I.T. was conducting his pioneer experiments with LSD when I became his patient in 1953, and I was aware of the drug at that time. Soon after that, my friends Aldous Huxley, Gerald Heard, and Christopher Isherwood, who were among its first white-collar users, invited me to try it, to test its effects on my experience of music. But increased sensory intensity, time dislocation, the altering of consciousness are the very last sensations I am looking for.

III

N.Y.R.: May we return to the question of the ineffectual, or non-existent, intellectual community? What is your notion of the 'intellectual' in the first place?

I.S.: *Not* the literary men, the philosophers, and the artists that my remark implied, but someone more like Gramsci's 'Everyman who outside of his own job shares a conception of the world, has a conscious line of moral conduct, and so contributes toward maintaining or changing that conception and encouraging new modes of thought.' (Elsewhere Gramsci forgets this Marxist idyll, noting that 'Intellectuals have been produced in numbers beyond what is justified by the social need.') The poems of the Manyōshū were written *by* 'Everyman' or at least by a representation of people extending from beggars to the Empress.

My remark was provoked by the kidnapping, in West Germany, of the Korean composer I Sang Yun, who was returned to Seoul and condemned as a communist spy. I was unaware of the evidence, and even unaware of Mr. Yun, who could have been the ghost composer of '*We Love Chairman Mao*' for all I knew (Mr. Yun's first names are good for a musician, less good for a spy). I signed a petition to reprieve Mr. Yung, nevertheless, for the reason that I do not believe in judicial murder. (Or any other kind; I should add that I am not a scrutator and that I tend to shirk my social duty of agreeing on one matter with people concerning whom I am in permanent disagreement about virtually everything else.)

Mr. Yun was spared, but whether because or in spite of our protest I have no idea. The only acknowledgement I have seen that the protest ever existed is a note from the American Academy of Arts and Letters, to whose care the cablegrams were mistakenly directed. It said that Academy policy excluded it from taking a hand in such recommendations; I hope that a 'policy' of that sort is a nuisance-avoiding expedient rather than an attempt to preserve the 'neutrality' of arts and letters.

N.Y.R.: And your idea of community? Do you agree with Durkheim that society, as a moral body, should be 'qualitatively distinct' from the individual bodies comprising it?

I.S.: No such society is making itself very conspicuous at present, in any case, nor is the perfectibility of the collective mini-mind showing greater signs of success than the perfectibility of the individual one. But I would be content with lesser ideals myself, even with a *less* 'human' and *more* mechanical system, but one capable of achieving a balance between the safety in numbers and the danger in numbers.

Whatever the relationship between the collective morality and the new instruments of communication, the double standard is now the one and only, at least in public life. No statement by any public figure not made under sodium pentothal or hypnosis can be taken as entirely candid, so long as the said figure is primed by popularity polls. As we are already in the second generation of 'lip service', moreover, the public figures of the near future will soon be unable to tell the difference, even under truth serums, between their own true opinions and their blue chip political investments, much less understand the fate of Ananias or the idea that silence can be a lie. Mr. McNamara's sudden change of occupation, for example, set me wondering whether a measure of personal victory might not have been salvaged from his defeat on the grounds that if it is impossible both to say what one believes to be true and to survive politically, then one should get on with the political suicide. To give Mr. McNamara the benefit of the doubt, he appeared to be merely dumbfounded. But it would have been interesting to know what a 'peace offensive' is really like, and who could have been in a better position to say?

And who now, what telegenic younger Senator, will remind us that our judgment against the Nazi War Criminals, a judgment independent of the differences between Nuremberg and now, was that even soldiers under orders are responsible for 'crimes against humanity'? That, after all, is what Captain Levy and others have had the courage to say. And somebody more highly and safely placed had soon better say it, too. In view of the vindictiveness toward Mr. LeRoi Jones, it begins to look as if we may have some Daniels and Sinyavskis of our own.

While and if he were about it, incidentally, the same spokesman might well repeat the no less pertinent question of Marlowe's Machiavelli: 'What right had Caesar to the empire?' Was it, I wonder, the right of self-defence?

IV

Since we are deprived of acquired experience and former practice by each new case, we do not know what to do.

AMIEL

And age, and then the only end of age.

PHILIP LARKIN

N.Y.R.: Do you ever think about the future of your works, Mr. Stravinsky?

I.S.: No. I have already seen some of their 'posterity'—as soon as a work is performed, that is what it belongs to, after all—and the more I see of that, the less I care about it. Of course it is satisfying to see settled estimates unsettled, and the removal of interdicts from works of unfashionable periods. But I care less about my 'works' than about composing. This is partly because one never composes exactly the piece one sets out to compose, just as I am not now saying exactly what I had in mind to say, but what the extenuating words that come to mind as I go along lead me to say. But the threat of posterity is worse now than it used to be, for other reasons as well. I have changed my mind, for example, about the advantages of embalming a performance in tape. The disadvantages, which are that one performance represents only one set of circumstances, and that mistakes and misunderstandings are cemented into traditions as quickly and canonically as truths, now seem to me too great a price to pay. The Recording Angel I am concerned with is not CBS, in any case, but the One with the Big Book.

N.Y.R.: And your own future, Mr. Stravinsky?

I.S.: I will have to stay closer to home, and my object world will be more limited. But I have been thinking of how Vermeer was able to reflect a world and live a life of perfect making in his own studio; and of how Chardin could display a richer representation of life in his kitchen than other painters managed with all Versailles. So I must try, in my smaller way, to look more closely close by, and to bring more life to my own still-life. One difficulty is that I am regarded as an object now myself, some priceless piece of porcelain as it may be, and this crockery is my greatest enemy. I hope nothing else befalls it for a spell, but if something does, that it comes 'during office hours'. As for the 'contents', our talents are not given to us with any tenure, and 'we' may well outlast them. I know, nevertheless, that I have more music in me. And I must give; I cannot live a purely receiving life.

Of the two greatest problems of age, the first is simply the lack of preparation, the lack of a natural or acquired provision of experience. All our lives we observe other people in the condition, but fail to learn biologically from the spectacle, and even fail to believe that the same thing can and will happen to us. When it *has* happened, the suddenness is like Levin's awareness, in the peasant village, that the sky had changed and that this change, like the transformation in himself, was unnoticeable as a process.

The more difficult problem is inevitability. It was put very gently by Augustine in his last sermon, and I would prefer to have him say it for me, as Mr. Peter Brown describes the scene in his *Augustine of Hippo*. After appointing the priest Eraclius as his successor, Augustine reminds the congregation that:

'As boys we can look forward to being youths; as youths to being grown up, and as young men to reaching our prime and, in our prime to growing old. Whether this will happen is uncertain; but there is always something to look forward to. But an old man has no further stage before him. Now I have grown old.'

But the end of the story reminds *me* of something, which is that I have been talking too much:

'Eraclius stood forward to preach, while the old Augustine sat behind him: "the cricket chirps", Eraclius said, "the swan is silent." '

Hollywood/Feb. 1/68

WHERE IS THY STING?

Crito: The attendant who is to give you the [hemlock]
wants me to tell you not to talk too much . . . talking is
apt to interfere with the action of the poison.
Phaedo, 63

N.Y.R.: When you went to Europe recently, Mr. Stravinsky,
we heard that you were intending to go for good.
I.S.: For the better, anyway. At the time I left Los Angeles it
already seemed too late for a phased withdrawal. The smog
was like Mace. But, then, the air, apart from radioisotopes, must
be better anywhere else now, even in a coal mine. A major
earthquake was predicted, too, not merely by seismologists but
by the religious-protection rackets, which were transferring east
to pray out the millennium and await the second option of
chiliasm there. Self-centred as it is to say so, in view of the
probable devastations to and from atomic and bacteriological
stockpiles, I would fall like Humpty Dumpty now, and being
unable to make a 'soft landing', break unmendably. A tidal
wave was expected also, and as a few heavy showers can turn
much of the city into 'slide areas' necessitating helicopter
evacuations, a really sizeable inundation would wash the whole
'songdom' and 'gemurrmal' out to sea. Yet despite these and
other catastrophes, actual and impending, no one got around to
designating the State a disaster area until the mid-winter
monsoons.

Even so, the most immediate hazard was the state of society.
Whatever they were 'on' about then, 'speed', 'soul', the recent
invention of 'youth', people with long, anti-astronaut hairstyles
were milling about my street in such numbers that the ambu-
lances—which siren by every few minutes normally, curtains
raised, presumably to give the emergency patient a last look—
had to find another route. Welcome as this was in terms of noise

141

abatement, it attracted still more of the armed and uniformed men who were already so conspicuous that the neighbourhood felt like occupied territory. Or worse than occupied territory. For the xenon beams that search the stygian gloom of the polluted upper sky ('the smog is lofting'—*Finnegans Wake*, 593), and that supposedly 'send up' film premières, give one the impression of being near, or in, a concentration camp.

High barriers exist, in any case—and not only figuratively, the fencing of at least one private estate hereabouts apparently having been modelled on the Berlin Wall. A social war foments around them, moreover, and it could easily break into a shooting one, *did* break into one shortly before I left, when the police out-gunned a man hardly three hundred yards from my house. At about that time, as well, the American Legion opened its campaign against my San Diego neighbour Professor Marcuse, an action I read as a warning to keep my peace about the war or risk being dealt with Chicago-style myself.

All the same, the final decision to leave came from a very different consideration. It was simply that I had begun to fear some City or State official might find out that I live there. This would almost certainly lead to an award, such as I have been receiving during the past sixty-five years from other cities, states, countries, kibbutzim, and tribes; and entail a ceremony, with a presentation speech by Miss Long Beach, or one of the Beverly Hillbillies. Something had to give, obviously, and it was me. I took the least frequently hijacked run to New York and Zürich.

N.Y.R.: What did you do in Switzerland, Mr. Stravinsky?

I.S.: Saw friends. *They* came not only to see but to touch me, though, as if I were a talismanic relic; I supposed that they were only double-checking, as the Great Leap Forward had checked on the tangibility of Chairman Mao by obliging him to swim. In lawful, orderly, and quiescent Zürich, however, and with distance lending enchantment, I began to miss the last-few-minutes-of-the-Roman Empire aspect of Hollywood, and the commotion ('Come to America where the action is') and campus 'unrest' (tanks, bombs, guerrilla warfare). The sound of hunters' rifles in the woods near the hotel one afternoon filled me with nostalgia for Sunset Boulevard on a Saturday night.

N.Y.R.: Where else did you go, Mr. Stravinsky?

I.S.: To Paris, to see more friends. I walked quite regularly, too, as much as I *can* walk, in Le Nôtre's paths at Chantilly and, less bracingly, in the corridors of the Trianon Palace Hotel, where some of the boarders might have been making an early Chaplin film: a white-gloved cigar-smoker; a spats-wearing walker of a small but ferocious dog; an alcoholically roseate old woman talker-to-cats. I did not go to concerts, but did hear some new music on tape, including one very fine piece by Gérard Masson, whose acquaintance I made as well. And, yes, I saw *Le Sacre du printemps*. This frolic was held in the Opéra, but it belonged at the Folies-Bergères.

I was in Paris during the monetary crisis, by the way, and was greatly impressed by the contrast between the success of the international bankers and the failure of the international peace negotiators. What is really important to 'the comity of nations', or, at any rate, to the people who really run the world, can and does get instant action.

N.Y.R.: We read that you had talked with French television officials, but did you see any television there?

I.S.: No, which must be why it strikes me as even more echolalic and mind-jamming back here than before. Yesterday I saw and heard a newsman, part green, part third-degree sunburn, say that 'Although General Eisenhower's condition has improved, plans are going ahead for his funeral.'

Television sells more than that which is so disastrously rated next to godliness, to be sure (in fact it sells vicarious existences), but the predominating advertisements seem to be those which imply that a dirtless, odourless, and inconvenienceless society is the ultimate goal of civilization. These somehow inadequate aims must be near fulfilment, furthermore, at least in the home, thanks to socially-up-to-date detergents ('DRIVE eats blood stains') powered by 'ultrasonic activated bubbles'. The 'technology of false needs' has turned to Nature now, in any case, and is already spraying it with defoliants, denudants, desiccants, deodorants, herbicides, germicides, pesticides. A new play about Adam in contemporary undress would already be obliged to represent the Garden without a leaf, let alone an apple. Now, too, the punitive and expiatory needs of puritan sanitation insanity are arousing expectations of cosmic retribution, in the contamination of other planets with terrestrial micro-organisms and of our own with lunar spores.

Which reminds me of the video highlight on my return, the Christmas-pageant space-show reconciling missile technology and *Genesis*. In fact the space capsule itself was turned into a teleological argument as the Three Wise Men astrobards, guided by earthshine, read Bible poetry to Sabbatarian earthlings. *Gott mit uns*, the Space Program was assuring us, but it must have been worried that a more prestigiously remote orbit had been destined as a pulpit for readings from *Das Kapital* on Marx's birthday.

N.Y.R.: What did your European friends think of our elections?

I.S.: They were unable to imagine the visage of the new President on Mount Rushmore, so they said, and not only because of the sculptural obstacles. And some of them questioned whether actual voting need take place any more, on the grounds that computerized public-opinion polls are reasonably reliable now, and in effect have already done the job; one friend, thinking of my own welfare, suggested that the saving in time, money, and fresh fertilizer, properly converted and applied, could be used to make Los Angeles inhabitable. Certainly an election by opinion survey would not destroy the illusion that by dropping a ballot in a ballot box and proclaiming the winner the people's choice (which he or she could be only by a concatenation of choices several million links removed), the body politic is exercising its freedom and democratic rights. After all, even so transparently suppositious an operation as the Chicago convention could not undermine *that* fantasy.

Vested-interested legislators may be an old story, but some of the territory they are now obliged to administer—the management of the scientific future, for one rather estimable precinct—is alarmingly new. Consider the field of genetics, with its limitless power and short timetable of disaster. Assume, too, that the 'new-mandarin' race-improving committees are 'humane', 'well-meaning', 'responsible', and that they can be entrusted with the elimination of diabetics, cleft palates, stutterers, the colour-blind and the tone-deaf. But what about mental defectives, and especially borderline cases?

Darmstadt, 1931

COSMOPOLITAN HOTEL

Ladies and gentlemen

PLEAS PERMIT ME TO EXPRESS TO YOU
MY SATISFACTION AND MY GRATITUDE FOR THE
INTEREST, WHICH YOU, THE ARTISTIC ELITE OF
DENVER HAVE SHOWN TOWARDS MY ART.

S. D. & I, HAVE UNITED OUR EFFORTS
IN THIS LIMITED BUT CONDESEDAND AND
POWERFUL FORM OF DUOS FOR V. & P, in
ORDER TO SERVE THE ESSENCE ITSELF OF
MY MUSIC, AND WE ARE HAPPY TO DEFEND
BEFORE AN ENLIGHTENED PUBLIC A CAUSE
WICH IS DEAR TO US.

CLUB HEADQUARTERS
ROTARY—OPTIMIST—ADVERTISING—TEXNIX

Text of a speech delivered to the 'artistic elite of Denver, at a concert in which the composer and SD' (Samuel Dushkin) happily 'defended the powerful form of Duos for Violin and Piano', 1935

Consolation of a sort is offered by the certainty that the administration of science by scientists would be even worse. When a debate opened up at the recent Congress of Genetics in Tokyo as to whether science could afford to be bound by ethics, one pro-ethics delegate clinched his argument with the epiphany that 'Although man consists of molecules he is not a molecule himself'; and a like-minded colleague added that 'The evolution of every species is certainly being modified very greatly by the presence of man.' That at least deserves a prize for litotes.

But this is high science, still for the moment unapplied. What is transpiring meanwhile with some of the applied kinds, with, for instance, the grafting, transplanting, implanting of those thirty-five spare body-parts? (What a relief to be too old for gardening of this sort!) Will those life-prolonging utilities be available to rich and poor alike, to the queue-forming as well as the well-connected? And by what means will donors be found? Euthanasia? Black Markets in dismembering? Body-snatching (of the still living)?

N.Y.R.: What were your friends' views of our Black Separatists?
I.S.: I have not worked out my *own* views yet. 'Now there are only the blacks and those who dislike them,' says Mr. Bond. But this is untrue and unhelpful. Nor will it help to ban Monostatos, or the Moor in *Petrushka*; they are Manichean characters, of course, but their absurdity apart from their music can only animadvert on white culture—they are little white lies—not on black. (Incidentally, the 'racial' motivation in Monostatos's account of his rape attempt resembles Mr. Cleaver's account of the same thing in *Soul on Ice*.)

As I cannot be certain that it mattered, I am being no less rhetorical than Mr. Bond when I say that the man outgunned near my house was black. Yet the origins of the black man's crime were to some degree rooted in the inequities which that circumstance introduces. The point is irrelevant in the near-sighted and compartmented eye of the law, which does not admit or apportion any dependence of the particular on the general, and which is only beginning to accept the idea, as old as the Encyclopedists, of diminished responsibility. But the law, after all, is a large constituent in the moral dilemma.

The shooting was a consequence of petty larceny. But was it

necessary to kill? Can trained marksmen do no better? Or are the Los Angeles Police (as they might at times appear to the incompletely manumitted people of Watts) underpracticed at certain targets because of over-specialization in the upholding of a prejudicial system? The system I mean is the non-distribution of wealth, thanks to tax shelters and other privileges whereby the rich may pay less taxes than their chauffeurs—which is why possession should be taxed rather than income, why we need an Onassis tax, and Rockefellow and Rothschildren taxes, and a tax on tax expatriots, and a not-likely-to-pass-through-the-eye-of-the-needle tax.

The solution to racism is genetic, but I no longer remember my Mendel and whether fusion can be achieved quickly or only after a long interregnum of sexual roulette. I wonder, too, if when it *has* been, racism will disappear, or whether it will then be a question of

> . . . I swear Beauty herself is black,
> And all they foul that thy complexion lack.

II

N.Y.R.: How would a contemporary musician paraphrase Mendelssohn's 'What a piece of music expresses is not too vague a thought to be put into words, but too precise a thought'?
I.S.: He might say that music is a non-analogous system—or several non-analogous systems: it is more of a Babel than a universal language. And if he had said that, he might add that the basis of intelligibility (music is not an encoded something else) is presupposed, self-contained, innate. The epistemological problem would thus be the same as it is with verbal language. The mode of knowledge is untranslatable but not private: it depends on other users. Which is Descartes's (superseded) 'other minds' argument: '. . . *qu'ils usent comme moy de la Parole . . . qu'ils le sont comme moy.*'

But *would* 'he' have said it, subscribed to the nominalism, in the first place? A sociology of music, the correlating of music and the whole of life, does not exist as yet, but studies in specialized

areas—in psychiatry, for instance, where patients who will respond to no verbal approach (*trust* no verbal approach?) both
respond to and participate in music—prove that it *is* understood
in correlative terms.

Does a world of the Beethoven quartets exist outside of
music, then, and is it possible to discover a reflective system
between the language structure of the music and the structure
of the phenomenal world? No, to the first, but to the second,
well, yes, perhaps, eventually. All the same, the music of the
quartets, and of *The Magic Flute*, accedes to an *in-extremis* importance in the human consciousness beyond the pleasure principle,
or divertimento principle, on which it nevertheless continues to
depend.

My further, personal, belief is that the quartets are a charter
of human rights, a perpetually seditious one in the Platonic sense
of the subversiveness of art. The charter is obviously no solvent
to the discarded humanity in Resurrection Cities, for whom, on
the contrary, the accessibility of such treasures to other people
must seem as unjust, and the use of them as tactless, in different
orders of value, as the Burtons' *ditto* with their new yacht. Nor
will it bring much balm to activists, for whom 'art' is a cant
word anyway, and 'aesthetic examples' a run-around in the
language game. (According to the Hindu *chakras*, the body-
centre both for the aesthetic feelings and the feelings of material
affluence is—did Freud know this?—the anus, which may have
something to do with the high incidence in aesthetes and collectors of a condition often if indecorously described as tight-
assed.)

A high concept of freedom *is* embodied in the quartets, nevertheless, both beyond and including what Beethoven himself
meant when he wrote to Prince Galitzin that his music could
'help suffering mankind'. They are a measure of man (I am
thinking of Professor Puccetti's extra-human 'persons'), and part
of the description of the quality of man, and their existence is a
guarantee.

N.Y.R.: Why *The Magic Flute*, even assuming that you mean to
limit it to the music?
I.S.: *Can* it be limited to the music? I believe in the entity myself. Certainly the *magic* is limited to the music, while the moral

meaning—the entity I believe in—would hardly be worth stating, if it could be stated, apart from it. Still, the music is not 'independent', and not 'pure'. In fact it seems to me that the intentional meaning of the opera, the triumph of Life over Death, is reversed at times in the depths of the music; in the brave little parade of Music through the gates of Death, for example, the flute charms the Keeper into a stay of execution, but the piece is a funeral march, nonetheless. Death is just beneath the surface in much of the other music as well, especially Pamina's, and in the great C minor fugato-chorale, which somehow succeeds in sounding Beethoven's *Eroica* note without Beethoven's display of superior will, the wings of the terrible angel are closer than they have ever been before in music.

Mozart's Masonic allegory-land is a more attractive country than the *dix-huitième* establishment countries of his other operas, at least to me, and not only musically. It is morally more generous, for one thing, and for another the dramatic terrain ranges more widely, partly because of the new and diverse elevations of the religious, the mystical, and the supernatural. In fact the greatest achievement of the opera is precisely the entity, the unity of feeling that embues all of the music from sacred choruses and magic spells to the proto-Broadway duet—except in musical quality—concerning the future propagations of Papageno and Papagena.

Unlike *Don Giovanni*, the opera does not include any extended scene, but neither does it 'lack' one. (It also does not contain, or lack, any bore comparable to Masetto.) And Mozart is more economical and faster-moving than ever, setting the stage for the final scene, for instance, with a single phrase. The simplest means are more effective, too, as in the device of the 'false' relationship, which occurs in all of his music, yet here (most vertiginously in Pamina's '*Mir klingt der Muttername süsse*') as if for the first time.

The most obvious anticipations are of Weber, Wagner, the Mendelssohn of the *Midsummer Night's Dream*. (The most obvious omission is Schubert, who had already been scooped in '*L'ho perduta*' from *Figaro*.) Wagner is everywhere, and all the way from *Tannhäuser* (the sixteenth-note violin figuration in the final *Andante*) to *Tristan* ('*Wann also wird die Decke schwinden?*' and '*jeden*

Tone meinen Dank zu schildern'). The Pamino-Sarastro scene is
Wagnerian, too (though Sarastro's own music more strikingly
resembles the music of Jesus in the Bach Passions), except that
Mozart stops at the point where Wagner, already heavy-
breathing, would have begun to overblow.

The forerunning, in any case and because I have somehow got
on to this dreary subject, is more remarkable in the *Terzett* (No.
16), and in the accompaniment to Papageno's final aria, which
plagiarize and improve upon *The Sleeping Beauty*; in the choral
parts and instrumental bass-line of '*Bald, bald, Jüngling*', which
have been lifted from *Rigoletto*; and in the introduction to '*Drei
Knäbchen, jung, schön*', which might have been borrowed from a
rainy-day mood-piece by Ravel.

N.Y.R.: What are the outstanding tendencies in music today, as
distinguished from a decade ago, when you said that Boulez and
Stockhausen represented them?
I.S.: Well, those two names are still an inescapable collocation,
and Stockhausen is still on the crest of the *Nouvelle Vague*, most
of the main rages of the moment either having been begotten
by him or else quickly taken under his wing. The one for the
re-employment of the classics (an idea as old as the quodlibet)
was popularized by his *Hymnen*, and the one for sustained-sounds
('. . . being all in one tone,' says Hawthorne, 'I had only to get
my pitch, and could then go on interminably') by his *Stimmung*,
a seventy-minute chord—Stockhausen's, time-scale is that of
Götterdämmerung—which to me indicates the need of a musical
equivalent to the parking meter; though *that* idea, I might add,
is as old as Purcell's *Fantasy Upon One Note*. The main lines of
many other Stockhausen novelties are laid down in his own
'concerts'. One of them is the blurring of the termini both *a quo*
and *ad quem*, or call it the blending of the aesthetic enterprise
with 'the world'. Another is in improvising electronic accompaniments to the ascents of balloons, which is rather like bubble-
blowing, pictorially speaking.

The handiest index of comparison from the beginning to the
end of the decade is not in the work of any composer, however,
but in the status of electronic music. It has moved in that time
from a corner of experiment to the centre of the stage, from con-

certs for hard-core colleagues to soft-centred films like *Candy*. And it has moved into and conquered academe. The young musician takes his degree in computer technology now, and settles down with his Moog or his mini-synthesizer as routinely as in my day he would have taken it in counterpoint and harmony (see dictionary) and gone to work at the piano.

As for the *live* new music of the decade, the main power struggle was between the pre-ordained and the lottery schools, even though so far as the ordinary listener was concerned this amounted to a stalemate, for no matter how polarized the differences, only score-readers and initiates were aware of them. In practice, the *ad lib* timing, the unfixed notes in fixed range, the mechanisms of choice, were not recognized as the freedom gestures they were intended to be, but as effects that might have been as despotically 'written' as any other.

Progress, or at least invention, might have been detected by the non-initiate in the new techniques for the movement of sound in space. But some of the other 'pioneering' of the period must have seemed to him like paring closer and closer to nothingness: the engaging of choruses in a variety of pranks not including any use of the voice, for example, and the performances on the woodwork of the piano (after the attractions of 'topless' pianos had been overexposed), and the exploitation of a principle of form based entirely on audience suspense in guessing how near the actual *cul* of the *sac* the promulgator really was. But the non-initiate may well have been wrong, and he may really have been offered

> . . . *imperishable presences serene*
> *Colossal, without form, or sense, or sound*

Progress was also measured, incidentally, or not so incidentally, when ephemerality was finally claimed as an objective. This may have seemed simply to be making a virtue of necessity, but it increased production to the point where the manufacturer could retire each new model to the used-car lot even before it had been driven around the block.

N.Y.R.: Have you followed the Boulez-Liebermann dispute on the present state of opera, or seen Laderman's letter in *The Times* on the neglect of American efforts in this form?

I.S.: Boulez assailed his targets so convincingly that I all the more regretted his reluctance to contribute his own example of the requisite new opera. But whereas Boulez rejects all contemporary operas except Berg's, Laderman does not even raise the value question. American operas should be performed because they are American. And in so far as opera composers require even more help than other kinds of composers, and American more than European, who would disagree? Except that what is the point?

In 1937 the Met could have been doing *Wozzeck*. What it did do was Damrosch's *The Man without a Country*, the indigenous opera in an acceptably bland style by a composer with the connections to get it performed. I did not hear it, but being in New York for my *Jeu de Cartes* at the time of the rehearsals, I heard some tattle about it. (There was said to be an unfortunate *fermata* on the first syllable of the last word of the title aria: 'The Man without a count . . . ry.') Judging by its traces, the performance did little for the Met, the composer, or the future of opera, which in fact seems more and more to be in the past.

N.Y.R.: How do today's new-music audiences compare with those of your own early years?

I.S.: The question is unquantifiable, and anyway, as practically the oldest audience alive, I am hardly able to speak for young ones.

N.Y.R.: Then what are the incomparables?

I.S.: In my youth the new music grew out of and in reaction to traditions, whereas it appears to be evolving today as much from social needs as interior artistic ones. I am unable to evaluate this development, but I retract my former, irrelevant objections, which were that if anything goes, then nothing *goes*, and if anything can happen, it cannot matter very much what *does* happen.

The status of new music as a category is another incomparable. It had none at all in my early years, being in fact categorically opposed, and often with real hostility. But at least the unsuccess of composers of my generation kept them from trading on success, and our unsuccess may have been less insidious than the automatic superlatives which nowadays kill the new by absorbing it to death. (By the same token, of course, the best hatchet jobs are done with pernicious praise.)

151

The largest incomparable is in the permissiveness factor. Twenty years ago, when Mitropoulos introduced Schoenberg's still rather steamy *Five Pieces* to New York, one die-hard Philharmonic subscriber actually did die from the shock. Surely a response of *that* sensitivity is no longer possible now.

N.Y.R.: How do the upper eighties compare with the lower, Mr. Stravinsky?

I.S.: Very unfavourably. I may seem like a 'kid' to a Struldbruggian like Bertrand Russell, and, in fact, next to the redoubtable sage I do not look very arctic. Still, eighty-seven years can feel like, as of course they *are*, an incurable disease. At that time of life one's corporeality and what is bizarrely called one's health are too important. Not only must one husband one's strength, but the most 'mechanical' body-habits have to be programmed by the brain, and at times even the simplest limb movements must be put through the mind. Which is part of the reason we no longer gallivant but only toddle—at the end as in the beginning, as I was reminded while posing for photographs with my two-year-old great-granddaughter not long ago. And this is the only certain 'wisdom of age' I am able to impart.

The perimeter of my epicurean pleasures, small as it was in the lower eighties, has shrunk further now, and my appetites have diminished to such an extent that everything except a gavage has been used to try to make me eat. Seek other satisfactions, doctors tell me, and the one that I have most earnestly sought of late is the satisfaction of surviving their remedies. This sounds churlish, I know, but I grew up, and old, in the days of general practitioners who did not expect a stipend or humanitarian award for each house call, or require the invalid to diagnose his own ailments. Competent treatment is available even now, no doubt, especially for illnesses uncomplicated by the necessity of considering whole human beings. But I mis-diagnosed one of my own maladies not long ago, and the doctors who likewise failed to classify it went about their search as if what they really wished to determine was whether I would prove as difficult to kill as Rasputin.

The more acute pains are the moral ones, that 'melancholy' which Dürer points to (*i.e.*, the 'spleen') in himself, in the draw-

ing evidently intended for *his* physician. But pain, in any case
and from whatever source, quickly becomes what we believe
in most completely. One of my most regular pains is induced by
comparing my present exiguous output even with that of the
by-no-means-bumper years of the mid-sixties. I am pained, too,
by sudden memory blanks, which is like waking at night in a
foreign hotel and not knowing where you are. And my memory
taunts me. I am unable to find the right address in it for an event
of a month ago, and yesterday is vague while last week might
have evaporated, yet much that was etched there three-quarters
of a century ago seems to lie on the tip of the tongue. These
memory failures are more disturbing than reduced engine power,
too, a car being able to run on one cylinder, after all, and a little
low-octane (not enough to flood the motor), so long as the
transmission works and the chassis gets enough servicing.

At least I do not dwell on the future. (Unlike Prospero: 'Every
third thought shall be my grave.') In fact the 'dying-trajectories'
in the Glaser and Strauss book bother me no more than an
insurance company's annual statement of earnings might have
done, even that vertical plunge at the end of each downward
parabola marking the point at which the person represented by
the graph had stopped creaking and, as the gerontophobes in my
neighbourhood so indelicately say, croaked.

It may be that the past *can* be recaptured, in sudden regurgita-
tions of memory with eidetic recall, provoked and abetted in
old people by moments of chronological suspension and confusion. I must have been in some such bemused state myself in
Lucerne one afternoon last fall, for I seemed to have re-entered
an earlier time-zone. I should mention that I have strong childhood associations with the city, and that its topographical
changes are comparatively slight even today. Horses and chara-
bancs have disappeared, of course, and the traffic police are
young women now, ex-Heidis in white rubber coats, apparently
weaponless though surely possessing secret ones, like Karate.
But the geranium windowsills, the swans waddling on the shore
(not in the least Pavlova-like, in drydock), the snow roofs and
log stacks, and much more besides are wholly unchanged.

The time trick occurred, of all places, during a visit to

Wagner's villa at Triebschen. The rooms themselves, the porcelain *péchka*, and the sash windows with pelmets, reminded me
of Russian country houses I knew in my youth. Looking from
them to the Lake (straight ahead because of encroaching fac-
tories and phalansteries), and hearing no sound but the wind—
no juddering tourist boat, even no yodeller—I was transported
to a similar and more naturally pristine afternoon on my first
Swiss holiday four-fifths of a century ago. I had returned from
a walk with my father that day, and as we entered the lobby of
our hotel, the Schweizerhof, he told me to look in the direction
of a beautiful lady he said was the Empress Elisabeth of Austria.
And he added, I think because it was only shortly after Mayer-
ling, that she was '*neschasna*' (unhappy). The picture of the
Empress, in any case, and of my father and the room, was as
clear and as real as the picture of Wagner's villa in which I was
actually standing.

Have I remembered this because of my father's word, which
I borrowed for my own miseries? *My* 'unhappiness', so I have
always been accustomed to think, was the result of my father's
remoteness and my mother's denial of affection. Then when
my eldest brother died suddenly, and my mother did not transfer
any of her feelings for him to me, and my father did not become
less aloof, I resolved (a resolution made at some time and for
one reason or another by all children) that someday I would
show them. But now that someday has come and gone, and no
one remains to whom it would mean anything to be shown
whatever is left to show, I myself being the last witness.

Restored to the present (and to resipiscence, if my 'normal' mind
can be described that way any more), I went from Triebschen
to the Schwann Hotel for tea. (In 1890 it was tea and ratafia in,
I think, the *Englischeviertel*.) Sitting there—where Wagner, not
yet amnestied, 'followed' with watch in hand the first performance of *Lohengrin* in Weimar—it seemed impossible that my own
childhood could be so far away, and impossible that that world
of feeling could be extinct except in me. Yet not how far away
but how close and how real; and how soon that question in
answer to which, like Lohengrin, I must disappear myself.

Hollywood/March 27/69

PROGRESS REPORT

And he was preparing to cry out to show that he wasn't
dead.
                              SOLOMOS, *The Woman of Zakynthos*

N.Y.R.: It is good to see you up and about again, Mr. Stravinsky.
I.S.: Thank you. But I am not 'about' very much. In fact the
problem of locomotion was one of the reasons I left New York.
As the streets there have become more like parking lots than
thoroughfares, and as I am unable to perambulate myself any
more, and would in any case be let out only on a very short
chain, I was practically marooned in my hotel. A litter or sedan
chair would be the only method of conveyance for me now, at
least in midtown.

Otherwise I might have stayed in New York. Such a clean
city. And everybody so polite and amiable. And always more
and more of those 'relating' new buildings filling the sky. And
the students learning so many useful things about explosives and
arson and barricades. And all those confidence-inspiring candidates for mayor. Mr. Mailer was *my* candidate. The city *should*
secede, and be re-annexed, if at all, as the fifty-second state—
following the moon, of course, as the fifty-first.

I returned to Los Angeles for a few weeks, although wondering
how *it* could last even a few more minutes. The usherettes on the
flight out were dressed in 'the Spirit of the Revolution' (of 1776!),
but the route—over Utah, where nerve gas killed thousands of
sheep last year; and Smithereens, Nevada, where the atomic
blasting is now measured in tens of kilotons; and California,
where (poisonous) methyl parathion is used for crop-dusting—
reminded me of more recent and forthcoming wars. Nerves are
destroyed in Los Angeles, too, I hardly need to add, but purport-
edly from 'natural', not noxious, causes.

N.Y.R.: What did you do in exurbia, Mr. Stravinsky?

I.S.: Lived dangerously. I was twice in hospitals for tests, and you know how risky that can be. The second time, incidentally, I was asked whether the 'Russian Orthodox Church', noted as my 'Religious Preference' on a former registration card, meant that I was Jewish. I explained that this would not necessarily be the case and added that a branch of the institution in question was only two blocks up the street, which would have been useful information if, as seemed likely, worst came to worst. I was thereupon invited to refile as a Catholic, but resisted, the advantages in that having diminished, in my view, since the Vatican dropped St. Christopher last spring. Finally I was put under 'U' (Unknown) 'because the computer only programmes Protestants, Catholics, and Jews'.

Dangerous, too, no doubt, was the near-by murder epidemic. Yet you can hardly help admiring the way Hollywoodians make the most out of their murders. Thus a press agent for the husband of the slain Mrs. Polanski managed not only to mention several of the prizes won by his employer's latest film, but also to puff a work in progress, all in the course of a statement describing the prostrate director's grief. Hollywood funerals, moreover, are like movie premières. Camera angles, which include crane-shots, are rehearsed for the most 'filmic' views of the attending 'personalities', and above all of the mini-skirted starlets as they debouch at the cemetery from motorcades of Italian sport cars and sashay toward the taxidermal exhibits of the 'Slumber Room' for the last, and in some cases first, look at the victim.

Almost daily 'smog alerts' were reminders of still another danger, but what one is supposed to do after being alerted I have never found out. Try shallow breathing? Only a mass asphyxiation leaving the area strewn like the battlefield at Ypres—except that in this case the gas would come from industrial cesspipes and machine exhausts—can provoke the long-overdue exodus of the not-yet-succumbed. When that happens, incidentally, the effect on *you*, distant TV-watcher, and the amount of sympathy expected from you, will be assessed by the 'medium' as if it were strictly a matter of your proximity to the scene of the catastrophe. Thus a famine in India killing millions is equated, in TV time, with a Freeway accident injuring two; and that, in turn, is rated as about equal to a minor fire on the next block, or the death of a favourite goldfish at home.

Whether dangerous or not in itself, the small green monkey that appeared by our swimming pool one afternoon was undoubtedly capable of causing heart failure. At first I took it as a sign of how far on the skids I must be; but at second, when it failed to dematerialize, I understood that it was an escaped pet. It nuzzled and tamped its head like Judy in 'Daktari', then swarmed up a vine to the balcony from which, half an hour before, I had been watching a neighbour in our pool practising the Chappaquiddick crawl. The SPCA, when we called, advised us to bang some pans together, forgetting that noise is a cruelty to monkeys and quite ignoring the plight of the animal. In fact a raucous blue jay eventually drove the timorous intruder off— to my regret, for it was not baleful, and in truth I would have preferred its presence to that of at least some creatures I can think of on *this* side of Darwin. Our aquatic neighbour thought it might be a reincarnation, incidentally, and he suggested we notify a society of metempsychosis (such a thing being bound to exist in Los Angeles), but I did not get any 'waves' myself. Only a month or so before, I might add, the police were looking for an escaped seal in the neighbourhood. Monkeys, yes, but a *seal*? How did it cross Sunset Boulevard? Did none of the rather remarkably hirsute pedestrians there, who would have *had* to see it, turn a hair?

N.Y.R.: Were you able to work while convalescing from your embolectomy last spring?

I.S.: Actually *two* embolisms were removed, and in addition to that a left lumbar sympathectomy, or shortcircuiting of the nerve, was performed. The incisions were large but the skin healed quickly. It was the skin of my teeth I was worried about. So were the doctors, and for a time I think they were convinced that I had gone down for the count. I was as pale as a dybbuk, and so thin that I resembled my former self like a photograph taken by a thermal camera, the former me having departed, so to speak, but leaving enough warmth behind to limn a human-shaped mirage on the print. But I was *unable* to eat, and for days I would sit at table as dead Roman noblemen sat at table in their graves, with meat and bread and cups of wine in front of them. I was not 'medically dead', of course, as no cessation was recorded (and as these *mémoires* have not had to be smuggled back, *d'outre tombe*, on strips of winding sheet); yet it would have been perfectly accurate to describe the state I was in as after-life.

But the lid was not nailed down. And I began to revive, feeling at first as if I had come unsoldered and, as economists are saying of the economy, held together by chewing gum. I managed to walk a few steps, too, by holding on to the shoulders of my nurse, who walked backwards—a *pas de deux*—although the knee of my operated leg did not respond to drumming by a rubber-headed hammer. For 'mental' mitigation I played cards, as old generals are said to do petitpoint, then read Solzhenitsyn, which helped to unfuddle me in a limited sense because of a new-to-me Russian vocabulary, and in a larger sense because the people in his 'ward' had and still have it so much worse, and by that I am not referring to blastomas and other oncological horrors only. The Solzhenitsyn prepared me for my own long-accumulated mail which, thanks to a news bulletin saying where I was, included a number of requests for autographs, some of them apparently posted even before I was out of the operating theatre and expressing no concern whatever about the reasons for my new address.

Finally, having been close enough to Kingdom Come to know that I wanted to co-exist a little longer, I began to work. My transcriptions from the *Well-Tempered Clavier* were finished in the hospital, and the next day, my birthday as it happened, I was paroled back to the hotel.

N.Y.R.: Will you tell us something about the Bach?

I.S.: I had planned to set four fugues—one each in two, three, four, and five voices—for solo winds (clarinets and bassoons), and to set their preludes for string orchestra. But the four-voiced fugue that I finally chose suited solo strings only, besides which I later doubled the instruments in the two-voiced fugue, for the sonority.

I hardly altered the music itself, and certainly it has not acquired any Technicolor or Stereo, but only a character of performance through phrasing, articulation, and rhythmic alteration.[1] The ornamentation is not florid, for even though under- not over-embellishment is the commonplace of mis-performance today, I am still mindful of the complaint of Mrs. Delany, the Handelian, concerning a performance of Corelli's *Christmas Concerto* in Dublin in 1750, that the final cadence, in-stead of being 'clear and distinct [was] filled up with frippery and graces. . . .'

As for my 'aim', if I must pretend to have had one, I simply wished to make the music available in an instrumental form other than the keyboard, which may also have been Mozart's 'aim' in transcribing five fugues from the same collection for two violins, viola, and bass. But I *could* not have done any more than that in the case of the middle pieces. The act of writing was probably the psyche's way of defending itself, and it was all that mattered then, not *what* was written.

N.Y.R.: What is the state of your health now, Mr. Stravinsky?

I.S.: Ask me another. I am not exactly thriving as you can see, nor are all of the late returns in. Still, for the moment—and sufficient unto the moment—it does not seem too bad. I *feel* awful, of course, like old Tristan Bernard when he saw a hearse in the street and hailed it as if it were a taxi, saying 'Are you free?' But medical discoveries are announced every day now (you can even get plastic eardrums if you are willing to live in a padded cell), and something may yet be found to help me, even perhaps in the enzyme racket when it gets over its laundry phase.

Nature *is* witty, as Peer says, but with age you discover that the wit is *méchant*. It gives you a vatic streak and denies you to-morrow; endows you with memory crypts and safe-deposit boxes for the past but locks them and throws away the keys; grants you eighty-eight years but at a rate of interest for the borrowed time that hardly makes the loan worth while. Then on top of every-thing it taunts you with being still 'too *young* to be told' what you most want to know. But if you were to protest to a court of Nature that none of this was part of the bargain, the answer would come back that it was all in that small print young people never read.

[1] This was partly the work of Mr. Sol Babitz. (R.C.)

And speaking of that vehicle from which Tristan Bernard tried to hitch a ride, I wonder if 'any resemblances to persons actually living or dead' were noticed in Robert Graves's latest rhymes:

> . . . *What envious youth cares to*
> *compete*
> *With a lean sage hauled painfully*
> *upstage—*
> *Bowing, gasping, shuffling his fro-*
> *zen feet—*
> *A ribboned hearse parked plainly*
> *down the street?*

Hollywood, 9/12/69

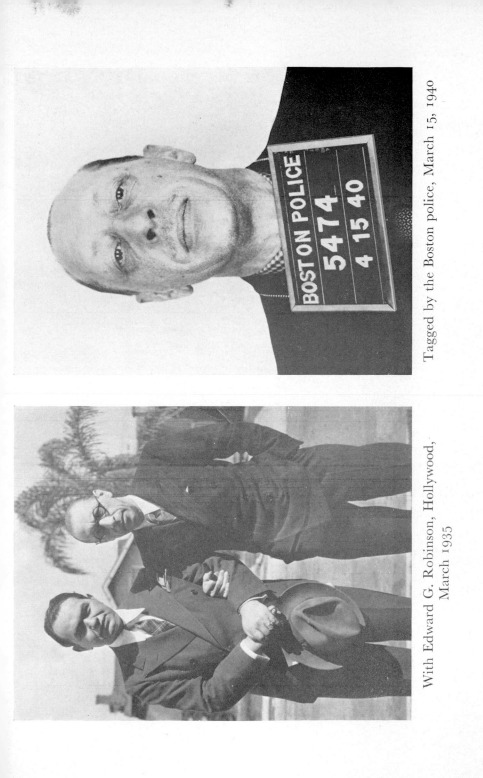

Tagged by the Boston police, March 15, 1940

With Edward G. Robinson, Hollywood, March 1935

With Fritz Reiner, New York, 1937

On the S.S. *Ile de France*, with Nadia
Boulanger, Mr. and Mrs. Samuel Dushkin,
Artur Rodzinski, May 1937

PORTRAIT OF THE ARTIST
AS AN OLD MAN (Cont'd.)

I

Eau d'Evian

> When I made the first incision [in the autopsy of a man who had drunk too much mineral water] the glitter of the stalactites in the poor fellow's gastric cavity positively blinded me—I had to wear blue glasses for a month.
>
> GEORGE MEREDITH

N.Y.R.: It is a year since we heard from you, Mr Stravinsky. You were recovering from an operation then.

I.S.: And allegedly still am. Meanwhile a crisis in another area was so portentously publicized that the sympathy mail has never ceased. The latest was a batch of letters from children in a Long Island school. 'You're a real cool guy,' one of the young correspondents said. 'And if you feel like it, you can write me back.' Another, foreseeing the boredom of the hospital but not that I would be watched to the point of harassment, advised me 'to look at the nurses'. Still another, whose logical approach to morality was evidently suffering the first collision between what is and what ought to be, said he was 'sorry a good composer like you is sick. *P.S.* My father is a doctor.' And another, an incipient music critic probably, expressed the wish that I would 'Get better and compose another operetta.'

I *am* better, thank you. European friends said that I seemed younger than when I was there two years ago—even if they *were* appraising the likelihood of events in the other direction. But at my age the compliment in 'younger' depends on how much. A rejuvenation of eight decades, for example, would definitely be overdoing it.

N.Y.R.: Were you in Evian-les-Bains all summer?

I.S.: Evian-*dans-la-pluie* would be more like it. Except that *'pluie'* is too gentle. It is an elemental place. A storm dervishes down the lake almost every afternoon. Evian the town is another matter. It offers a choice between a fast death in the Casino and a slow one by mineral water. Evian is definitely *not* 'where it's at', or ever likely to be. It has kept pace with the times, in fact, only in that the lake is polluted and the *truite* mercury-poisoned *à la carte*. But perhaps even that is not so new. As early as 1400 the lakeside Château de Ripaille was renowned for distilling essences *'contre les miasmes'*.

N.Y.R.: Did you live near the lake?

I.S.: Just above it, in a hotel for octogenarians. But in contrast to Auden's friend in his *'Old People's Home'*, none of my fellow guests was praying for a 'speedy dormition', I think, though possibly for a painless one. (Auden dislikes abeyances: if made Director of the Voluntary Death Programme, he would quickly clear out all such God's Waiting Room establishments.) In fact the only disease these venerables wanted to die of was more life. And, being French, more meals. Moribund as they might appear between times, they would positively scamper into the restaurant, or be trundled there at a fast lick. Moreover, all of them ate like pregnant women, and though they invariably complained that the meat was *'dure'*, it almost invariably *was*, teething troubles apart. (Small wonder, in view of the time devoted to swallowing that the French are virtually monoglottal; a large wonder, at least to me, is the extent of their monarchism. Even the preferred *pâtisseries* were *le désir du roi, caprice du roi, la couronne, rondure royale*, etc.; no doubt busts of one Louis or another can be found in their bathrooms.)

If old people look dour and even hostile, experience is probably a lesser cause, reasonable as that would be, than physiological degeneration—Circe's terrible island of change. Thus the narrow pursing of lips—the lockjaw look—is due in greater measure to dental vacancies and instabilities, it seems to me, than to bitterness and enmity. Likewise the silence of the elderly must be attributed more to poor hearing than to critical disapproval; and the fitful speech of the very old to their own struggle to enunciate, rather than to ill-humour, for old-age tongue-ties. So, too, if the aged are annoyingly finical, complaining of the slightest perturbation, physical weakness is primarily to blame. Thus, the two antediluvian spinsters at the next table, who were greatly concerned with the beverages on mine, may not have been the Brothers Grim at all but quite genial (and thirsty) old souls, whose countenances—'Is thine own heart to thine own face affected?'—simply did not register any semblance of their 'inner dynamics'. So I would like to believe, anyway, as I agree with Mme. De Nino that, 'After the age of eighty all contemporaries are friends.'

N.Y.R.: What did you do in Evian?

I.S.: Received visitors. One is less plausibly 'not in' in an isolated hotel than in a city. *Not* receiving research academics took some time, too. In fact I could have filled the summer simply reading their inquiries. I did some research of my own, looking for my old residences in Montreux, Clarens, Vevey: they seemed very dinky now in their new, overbuilt neighbourhoods. The views are superior from the Swiss side, incidentally, but I was so conditioned by the spectacle of my fellow guests at the hotel that even the Dents du Midi looked snaggle-toothed.

A new time-consuming menace has arisen with the immanence of another round-number birthday, whether or not I live to see it; the Elba Festival, for instance, is asking for a commitment. But a greater nuisance is in the very lively business being done with one's demise. I have already been consulted about the contents of memorial concerts, posthumous record albums and TV programmes; and offered good fees, too, though I would like to know how I am supposed to collect them. I have even had a bid for a monument, but decided to hold out for something better, perhaps by fanning the competition among newer, more avidly culture-climbing countries.

N.Y.R.: And the visitors?

I.S.: Some came simply out of curiosity, I think, for they regarded me as if I were a phenomenon rather like a stone, still warm for a while after sundown; no doubt, too, they were thinking that they themselves would be content to stop at 60 or 70, as no doubt they would, until the time came. Others were on professional visits: a dentist from Geneva who, as it happened, knew every note of *Les Noces*; and Lord Snowdon, who took photographs. (I was greatly relieved that he found me, a secretary having rung up the day before to ask 'Where exactly *is* Avignon?')

But largely they were old friends, and from as far away as Los Angeles and as near as the other side of the lake. One of them, I might add, was a Parisian 'intellectual' of the older generation —meaning an almost extinct type of moral philosopher, well grounded in mathematics and the arts, trained in and still conversant with a science, fluent in five modern and two classical languages. I say this to distinguish him, first, from today's endemic Parisian 'structuralist' who, like his transatlantic colleague—experiments so far limited to mice—appears to know everything about language except how to use it; and, second, from a peculiarly American species of pilot-programmer, systems-analyst, futurologist.

But I have strayed. The most interesting visit was that of my niece from Leningrad. She said that my home in Ustilug has been restored and made a museum; that my letters in the USSR—now in the Pushkin House, the Russian Museum, the Institute of Russian Literature, the Rimsky-Korsakov Archives, the Leningrad Public Library, the Leningrad Institute of Theatre and Music—have been published (presumably under Proudhon's law that 'property is theft', and there to be stolen); and that a biography of my father has appeared—by Kutateladze and Gosenpoud (Hamlet's student friends, in a garbled translation?). In short, prophets are unhonoured in their own countries only if they fail to survive or turn out not to have been prophetic enough. Not ideological waywardness, but true Russian-ness is all that matters. And in this regard it is probably safe to predict that the best-known romance by my compatriot across the lake will soon attain the status of a Soviet classic, the Russian nymphet herself enshrined in the national folk mythology. Still, it is nice to know that one is wanted back, as my niece assured me I am, and even nice to learn of the confidence the USSR is now showing in my music, to judge by this story in the *Sunday Times*:

Most of the West's NATO and scientific secrets were passed to Moscow through Mrs. Lindner . . . and Mrs. Schultz, the personal assistant to two Bonn Ministers of Science. The third member of the espionage ring, Dr. Wiedermann, and the two women frequently dined out together in Bonn, and the last occasion when secret information is alleged to have passed was just over a week ago, during a performance of Stravinsky's ballet *The Firebird*.

N.Y.R.: Then why did you return to New York?

I.S.: To be able to leave all over again. And to keep in touch with the 'now' scene in music—*i.e.*, knowing which people are going up and which down, who may have 'peaked' too soon, the latest PR jobs. And because I am now used to, and hence to some extent dependent on, the toxic air, the 100-decibel noise-level, the coronary anxiety-level. In Evian, the ventilation was exaggeratedly pure, the quiet almost too perfect, the abatement of tension too total; such an extreme change cannot be very healthy. (My next breakaway will have to be more gradual and include a week or so in Chicago en route.) What with the impending breakdown of the technology, the overgrowth (even the 'holding-patterns' over the airports are becoming permanent), and the revival of casuistry—will tomorrow's photo-chemical smog-cloud be 'dangerous' or merely 'hazardous', 'acceptable' or 'unacceptable' (and what then?)—the New Yorker is like the man tied to the railroad tracks in the silent film. He waits helplessly for the outcome of the race between a probably-too-late rescuer and an unstoppable locomotive.

N.Y.R.: And New York's cultural attractions? The theatre? Opera?

I.S.: Really? You could have fooled me.

II

Eau de Vie

N.Y.R.: You have shared some of your views on the Beethoven sonatas and quartets but not those on the symphonies.

I.S.: Because we have no perspective on music *that* popular. Also while negative criticism does not interest me, the affirmative kind is too difficult—which is like Professor Popper's argument that the hypotheses of science can be proved false but not true. And, finally, because the symphonies are public statements, the sonatas and quartets—especially the later examples—private or at least more intimate ones, to which I am more drawn.

Except the *Adagio* of the Ninth, which I probably say because I have been so deeply moved by it lately, a confession that seems to make me guilty of the Affective Fallacy. But in fact I have always tried to distinguish between the musical object and the emotion it induces, partly on the grounds that the object is active, the emotion reactive, hence a translation. Not that I ever believed in separations of the sort; or believe now in those fashionable leucotomies of 'sensibility' and 'intellect', the so-called 'new' and 'old' brains. My point was simply that *your* feelings and *my* feelings are much less interesting than Beethoven's art. And that Beethoven, in the first place, was not conveying his 'emotion' 'but his musical ideas'; nor do these necessarily 'translate' whatever emotions he may have had at the time, although they may have transferred them. In other words, I stood (and stand) exactly opposite Diderot, who asked that a painting 'move' him, 'break' his 'heart', let him 'tremble' and 'weep', but only 'delight' his 'eyes afterward'. In short, never mind the *art*.

N.T.R.: What constitutes an idea? What are you aware of first?

I.S.: Intervals, intervallic combinations. Rhythm, being design, tends, if not to come later, at least to be subject to change, which intervallic ideas rarely are. In my own case, both generally occur together. One indispensable attribute of the composer's imagination is the ability to recognize the full potential of his idea; to see at once, for example, whether it is over-complex and requires disentanglement, or too loose and requires concentration. Perhaps force of habit plays a larger part in this than the composer himself realizes.

I have never seen the sketches of the first movement of Beethoven's Fifth Symphony but cannot believe that interval and rhythm were conceived separately; certainly they cannot be regarded as other than perfectly congruent in the finished composition. (Or as 'Two Natures' theologians used to say, 'without separation or confusion'.) The most remarkable aspect of the movement, nevertheless, is the rhythmic. Firstly, the *irregular* durations are confined to the *unsounding* music, the varying-in-length silences. Secondly, the *sounding* music is articulated in only three—and these even-number—rhythmic units: halves, quarters, and eighths (no iambs! no triplets!). Thirdly—the most surprising delimitation of all—the movement is without syncopation.

Beethoven follows these conditions so strictly, moreover, that one almost suspects him of imposing them for the 'game'. But so far from restricting his invention, it is *as* prodigal and *more* radical than ever. In the wind and string dialogue from m. 196, for instance, no fewer than thirty-two half-notes succeed each other with no *rhythmic* relief, whatever the other kinds (the harmonic movement, the weight-shifting instrumentation, the changing phrase-lengths). And not only is the passage not rhythmically monotonous, it has as much tension as any in *Le Sacre du printemps*.

The second movement, for comparison, falls so thumpingly *on* the beats in the *wrong* sense—inevitability—that rhythmic tension scarcely exists. Besides, Beethoven does not always resist the temptation to over-extend (*cf.* the woodwind music m. 129–143). After the first movement, the symphony is a little hard to take.

N.Y.R.: Which symphonies *can* you take all the way?

I.S.: Two, Four, Eight. But Six not at all; the music is 'beautiful', of course, but no more. No doubt the tonal and metrical uniformity suit the simplicity of the 'scene'; but does the 'scene' really matter? The 'brook', though Danubian in length, lacks incident (rapids, falls, whirlpools), and few episodes in the great composer's work are less welcome than the return of the second theme at m. 113. Yet a melodic character related to the *Pastorale* is found in earlier and later symphonies as well; in the *Adagio* of the Fourth (m. 34), for example, and in the *Andante* of the Fifth (the theme itself, but most conspicuously in the 32nd-note variation), and, surprisingly, in the final climax of the *Adagio* of the Ninth (m. 147).

The first movement of the Second is one of Beethoven's most relentlessly brilliant pieces, but besides that it establishes many of the features of his symphonic style: the hammer-blow upbeats, and the sudden pauses, sudden harmonic turns, sudden extensions and truncations, and sudden reversals—or witholdings— of expected volumes. The other movements, too, serve as models for later symphonies, the *Larghetto* for the *Andante* of the *Fifth* (*cf.*

from m. 230, especially), the *Scherzo* and finale for their counter-
parts in the Fourth. Apart from Haydn, in Number One, the
symphonies rarely disturb the ghosts of predecessors. Yet one of
these rarities, is the episode at 'A' in this Finale; it might have
occurred in a Mozart opera-overture.

N.Y.R.: And the '*Eroica*'?

I.S.: The first movement is usually so mangled by conductors'
delayed beats and soggy retards that I seldom listen to much of
it. The same can be said of the Funeral March, which conductors
may come to praise but only succeed in burying. And, finally, the
let-down of the last movement—this *not* the fault of the performer
—is all the worse for following the most marvellous *Scherzo* for
orchestra ever composed.

The Fourth (with the Eighth) is the most evenly sustained of
the symphonies, but conductors generally miss the point that one
measure of the Introduction equals two measures of the *Allegro*
(just as the sixteenths at the end of the *Introduction* to the First
Symphony equal the sixteenths of the *Allegro*, *i.e.*, should be
played as sixty-fourths). Yet the first tempo is taken so slowly,
as a rule, that an *accelerando* is needed to accommodate the
chords at the end. The incomprehension of Weber before this
Introduction is all the odder, incidentally, in that the clarinet
cantabile in the second movement is so close to his own music.

N.Y.R.: And the Ninth, as an entity?

I.S.: The *Allegro* contains many new things (the Wagnerian bass
at m. 513, for one), but the principal theme ends with a bump,
and the dotted-note theme is stiff-necked (*cf.* the eight *fortissimo*
m. before the *da capo*). The *Scherzo*, though the best part of the
Huntley-Brinkley programme, is too long, like the *Scherzo* of the
Seventh. Moreover, it is always wrongly played. A measure of
duple time should approximate a measure of triple time. And if
this were not already obvious from the *stringendo* lead-in, it
would be from the *Presto*, which is a more reliable marking than
the metronome, and which, unlike it, could not be a misprint.
Clearly the relationship is roughly the same as the one obtaining
between the duple and triple meters in the *Scherzo* of the *Eroica*.

Concerning the great-untouchable finale, however, one still
hardly dares to tell the truth, and that though the composer
himself seems to have recognized it (according to Sonnleithner

and others). The truth is that some of the music is very banal—the last *Prestissimo*, for one passage, and, for another, the first full-orchestra version of the theme, which is German-band music about in the class of Wagner's *Kaisermarsch*. The banality weighs heavily, too, perhaps disproportionately so. Still more of the truth is that the voices and orchestra do not mix. The imbalances are a symptom. I have not heard a live performance since 1958, when I conducted a piece of my own on a programme with it; but I have *never* heard a balanced one. The 'wrong' notes stick out wrongly in the 'apocalyptic' opening chord, despite recording engineers, nor can all of their periphonic faking pick up the string-figuration in the '*Seid umschlangen, Millionen!*' the failure being not electronic but musical. Yet the greatest failure is in the 'message', hence, if you will pardon the expression, in the 'medium'. For the message of the voices is a finitude greatly diminishing the message of the wordless music. And the first entrance of the voice is a shocking intrusion. The singer is as out of place as if he had strayed in from the prologue to *Pagliacci*.

N.Y.R.: And the *Adagio*?

I.S.: I cannot argue the 'rightness' of it, as I said. Nor can I affirm it so precisely as the deaf man's nephew. 'How well you have brought in the *Andante*, uncle', he remarked in a conversation book, and with far wider meaning than he knew, for the shape of the theme and its counterpoints, the lilt of the three-meter and its over-the-bar suspensions were to become properties—at times stage properties—of the 'Old', meaning a new Vienna. The so-called Viennese style, some part of a common language of composers as different as Brahms, Strauss, Wolf and Mahler was, in fact, not merely forecast but invented in this music. Particularly Mahler, whose evocation in the wind-serenade centrepiece is truly uncanny; except that Beethoven was always the most observant messenger from the future, at any rate the future *I* care about. But enough. Go and listen. The whole movement is a sublimely sustained melody by the composer who, perhaps more than any other, 'Doth refine and exalt Man to the height he would beare.'

New York, September 1970

RAP SESSION

I: Fun City: Neighbourhood Notes

When I begin to be over conscious of my lungs I go to sea
. . . for the pure air . . . quitting the good city of old
Manhatto. . . .   *Moby Dick*

The isle is full of noises.   *The Tempest*

N.Y.R.: *The Times* said you had chosen to live in New York, Mr.
Stravinsky.
I.S.: Chosen? Well, yes; I can see what they mean: rather than
the Galápagos. In fact I am here because I can manage to be
looked after medically, though if I weren't here I might not
have to be quite so often. Still, one adapts, perhaps even to
environmental poisons: the argument of mithridatism which the
ecological bores may be overlooking.
N.Y.R.: *The Times* also said that you were selling your manuscripts and papers.
I.S.: Hoping to. Without concerts and recordings, my income has
dwindled; and while the popular part of my catalogue is free
in the United States (which did not sign the Berne Convention),
the unpopular, judging by the present rate of progress, should
be able to 'fund' my pharmacy bills by about my hundred and
second birthday. Yet the apparent assumption behind the new
tax laws is that composers are likely to be richer sources of
revenue than all those still-untapped oilmen. The latest decrees
not only forbid gifts of manuscripts to libraries and universities
in exchange for tax deductions, but require the giver to pay a
tax himself; thus are one's assets turned into one's liabilities.
In my case the only recourse is to sell, if I can, though the com-
missions and the tax 'bite' (crapulous, needless to say) would
leave only a fraction of the sum the newspapers report. But all
may not be lost. I have been offered as much to appear on a TV

talk-show—or was it 'What's My Line?'—as I have earned from
my life-work as a composer.

N.Y.R.: But *The Times* said you had bought an apartment.

I.S.: For economy, so the argument runs. Besides, I need more
room for books. I am like the bookclub subscriber who discovered
that it was impossible to unjoin, and who escaped biblio-suffoca-
tion only by moving. My father had the largest private library in
St. Petersburg, so I learn from the latest issue of *Sovietskaya
Muzyka*, which also reproduces an early painting of mine, and
some drawings of views of Königstein, the Höchst Spa, and other
nineties resorts.

N.Y.R.: Why did you move from Central Park South?

I.S.: I needed a change of statuary. (The new apartment is not
far from that alfresco Hall of Fame, the Mall.) Consider Fifty-
ninth Street, beginning at the Fifth Avenue corner. But first,
who *is* that mounted warrior led by the palm-bearing female
angel? The pharisaism of the combination is up to date, to be
sure, but the style and means of transportation are more like
Civil War One. Could it be Whitman on foot, then, and
Gertrude Stein the man on the horse? I suspect that the answer
is known only to those who have actually consulted the lettering
on the pedestal. The peace-bringer is General ('scorched-earth')
Sherman.

But does anyone ever look at these statues? Do they satisfy
any requirements?—apart from dogs, whose tokens of preference
(to the broader abutments of the surrounding streets) may be a
source of *toxacana canis* but are also homage, of a sort, to human
scale.

The fountain across the street is even more of a riddle, due in
part to hydraulic failure (neither trickle nor gurgle within living
memory—mine, at any rate). But who *is* the nymph in the
centre of that imaginary spray? Modesty? (One crucial garment
is not entirely shed.) Diana? (The place is abundantly favoured
by the hounds.) The ornaments are no less of an enigma, being
at the same time vaguely astrological—a winged Aries—and
manifestly pelagic—mollusks, turtles, and, well, that unknown
bathing beauty. But like every other block in the neighbourhood,
this one is being torn up. 'The Rehabilitation of Pulitzer Plaza'
says a sign, compounding the mystery. Rehabilitation? Why not

just return it to that Thirty-Fourth Street Bargain Basement?

The southern shore of the Park mainland, on the other hand, is unambiguously consecrated to Good Neighbours, Cuba above all. Except that the monument to the 'Maine', at the Columbus Circle side, must be a leading contender for the 'City's Most Underwhelming Sight'. The sunken ship, represented by a three-pronged prow of the gondola class, is decked with mourners; at least that is what I think they are, though they could be hanging their heads in artistic shame; or simply be cowering from the pigeon plaster, the soot, and the besmirchings by other, more polychromatic pollutants. No wonder the statue of the great, if misinspired, mariner responsible for it all, now marooned in the whirlpool of traffic named for him, looks in the other direction.

N.Y.R.: And Bolivar Plaza?

I.S.: Even to call it an indentation is stretching a point. In fact the allotted Real Estate is so stingy that the three equestrian counter-Conquistadores are practically invisible to anyone on the same side of the street. Another factor is that the plinths are unscaleably high, for the same reason that shallow-rooted trees in the Park are now chained to the ground. But, then, the plinths are the most valuable parts of the statues. For in the guerrilla warfare of the near future, when the one of José Martí (that horse on its hind, not to say last, legs) is in the direct line of fire from the trenches in the Park, his Martian followers (or whoever) can at least shelter behind that marmoreal foundation.

But how preposterous these Latin American cavalrymen are, especially to drivers debouching past them and into the Park! Not that the subjects of portrait sculpture matter, of course (though they are somehow expected to excuse its worst examples); and not, certainly, that any of this *is* sculpture, which would be asking too much since, unlike Bartolommeo Colleone, we do not live in a horse age, or an age of portraiture, or even, as it may be, in an age of art. Justification, if anyone requires it, is surely best sought in something closer to our own line. Extinctions of species, for example. Now in *that* context the statues could someday acquire a certain zoological interest; or even mythological, for horses, hereabouts, are very likely destined to become as rare as unicorns.

Speaking of statues, I saw a robot recently, the first real one—
i.e. non-human (I have seen political candidates programmed by
opinion polls)—in my experience. The electronic mannequin
was flagging cars from one lane to another on the George
Washington Bridge. And it was dressed in luminous cap and
jacket, partly because the success of the task depended on the
verisimilitude of the disguise (no system of arrows or other signs
having the same authority), partly because of the thickness of
the 'canopy of air', for Hamlet's word now sounds ominously
fatidic. Nor was the imitation man immediately recognizeable
as such. The give-away was its cruel tirelessness, and no doubt
future models, benefiting from more 'cyborg' and 'exosomatic
evolution', will 'build in' a degree of dilatoriness. Still, its facelessness, close-up, shocked me. And, again, shouldn't have.
After all, we adjusted very quickly to 'Walk', 'Don't Walk'.

N.Y.R.: But to return to those horses. A few are still left, you
know—the hansoms, the fuzz, perhaps an equitation academy.

I.S.: But I see other horses myself only on weekends when the
Park is closed to automobiles and might be a movie set for a
scenario of *c.* 1900. So far, that is, as bicycling, jogging, skating,
and hansom-riding are concerned. The clothing is something
else. I have also seen Quakerish male hats, of the same period as
the black female bonnets of the hansoms; ruched, gypsy-like
skirts; pelerines and even crinolines; and these together with the
latest from Bloomingdale's St. Tropez Department, as well as
examples of buyers-in at every fluctuation of the hemline stock-
markets, with their daily averages of sales above, at, and below
the knees (the only sartorial sign of the times with any claim to
universality is—I hope not significantly—the boot). But, New
York being New York, the bicycles tend to jam, the joggers to
jostle, the hansoms to form funeral-like-trains, and the skaters
—more loudly sibilant than in Wordsworth

> . . . *all shod with steel*
> *we hissed along the polished ice in games* . . .

—to bunch together, runner to runner.

N.Y.R.: Yet even the partial closing of the Park to automobiles
is a victory in the struggle to wrest something from total
mechanization.

I.S.: Will it stop the construction of skyblocks on Fifth Avenue—
the demise of Best and Company having exposed the question of
upper air-space ownership? And will it compensate for the new
missile-silo and filing-cabinet architecture on the Avenue of the
Americas, which is rather, it seems to me, a victory for think-
tank thought? In fact these in- and anti-human buildings
affront the needs of real, *vs.* blueprint, people, who are banished
even from the vicinity of them at night, as if by curfew. It is hard
not to sympathize with the Weathermen.

As for mechanization, in my neighbourhood even the graffiti
have become mobile. Heretofore confined to the hoardings
around building excavation sites, and to cloacal language and
subject matter, it now travels on the bumpers of automobiles and
says what it pleases. And the texts frequently recall the scandal-
mongering of the eighteenth-century underground pamphlet
(except that in one of the most popular examples of the new
sticker literature that I have seen—'Buy a Ted Kennedy Scuba
Suit'—it might be more accurate to say underwater).

N.Y.R.: Statuary apart, in what way does your new neighbourhood differ most strikingly from the old one?

I.S.: The social stratification by avenue is more marked than it
was directly below the Park, at least on Fifty-ninth Street. But
the radical segregation, not merely by area but from street to
street, has to me always been one of the phenomena of this
symmetrically reticulated city. For in spite of the perpetual
movement and commotion (no siestas and hardly any night),
the pedestrian populations of each East or West block remain
distinctly different breeds. Which may be saying no more than
that people can be computerized in terms of the kind and price
of the merchandise they consume, whether it be from the pubs
and antique shops of Third Avenue or from the ponces and
pushers, the muggers and stick-up men on Avenue Eight. Now
of course the lines are not really so rigid as I am making them
sound; but to whatever extent they are infiltrated, the numbers
are not large enough to blur the character.

N.Y.R.: How do you feel about the new atavistic life-styles?

I.S.: I have no inkling of what they are about. But the other day
I saw one of those toga-and-sandal salvationist types, and was
struck by the transformation from a generation ago. At that

174

time he would have carried a pilgrim's distaff or a placard ('The End is Nigh') and been distributing tracts for or against fluoridated water or Seventh Day Adventism. But his successor on a corner of Fifty-fifth Street the other day was grimly messageless, and he stood as stiff and remote as a cigar-store Indian. Moreover, instead of a distaff he was brandishing a very business-like spear.

II

N.Y.R.: Have you heard any concerts this winter?

I.S.: Only in my own living-room and only of escapist music. Not that I no longer want to keep my hand, or ear, in, or no longer need live music. For one thing, most new products tend to be 'visually oriented', coming under the rubric of spectator sports. And not only the new. Conducting has become ever more spectacular as audiences have become less and less auricular. The poor *chef* is obliged nowadays, even in Haydn, to gesticulate like an Armenian rug salesman, and jump at each *tutti* as if he were auditioning for Moiseyev. Mr. Bernstein used to be an impressive jumper, incidentally, even, like vodka, leaving you a little breathless. I have never seen him jump in *Les Noces* and regretted missing his performance last fall. Besides, I wanted to express my sympathy for the bruises he incurred in the affair of the *beaux ténébreux*—a return visit, for Mr. Bernstein was as thoughtful and attentive to me as any of my musician friends during my illnesses last year and the year before.

N.Y.R.: And your living-room concerts?

I.S.: I have been listening to the new recording of *Pelléas*. But the performance is disappointing and will no doubt increase the demand for the old Ansermet album. A non-French-speaking cast imposes too great a handicap, *Pelléas* being the unique opera in which diction is a decisive element. The diction, here at least, affects not only colour but pitch and rhythm. And while the performance is stylistically questionable in other ways—it over-accents and over-articulates (the dotted notes in the Interlude between the first two scenes of Act Two are too short and too bouncy); substitutes *forte* for *pianissimo* (*cf.*, the winds at 35, Act Two); *etc.*—the singers are the main problem. The brat Yniold is the only one wholly free of a pitch-blurring vibrato, but his performance—that puling '*petit père*', and whining '*oh, oh*'—is unbearable in other ways. Besides that, the accents and mispronunciations—Mélisande's '*un*' and '*une*' are indistinguishably masculine; Golaud's '*vous*' rhymes too perfectly with the word used to represent the vocalizing of cows in children's books; *etc. etc.*—attract too much attention to the words. And what words! How could Debussy, the friend of Mallarmé, stomach Maeterlinck, let alone underline some of his most irritating mannerisms? Those expletives and short phrases, for instance—'*oui, oui*', '*loin, loin*', '*tous, tous*' '*où est-il, où est-il*', '*la verité, la verité*', '*ne me touchez pas, ne me touchez pas*'—which everyone reiterates as if it were a nervous tic common to the region and the time. Debussy makes the tic all the worse by separating the words with evenly-measured rests. Thus '*Oh*' [rest, rest] '*Oh*', must occur a dozen times even before Mélisande drops her ring —and with it her second '*Oh*', a loss that bothers the by-now conditioned listener more than that of the heroine's jewelry.

Of the two inexactnesses of the singers, in rhythm and intonation, the former is the more surprising. Not that exactness is all; but suppleness comes after, not before, fidelity to the written rhythmic values, and each of Debussy's distinctions does its bit. Yet the singers do not always observe them. For example, more often than not the duration of the upbeat, or first note of a phrase, is doubled. Thus, choosing at random, Pelléas's '*mais il y a longtemps*' (beginning of Scene Two, Act Three) is set to five sixteenths but sung to an eighth and four sixteenths, nor is the emendation desirable. The singers' rhythms are slack not only in isolation, however, and so far as their own parts are concerned, but also in conjunction, or lack of conjunction, with the orchestra. This is no great matter in a *récit* punctuated very simply by chords, but when the rhythms are intricate, as in Geneviève's music (*cf.*, Act One, Scene Three, measure four) the result is a long way from any kind of *clarté*.

But enough. What beautiful things the score contains! I limit my judgment to the music though, no longer being able to 'see' the work as an opera. And my impression of the musical whole is of a decline in effectiveness after the '*Hair*' scene, when the quiet gloom of the earlier acts is dissipated by Golaud's melodramatics. Moreover, certain moments in the later scenes seem to me less than perfectly calculated—the musically perfunctory Fourth Act curtain, for one—but, then, the idiom itself, like a drug, wears off with time. Is it a too-confining one for an opera of this length? For though it ranges from Wagner—without, however, anything like Wagner's range—all the way down to *Petrushka* (the bassoons and clarinets in seconds in the Interlude to the second scene of Act Two), the later scenes are musically claustrophobic. Simplicity and restraint turn into limitation and constraint, beautiful monotony into just plain monotony. In fact, the opera is too long by the Fifth Act, though the death (puerperal fever? ennui?) is one of its most beautiful events.

Virgil Thomson has remarked that I 'scared the daylights out of Claude Debussy'. Sorry about that. Recently I came across an eyewitness account that I had not seen before of another of Debussy's reactions to me, or rather to a work of mine. Shortly after I first heard *Pelléas*—sitting with the composer, which, incidentally, I must be one of the last people, still more or less about, to have done—Debussy was listening to my *Sacre du printemps*. The dramatist Lenormand, was watching him, and apparently with more attention than he was giving to the music. 'Debussy's face was distressed', Lenormand writes.

It showed a grief impossible either to master or to hide: that of the creator before whom opens a world wholly different from his own: the sadness of being left behind, the suffering of the artist in the presence of new forms which reveal his place and his limits.

Debussy, one must remember, did not know that *Le Sacre* was already in a sense the pinnacle, the one piece in which I am still generally thought to have 'got it all together'. And apart from that, *Le Sacre* should not have been all that new to Debussy, who surely must have heard his own share in it. Yet the groundswell *was* new, and to Debussy, no doubt premonitory. But I think Lenormand's reading of the great composer's face was right; for those reactions are part of the reason why Debussy is, in all senses, the century's first musician.

New York, January 1971

BORBORYGMS
(fragments of an interview)

I

Thou shalt not kill; but need'st not strive
Officiously to keep alive.
ARTHUR HUGH CLOUGH

N.Y.R.: What are your thoughts about the new euthanasia movement, Mr. Stravinsky?

I.S.: First of all, I noticed on their appeals that the two leading promoter organizations share the same building as *The New York Review*; which, I hope, affords you a little cold comfort now and then. I hope, too, that they are merely passing the hat around, and that the contribution they want is not *me*.

Surely many or most of us believe that when we lose control, it would be better not to come in from but, rather, like Eskimos, to go out into the cold. The rub is that we also lose control of that belief. A friend of mine, a lifelong proponent of 'voluntary death', was stricken some years ago by paralysis which, however, apart from some speech impairment, did not cripple his faculties. His friends, knowing his state of awareness, expected a quick surrender, since he obviously could have given up the ghost and was in the first place, or so it seemed, possessed by a 'death wish'.

But was he? Is he now? And can we ever know very much about the life incentives of people in his condition? The American Sociological Association reports that deaths decrease in the month before a birthday and increase in the month after it, and people appear to postpone their deaths until after an election, or other event of general, even if possibly quite trivial, interest. No doubt the moon landing kept many people alive; and I

178

might even derive another few years myself from further short-cuts, such as Cambodia and Laos, to the end of the war.

'I want to die with dignity', the euthanasiast says. And, 'I don't want to leave my family with the image of deterioration'; which sounds like the speaker's fear of deterioration. But these are present sentiments, and future ones are not predictable. Deterioration, moreover, is insidious, and the lines shift or become indistinct. What if, after committing someone else to draw them for us, we feel ourselves to be less concerned about our dignity than about even a very little more life? I once thought that my own criterion for a proper time to pull the plug would be the moment when my more and more furtive memory had retreated to a point where I could no longer recollect which of my coevals was alive and which dead. But I have long since passed beyond that, and now simply, and on the whole correctly, assume that they are *all* dead.

Finally, the 'modesty' of some of the proposals of the right-to-die lobbyists is as horrifying as Swift's. One doctor has stated that 'anyone over sixty-five should not be resuscitated if his heart stopped'. (But Schoenberg dramatized his own resuscitation by a needle directly into the heart, at an age well beyond that, in his *String Trio*.) And another doctor has argued that our already overstrained medical resources should not be wasted on anyone over eighty and very ill. (But I was both when I wrote my *Variations* and *Canticles*, and they are superior, I think, to some of the music I was writing in my early seventies.) And why not increase the medical resources, even at the cost of diminishing some of the military ones? Or slow down on Project Methuselah? For the fifty-year increase in life expectancy by the end of the century, thanks to anti-oxidents such as BHT and hormone rejuvenators such as prednisolone is surely the grisliest of all the fates in store for the future beneficiaries of our current medical miracles. In short, gerontological retrogression is as important as euthanasia, if ounces of prevention are worth their proverbial weight in cure.

March 1–2, 1971

179

II

N.Y.R.: Is your interest in new medical developments largely the result of the disasters that have befallen you in that line? *I.S.*: It certainly got a boost from them. Thus an unfounded prognosis, a year and a half ago, of atypical tuberculosis naturally aroused my curiosity in the whole subject of atypical diseases. Thus, too, my interest in fluorocarbons and synthetic blood substitutes may be attributed to years of contradictory and conflicting treatments of my own blood disease. And thus my confinement last year in a cardiac unit—the wrong department for the illness from which I was actually suffering—greatly stimulated my interest in auxiliary hearts and in defibrillators, pacemakers, vitallium mitral valves. The latter are not yet soundproof, and the man who has one installed, like the crocodile with the clock in *Peter Pan,* is unable to hide himself—or, worse, *from* himself—though undoubtedly the thought of this tell-tale heart is more distressing to a metronomically minded musician than to other people.

Numerous unsuccessful experiments with behaviour modification drugs have had a deleterious effect on me, but they have not shaken my faith in that boundless domain. The effectiveness of lithium in constraining our manic friends during their cliff-hanging phases has already been demonstrated, after all, and probably more of our other friends than we suspect are kept going by amphetamines. And in spite of all the failures in my own case, I prefer to attribute my depression to a so-called sodium leak into the cells, rather than, say, to 'the state of the arts' or the 'philosophical overview'.

Another malady, but this one not my own, is responsible for my keen interest in the science of diagnosis by smell. I think it was Coleridge's 'Every teacher has a mental odor' that first drew my attention to the subject. Then, recalling what my Danish nurse had said about Følling's detection of a metabolic disorder in babies from an odour in their urine; and remembering that the perspiration of schizophrenics is distinguished by an odour (trans-3-methyl-2-hexenoic acid), I began to wonder whether other biochemical disturbances might identify vocational aptitudes and inaptitudes. Music critics, for example. That most of them 'stink' is obvious, of course, but what is the chemical basis?

Perspiration may be a primary odour, by the way, since some people are 'odour blind' to it. But unlike the primary colour receptor sites in the eye, the primary odour receptors in the olfactory tissue—which could conceivably identify by shape, on the grounds that molecules with different chemical properties but similar shapes possess similar odours—have not yet been isolated. And we should be grateful for that, otherwise television would come not only in deadly colour but with the living smellies as well.

March 6–10, 1971

III

N.Y.R.: How do you feel since your return from the hospital, Mr. Stravinsky?

I.S.: Worse, thank you. And apart from being fleeced, I do not know what happened to me there. 'Recycling', perhaps, to borrow the term for reprocessing discarded containers. But the doctors say that worse means better, since it indicates that I am more aware of how bad it is. And by that logic I could hardly welcome a euphoric sense of improvement.

N.Y.R.: Is life more pleasant in your new neighbourhood?

I.S.: It is safer, I think, judging by the numbers of prams for both age extremes, and by the relative absence of suspicion among them, as standards of paranoia go in the rats-in-over-crowded-cages neighbourhoods. The atmosphere is no purer, though, and in fact the incidence of emphysema is reported to be about equally high among zoo inmates (ophidians are especially susceptible) in all of the boroughs. Woe to anyone who comes here to 'take a breather'.

But whether the noise is less or I am deafer, I cannot tell. There are no wrecking balls and no Hell's Angels, but the street is the City's parade ground, the line of march for all militant 'minorities'. I expect to hear more Sousa this spring then any other live music. Night noise *is* lighter, but it is not of the sleep-inducing—crickets, town-criers (*'Oyez!'*)—kind. As a substitute for sheep-counting, I have tried to disentangle it strand by strand, from fire engines trying to break the sound barrier down to burglar alarms and buses changing gears, but without success (*i.e.* sleep). And the noise hazard is still the strongest argument for emigration. It not only fatigues, destroys concentration, and causes premature presbycusis, but it can be fatal. 'Infra-sound', if it comes to that, is more destructive to the cells than atomic fallout, and noise machines already exist that can homogenize you, whatever that means. Already now we need an absorbent, like the moth's fur, which diffuses the shrieks of the bat.

April 1–2, 1971

IV

> You must write the variations in a familiar, easy and brilliant style, so that the greatest number of our ladies can play and enjoy them.
> G. THOMSON of Edinburgh to Beethoven (!)

N.Y.R.: Have you heard any new music this winter?

I.S.: I seldom listen to new music any more, in fact not since my own Muse went out on a wildcat strike; and by preference never. Nor have I kept track, let alone 4-track, of Stockhausen. So much of it seems arbitrary to me, which all true art is, of course, but by my lights—dim as they are by Day-Glo—must not *seem* to be. So I must ask *you* what is new? Who are the leading Ivy League composers now? Am I the only listener who finds *Pli selon pli* both pretty monotonous and monotonously pretty? And do the new starlets of the podia lean as heavily on the music here and there, by way of 'interpretation', as their elders used to do? And what kind of beat is 'in' now, small and power-steering? And is Mr. Bernstein still the man for all channels?

N.Y.R.: What do you think of Liszt and Berg as material for exploration by the Philharmonic?

I.S.: Not very promising. Berg should be played more regularly but is hardly unknown. Besides, his orchestral music, apart from the opera excerpts, fills no more than a single, rather suffocating programme. A Berg 'retrospective' *is* needed, but in the opera house, an undertaking the local establishments will continue to avoid; and could avoid with a good excuse, namely, that they are waiting for the third act of *Lulu*, if they had ever heard of it.

The pertinacity of Liszt's orchestral music, on the other hand, wholly eludes me. The *Dante* Symphony is hell, and the tone poems can survive only by constantly renewed neglect. A precursor? But that is pedagogy; and, anyway, who wasn't? (To my mind the *Faust* Symphony, one of the better pieces, and *Tasso*, one of the worst, precurse Wagner less than they do Tchaikovsky, which I think is not the Philharmonic's point.) An inventive harmonist? Well, he contributed more than he stole, but we cannot listen to music one element at a time. A master of the orchestra? Yes, again, but not always; his lower brass parts are unwieldy, and on at least one occasion (*cf. Mazeppa*, pp. 40–41) he does not know how to deploy the strings in a middle-to-low range and maintain a balanced volume. His colours are sometimes novel (the organ in *The Huns*, for example), but tinted bathos is still bathetic. The *Christus* is reputedly superior in orchestral technique—I have not heard the Frankfurt tape and cannot vouch for it—and a performance of that opus is probably at least warranted, if not, by my prejudices, altogether urgent.

A Grade B, no-budget-for-music film company will find richer ore for its purposes in the poems than the Philharmonic, from accompaniments for cavalry chases (*The Huns*) and nick-of-time rescuing armies (*Mazeppa*), to music for flights of souls *not* rescued in time (the harp arpeggios in virtually every piece) and brass band, Salvation Army piety, wrong notes and all (the '*Andante religioso*' in the *Mountain* Symphony). The parodistic possibilities, moreover, are unlimited. (The fugue in *Prometheus* is surely intentional parody, but of what? A fugue?) Which is the reason that the most astute critic and truest prophet of Liszt's music is that unhonoured genius of the radio era who branded the 'Lone Ranger' with *Les Préludes* (and vice versa). *Les Préludes*, by the way, is the only one of the poems, together with the brief and quiet *Orpheus*, that I can get all the way through. It is also the only one in which galumphing rhythms, nagging sequences, turgid developments, lifeless pauses, and bombastic triumphs fuse into a really winning piece; in fact, it is one of the rare works in all of Liszt that I can take—though the expression may sound somewhat personal in his case—'warts and all'.

March 15–16, 1971

V

N.Y.R.: Does the state of the arts really depress you?
I.S.: Oh no. We live in a very exhilarating time, a little short of a Golden Age, perhaps, but, well, consider, in the visual arts, the recent Warhol retrospective at the Tate; in the dramatic arts, Broadway category, the revival of the Betty Boop period; in literature, the new genre of reality recalled on tape (best-selling fall title: 'Manson's Love Life As Told By His "Family"'); and in music, the increasing involvement of everybody except the composer. And these developments have in turn produced a great critic, Jimmy Durante, who described it all very accurately when he observed that 'Everybody is getting into the act'.

March 17, 1971

VI

The fair lords
That were the clients, are the
lawyer's now
BEN JONSON

(*unfinished*)

PART THREE

PREFACES

Some Perspectives of a Contemporary[1]

I have no synoptic view of our century's music to offer, or at any
rate none that I wish to expound or impart. The countenance
I would put on the period must necessarily and too closely
resemble my own, which means that it would also and inevitably expose my deaf spots—such as that I know nothing
whatever about electronic music, or any kind of popular music
save that all of it is very loud. Finally, and disqualifying myself
beyond rehabilitation as an 'objective' historian, I confess that
my recollections of some of the many different stages of musical
development since 1900 have become addled, not only in
general but even in my own work. In consequence, my remarks
shall be restricted to what I see as the principal contrasts between
the beginning and end—arbitrary divisions but conveniently
defining my own life in music—of the seven musical decades.

First and most important is the disappearance of the musical
mainstream. (Whether it really *has* disappeared is a contention
requiring analytical substantiation of a kind I cannot produce
here, but I have promised no more than a personal view.) The
problem imposed by this absence is the same as the problem of
man without God: irresponsibility; which in the domain of art
is translated to that emptiest of goals, total freedom; as if the
outmodedness and unserviceability of the laws and premises, the
techniques and systems embodied in the art of the past invalidated the need to search for new ones.

Composers continue to be generated by traditions, nevertheless,

[1] Preface to: *Storia Della Musica*, Vol. IX: *La Musica Contemporanea* 1900–
1970, Fratelli Fabbri Editori, Milano, 1967.

187

even if vestigial, splintered, and transparently self-fabricated (by
the adopting of ancestors and the pasting together of assorted
bits and pieces of the past). All works of art, and anti-art, must
have antecedents, though these may not be readily apparent, and
though connection may be discovered or created only after long
periods of time. The *'Beklemmt'* episode in the *Cavatina* from
Beethoven's opus 130, for example, acquired a new dimension a
full century later because of the rhythmic rediscoveries of
Webern and others. And this should warn me. The future will
undoubtedly provide connecting links with what (to me) is
most disjunct in the music of today.

A major cause of the evaporation or fibrillation of the musical
main-current is the dislocation of Western music from the West.
Europe's musical boundaries have been continually and ever
more rapidly crumbling during the whole of the seventy-year
period, and it is now safe to predict that the promised symbiosis
of new musicians and new media in the Future Welfare State
is as likely to occur (if it does occur) in Japan or the Americas as
in Russia or Europe. But the diaspora of the European musical
heritage must also be attributed, in part, to an increasing fusion
of East and West. Initiated in Europe and sponsored by Debussy
(among more superficial investors), this fusion is best exemplified
today in Messiaen, who both as teacher and in his compositions
has been a dominant influence on the 1960s. At the same time,
while music is reputed by its nature to transcend its own national
imagery, and while the new techniques and new media are, by
their nature, ethnically neutral, the nationalism of musicians
themselves is as rampant as ever. Nor have the new communica-
tions achieved anything in the way of overcoming this obstacle
except to substitute an airport culture for a stay-at-home one.
It is this transcendent (or 'abstract' or 'self-contained') nature
of music that the new so-called concretism—Pop Art, eighteen-
hour slices-of-reality films, *musique concrète*—opposes. But instead
of bringing art and reality closer together, the new movement
merely thins out the distinction; to my mind, at any rate, though
I regard the struggle between language and reality as mercifully
unresolvable. To my thinking the most concrete art is simply the
most perfectly made.

Cut off from its historical tradition, is Western music at an end? By any other name the music of the future will not sound any sweeter, in any case. But whether or not the Marxist argument of utility has proved its point, and the creative tradition of Western music is obsolete, Society certainly appears to prefer its new playthings; such as television, which is incontestably more interesting than any creative use of it. The ever improving tools of reproduction (in this age of the self-replicating molecule), together with the exponential increase in reproductive 'art' suggest that the hominids of tomorrow may well outgrow the need for creative art. It seems to me, at any rate, that the selling of the music of every era and culture in canned form—always in prettier and prettier cans, of course ('advertisements are truer')—can hardly encourage creativity.

The music of the 1960s—what I know of it—has been characterized by vastly greater diversity than the music of the first decade of the century; by a greater degree of experimentation; and by a facelessness and blurring together of its composers. It is characterized as well and at more profound levels by new measurements, such as a different specificity of time (and hence of the tempo of ideas); and by reflections (often naïve) of the ideas of the *Zeitgeist*, such as the attempt to incorporate elements of chance (which I understand hardly at all myself, for the reason that chance, being subjective, is non-communicative at the level of causation, which is where involvement must begin).

But the above impressions were formed under the sign of past perspectives. In another seventy years, another observer, surfacing about now, may well characterize the same period as one of synthesis, of the comparative toning down of the experimental, and of the emergence of strongly delineated individual personalities. Even now, my younger colleagues—and this is the measure of a gulf—are able to hear necessity where I hear only randomness, and to perceive Ariadne's threads (as mollusks perceive colours beyond the range of human awareness) where I find only broken bits of string.

Do these seventy years constitute a period of high musical achievement? *I* think they do, at any rate, and I would rank the

189

highest flights of the time (*Jacobsleiter, Pierrot lunaire*) with the greatest achievements of the past. It is true that no river of music comparable to the rivers of Bach, Mozart, or Beethoven has flowed from any original composer of the period (the adjective eliminating the many prolific reproducers in synthetic traditions); but, then, neither the age nor the nature of the new music is conducive to fluency.

In spite of my title, and indelicate as it is to speak of myself, I must explain in conclusion that I have never thought in perspectivist terms concerning my own participation in the century's music. My activity—or re-activity, as my animadverters would describe it—was conditioned not by historical concepts, but by music itself. I have been formed in part, and in greater and lesser ways, by all of the music I have known and loved, and I composed as I was formed to compose.

August 4, 1967

Gesualdo di Venosa: New Perspectives[1]

Musicians may yet save Gesualdo from musicologists, but the latter have had the best of it until now. Even now he is academically unrespectable, still the crank of chromaticism, still rarely sung.

Two new publications, Professor Watkins's monograph and the CBS recording of the sixth book of madrigals, should help to scotch the prejudice of the scholars. Professor Watkins provides the composer with surrounding scenery not previously in view, and into which he does not fade but stands out more vividly, if in different colours, than before. The recording, on the other hand, corrects the view of the music as a case of samples, simply by providing it with its own context, the largely tendentious interest in Gesualdo heretofore having deprived him even of his own 'normalcy'. Together the two publications fill in the lacunae to the extent that apart from the continuing search for the lost book of six-voice madrigals, the major goals are reduced to

---

[1] Preface to: *Don Carlo Gesualdo: The Man and His Music*, by Glenn E. Watkins, Oxford University Press (scheduled publication 1973).

two: the recovery of performance style (a by-no-means-impossible quest), and the recording of the complete music.

Seeking Gesualdo's origins in the Neapolitan school, Professor Watkins discovers Pomponio Nenna in the role of principal model. At least six of Gesualdo's texts, including *Ancide sol la morte*, *Mercè grido*, *Tu segui*, and *Deh, coprite*, were set by Nenna first. Apart from this coincidence, if that is what it was, Gesualdo appears to have helped himself to elements of Nenna's chromatic style and to have pocketed harmonic progressions verbatim. In fact, Gesualdo's imitations are so sedulous in some instances as to appear to us like light-fingering. Perhaps that was how they were thought of at the time, too, but the ingenuous opinions of a powerful prince's not-so-fellow musicians are unlikely to have been committed to paper. And, anyway, apart from a missing credit line in history, no monstrous injustice has been done. Nenna never received the touch of Zephyr. He is as devoid of musical interest, compared with Gesualdo, as Holinshed is of poetic interest, compared with certain plays based on him.

It has been known since at least 1934 (Pannain: *Istituzione e Monumenti*) that Gesualdo's sacred music (what was then known of it) shared a style formed by Nenna, Macque, Trabaci, and others. But *ante* Watkins almost nothing was known of Neapolitan influences on the secular music. Its radical chromatic tendency was linked to Wert, Rore, Luzzaschi and other madrigalists of the Ferrara court, though to judge from the little I know of these composers, Luzzaschi alone comes close enough to have been warrantably put forward as a stepping stone. Now, with Professor Watkins's discovery of the Nenna examples—as with the discovery of Linear B decipherment, the discovery of the Oldowan Fossil Cranium, and any other discovery involving contingent systems of classification—the entire history of the subject must be revised or scrapped. As discovery breeds discovery, too, Professor Watkins's should provoke explorations through the whole of sixteenth-century Neapolitan music. For a beginning, one would like to know more of some of the shadowy figures in Gesualdo's own circle: Luigi Tansillo of Venosa, for example, and Giovanni Leonardo Primavera, whose seventh book is dedicated to the Prince. And what of the madrigal style of the '*infelice*' Troiano, who was not merely shadowy but umbrageous, being the first of the composer-murderers who were to enliven the peninsular musical scene down to and through Alessandro Stradella, and whose fraternity was soon to include Gesualdo himself? Can any particular of Gesualdo's settings of the word '*uccide*' be traced to him?

For the rest, Professor Watkins surveys all of the forms, sacred and secular, as the composer inherited and bequeathed them. He ably anatomizes the complete music, too, and not only the music but the texts, for the musico-dramatic gesturing of the secular pieces depends on devices of oxymora, sexual symbolisms ('I expire', 'I die'),[1] and other conventional insipidities. Further and finally, Professor Watkins newly maps the composer among the peaks of Mannerism, and concludes this first sensible study of him with a fully documented history of the misunderstandings of his music down to *c.* 1970.

As aforesaid, the most novel perspectives extending from the CBS account of Book Six are of the composer himself. Before the appearance of this admirably crammed grammy-award contender ('I am dubbed,' says Shakespeare's Philip the Bastard), our musical bees had been extracting the composer's headier harmonic pollen as if he had cultivated only a single kind of flower. But the complete book shows him to be a composer of always strongly characterized and expertly made 'normal' music, whose special inventiveness lies in such other areas as rhythm and the intensifying of vocal colour by means of unusual combinations in extremes of range. (I wonder whether some of these 'normal' pieces are not more gratifying to sing than the chromatic ecstasies of *Moro lasso*, in which the demands of the ensemble must all but extinguish the performer's individuality?) Finally, Book Six, which represents the apogee of the radical chromaticism of the era, also reveals the composer as anomalously conservative-minded, at least by the lights of those contemporary aesthetes and *précieux* for whom monody had gained the inside

[1] 'Drowning' is a veil of the same sort in the Elizabethan madrigal—the seafaring English—and it may be one, too, for example, in Bennet's:

> O when, O when begin you
> To swell so high that I may drown me in you?

track, and contrapuntally voiced harmony of Gesualdo's brand was disappearing from the course.

Whether Book Six was the most propitious choice with which to inaugurate a new Gesualdo series is hard to say, but the larger physical requirements of the other music may have borne on the decision: Books Three and Four include six-voice madrigals; Book Five varies more widely in *tessitura*; the sacred music uses five-, six- and seven-part choirs. In any case, the stringencies of Gesualdo's madrigal form in no matter which volume may deter all except the doughtiest listener. Extraordinary absorptive powers are needed to digest a succession of twenty-three complete statements, each of great compactness—for if Gesualdo does not expand, neither does he dilate, and if his form is small, it is at the same time never elliptical. Another obstacle for modern listeners, if merely an implicit one, is in the limited possibilities of harmonic extension through key-relationships. To some extent this is offset by novelties of sequence and juxtaposition, but the music will seem inexplicably static to some, nevertheless, and as little satisfying, to dumpling-lovers as a dinner of twenty-three canapés of caviar.

Nor are Gesualdo's most overt means of keeping awareness of formal limitations at bay invariably the most successful. In fact, the most completely satisfying madrigals tend to avoid contrast for its own sake (Pope: 'The lights and shades, whose well-accorded strife') and either confine themselves to a single mood or follow the free run of the composer's death-wish, in which, musically speaking, he clearly knew his way around. Monotony threatens, in any event, only when, pretending that matters are looking up, he pays too many courtesy calls on the happy ending. Finally it must be said that, as Gesualdo's mode of expression is dramatic, highly intimate, and very much in earnest, he weights the traditional madrigal of poised sentiments and conceits, of amorous delicacies and indelicacies, with a heavy load. But this is in-theory criticism. In practice, which is to say, while listening, no unattached faculty remains with which to question the balances and proportions of 'form' and 'content'.

The extraordinary unity of character and style in Book Six—it would be impossible to exchange any madrigal with an example from the earlier books—opens the suspicion that the

composer himself may have been responsible for the selection
and ordering of the pieces. For one thing, the ingenious grouping in several kinds of pairs would seem to have been arranged
by an 'inside' hand. Thus the first two, and the first and last, and
numbers four and five, eleven and twelve, thirteen and fourteen,
eighteen and nineteen, are paired by 'key'. Pairing is likewise
effected by *tempo* and mood; by the incidence of *ballo* meters
(nos. 22 and 23) and pastoral modes (*Al mio gioir* and *Tu segui*);
and by similarities in initial canonic departures (*Ardo per te* and
Ardita Zanzaretta), final cadences (nos. 11 and 12), 'instrumentation' (the two-tenor madrigals, nos. 18 and 19). Changes of
tempo are managed by doubling or halving the unit of beat—the
practice of the time—but rhythmic irregularity is introduced in
about half of the madrigals by the use of meters of unequal
length. An example occurs on the first page, in the partly-in-six,
partly-in-four *Se la mia morte brami*, where the effect is strikingly
similar to the effect of Wilbye's enlargement of the meter to drag
the musical pace at the words 'whereon man acts his weary
Pilgrimmage'.[1] The rhythmic inventions throughout Book Six
are a match for the harmonic ones, in fact, and in such instances
as the virtually meterless beginning of *Quel 'no'*, and the lashing
syncopations with the word *'tormenti'* in *Càndido e verde fiore*, they
are as 'revolutionary'.

The chief obstacle to the recovery of performance style is pecun-
iary. In a few hours' leave of absence from a breadwinning
routine of taping television commercials and disposing of seasonal
oratorios, even the most excellent singers cannot achieve the
blends, the exactness of intonation, the diction and articulation
that the Prince's singers would have had to master by edict and
as a result of living with the music the year round. (And probably
under threat of flagellation, too, though the composer, a votary
of *le vice anglais*, seems to have preferred *that* in reverse, Marsyas
flaying Apollo, so to speak.) In short, the world is in need of
permanent madrigal consorts, and of Martha Baird Rockefeller
Grants to sustain them. Only then can the styles be reborn, not

---

[1] The 'Ay me' in Wilbye's *Weep, Weep, Mine Eyes* is so like a Gesualdo
'oimè', incidentally, as to suggest direct connection.

only of the Prince of Venosa, but of Marenzio and Monteverdi, Wilbye and Weelkes.[1]

In the case of the *Musica Riservata* style, edifying descriptions by ear witnesses abound. Thus Cerone reports that 'The madrigalist does not sing in a full voice, but artistically, in a *falsetto* voice or *sotto voce*'; to which I would add that pitch clarity in the denser harmonic coagulations can be attained in no other way, certainly not with woolly *vibrati*. Zarlino (whose theoretical writings influenced Nicolas Poussin)[2] affirms that 'the madrigal singer must perform his part just as the composer has written it'—*i.e.*, without embellishments, and *a cappella*; the *concertato* madrigal introduced in Monteverdi's fifth book was without issue in Gesualdo. Padre Martini further informs us that 'madrigals are to be sung softly' and that 'bold dissonances were permitted in madrigals because perfect intonation was easier to achieve by a few singers than by the crowd of singers in church music'. Finally, Mazzochi's reference to Gesualdo might be taken to infer that our composer employed *crescendi* (and the regraduation), as well as other dynamic shadings (*sfumato*) himself. The grounds for this illation are simply that Mazzocchi had invented a system of notating dynamics, and that what he praises in Gesualdo is his exactness in notation. But the question is fodder for a thesis, and that is where I must leave it.

My own attentions to Gesualdo between twelve and ten years ago led to a number of ramblings, musical and otherwise. Twice I visited the seat of the composer's family name, an unpicturesquely squalid town, the more so after Acerra and the other architecturally attractive villages of the Campania. On the first occasion, a listless day in July 1956, I had come to Naples by boat—my last such expedition, I resolved. The debarking ordeal alone took longer than a transatlantic flight, not to mention the simultaneous marathon concerts by competing brass bands, the continuous pelting by paper streamers, and the orgies of

---

[1] *Cf.* Gesualdo's *Beltà poi* and Weelkes's *Cease Sorrows Now*, at the words 'I'll sing my faint farewell'.

[2] As late as the eighteenth century the architect Vittone was illustrating his exposition of the Renaissance ideal of proportion with analogies derived from music theory.

weeping by separating and reuniting Neapolitans. I remember that on the way to Gesualdo we visited the Conservatory of San Pietro a Maiella, and the fish stalls near the Porta Capuana; and at Montevirgine, we watched the procession of a parthenogenetic cult, a parade of flower-garlanded automobiles led by boys carrying religious banners and running like lampadephores.

. Gesualdo's castle was the residence then of some hens, a heifer, and a browsing goat, as well as of a human population numbering, in that still Pill-less, anti-Malthusian decade, a great many *bambini*. None of these inhabitants had heard of the Prince of Venosa and his deeds, of course, and in order to explain our wish to peek at the premises, some of his lurid history had to be imparted to at least some of the tenants. A result of my own attempts to do so was that I soon became the object of very alarmed looks, the audience having confounded the composers in the story (blame my poverty-stricken Italian) and mistaken *me* as the murderer of *my* first wife.

The castle is measly. Apart from the lion rampant emblazoned in the *sottoportico*, and the well-known inscriptions on the courtyard wall, there was little evidence of occupancy at any time by an armigerous prince. The interior appeared to be furnished from the Apennine equivalent of Woolworth's, but as it was greatly in need of a dispersion of aerosol, I did not see much of it. In short, it was difficult to imagine the high state of musical culture that once flourished on this forlorn hill, the singers, the instrumentalists, the church choristers, and, not least, the great if emotionally disequilibrated composer whose last madrigal books were first printed here.

The portrait of the composer in the Capuchin church was dirty then but undamaged, whereas on my return three years later the picture had been cleaned but the lower left corner of it, just above the composer's head, was torn. (You can't have everything.) We were met there by a Padre Cipriano who said he was gathering materials for a biography of the composer, and that the most interesting of the documents so far turned up for inclusion were some verses by Gesualdo's ill-fated wife. I did not doubt this opinion; in fact if the lady's writings describe her amorous experiences in any detail, Padre Cipriano's book, if he ever wrote it, could become the first musicological tome to be published by Grove Press. The Padre served some thimblesful of the local liqueur, but, while we were swallowing this furniture polish, complained of the American occupation of the town in 1944. His story has been repeated in kind a great many times since then, of course, and throughout the world, but in the case of the Sack of Gesualdo, my sympathies were entirely with the G.I.'s.

I visited other sites associated with the composer after that, but not expressly, not on his trail. I was in the Este Library at Modena, and in Ferrara several times, but on behalf of the Schifanoia frescoes and the Etruscan Museum, and incidentally to drink Lambrusco. I even went to Mesola once, on an excursion to Pomposa Abbey and Comacchio, the latter loud with the clack of wooden shoes then, but now stranded in the ooze of the newly drained delta; other visitors be warned that Mesola, the Xanadu of the Estes, celebrated in a madrigal by Tasso and Wert, is now a very dreary town hall. As for Venosa, Horatian Venusiae, the city of the composer's principality, I have been no closer to it than Brindisi, perhaps not even that close, technically, as I did not leave the Greek ship—so overcrowded that tents were pitched on its main deck—which had called in its harbour, and on which I was bound for Venice.

The purpose of my next trip to Naples, in October 1959, was to conduct a programme of my music in the Teatro San Carlo.[1] Neither Gesualdo the place nor Gesualdo the musician had any part in my itinerary. (Deliberate sightseeing was limited to Sperlonga, a pool shivering with eels in a grotto that surged like a sea shell.) But I did go to Gesualdo again, finally, and, back in Naples, sought out the composer's tomb. It lies in the pavement of the Gesù Nuovo (whose *diamanti* façade is the most equable of pigeon roosts—a facet for each bird—whatever the pecking order), in the vicinity of some very grand mausolea. '*Carolus Gesualdus*', the epitaph begins, but it is entirely devoted to genealogy, failing to mention any contributions to music, or even that the interred was a musician at all. But then, very little

[1] Named for the composer's maternal uncle. The composer's paternal uncle was Cardinal of Santa Cecilia in Rome and a witness to the notorious trial of the Prince of Mantua's potency, popularly known as the congress of Venice. See *The Prince's Person* by Roger Peyrefitte.

attention has been paid to the music for four hundred years. And, come to think of it, that burial plaque is still in excellent condition. Perhaps, after all, 'The Gilded Monuments of Princes *Shall* Outlive . . .' their powerful madrigals.

Hollywood, March 7, 1968

Svadebka (*Les Noces*):
An Instrumentation

Hearing two of my discontinued preliminary versions of *Svadebka* (*The Wedding*) for the first time recently, I was reminded of a unique but long-forgotten experience of music-making fifty years ago. I am no longer certain how many versions I may have begun, or how extensive each fragment may have been; I have lately discovered a complete score for four pianos without vocal parts, of which I had no recollection, and other scores and sketches might still be excavated among the manuscripts I gave to people in return for financial help during the war. Nor am I certain of chronology, except that the ensembles were pared down over the years from a super-*Sacre* orchestra (I still possess sketches for this) to one for two cimbaloms, harmonium, pianola, and percussion, requiring only five players in all.

This last version, composed in Morges in the winter of 1918–19, is the most polished of the abandoned ones, and the most authentic, more so in some ways than the final score, which, though streamlined, stronger in volume, and instrumentally more homogeneous, is also, partly for the same reasons, something of a simplification. (For other reasons as well, one being that the figuration in the unfinished version is generally more elaborate, and another that it reveals a contrapuntal tendency, *viz.* the canonic treatment of the principal line at *54*, which seems wrong stylistically in the light of the final score but might have seemed otherwise if the earlier one had been continued.) The manuscript is complete in detail to the end of the second tableau, except that repeated passages are not written out where the instrumentation is unchanged. At this point I was interrupted by the rush-order commission for *Pulcinella*, but I must also have begun to realize that the problems of synchronization with the

198

pianola and the near impossibility of finding competent cimbalomists had made my instrumentation impracticable.

It is, nevertheless, the most practical score, in the technical sense, that I have ever written, every note having been sound-tested in my own proving grounds. I had packed all of the instruments into my little musical pantry and learned to play all of them myself, spending as much time practicing them, in fact, and tinkering with and tuning the cimbalom, as I did composing. But what I did write came directly from the instruments, while the sound was still hot. I am no mystic; I need to touch music as well as to think it, which is why I have always lived next to a piano, why in this instance it was necessary for me to manipulate the cimbalom sticks, familiarize myself with the harmonium registrations (a two-manual instrument: I still have my receipt for a year's rental), try out flams and rim shots on the snare drum, and even shake the tambourine ('raaaaaaaise your voices'). Risky as my memory is, too, in matters of dates and places, I am certain of the position of each of the instruments of this little orchestra in my room, which must be because my acoustical reality—bilateral in my case, not circular, as I am aware when hit in the nape of the neck by 'spatial music'—is a part of my biological reality.

The instrumentation exposes lines of descent from *The Nightingale*, hitherto unnoticed, at least by me. The music from the first entrance of the tenor, for example, seems to devolve from the opera not only in rhythm and harmony (parallel chords emphasizing fifths), but also in vocal style; and the twitterings in the pianola part during the bride's lament are unexpectedly revealed as an inheritance from the ornithological ornaments in the opera. Both works employ orientalisms, too, in *Svadebka* most conspicuously during that same lament, where the cimbaloms might be Japanese plectrum instruments accompanying a scene from a Kabuki play.

The pianola part was not intended for human hands but for direct translation into the punch-card language of the automated poltergeist. It exploits the superhuman (and multidigital) velocity of the mechanically programmed instrument to the extent that three pianists are required to encompass all of the notes—*if* all of them *can* be played, at strict tempo. (My *Etude for Pianola* would require the same number of players, incidentally, if read from the six-stave original score.) I might add that I did not choose the pianola only for economy, but also because the tinny, nickelodeon-like rattle of this primeval jukebox suited my scheme of sonorities; it compares with the glossy, emulsified 'tone' of a Chopin recitalist's Steinway somewhat as a Model-T Ford compares with a six-door Cadillac. What defeated me, as I said, was the problem of synchronization, in pitch as well as *tempo*, for the instrument could make one's flesh creep, partly because of the spooky absenteeism of the player, but mainly because it was so grossly, irremediably, and intolerably out of tune.

The harmonium part was the most difficult to write. I did not trust the instrument acoustically, and in fact composed alternate versions for many passages, hoping to allow for the varying resources of different makes of instruments. Harmoniums were popular in that hymn-singing age, but are virtually extinct now, replaced by the electric organ, which I reluctantly admit as a substitute in my own ensemble.

No substitute, no thumbtacked or otherwise doctored piano, is admissible for the cimbaloms, the scarcity of which constitutes the chief obstacle to performance. A rare animal to begin with, and one that is even more rarely tamed—played by people who read music—the chances of capturing two of the species, then of corralling a pair of competent players, are astronomically poor, comparable, in fact, to zoologists' chances with Chi-Chi and An-An. But its sound is so winsome that a society for the preservation of musical wildlife must be persuaded to endow one of the schools both with the instrument and with scholarships for its study. The music bounces, glittering delicately when articulated with felt sticks, and becoming more protrusive and as compact as billiard balls with wooden ones, which I prefer ordinarily. Both timbres are effective antidotes to the murky acoustical presence of the harmonium, and both combine ideally with the wiry playerless-piano (as it should have been named).

The role of the *batterie* was another novelty, at least in 1918. Percussion sections had long served the orchestra as arsenals and sound-prop departments, and supplied it with extra colours, articulation, weight. But before the *Histoire du Soldat* and this *Svadebka* version, in which the percussion is a continuing and internally consistent element, the 'drums' had never really been given their heads. The character of the music itself is percussive, moreover, and that character is part of me, another of my biological facts. To bang a gong, bash a cymbal, clout a wood block (or critic) has always given me the keenest satisfaction, depending on the resulting qualities of sound. In fact I am still tempted at dinner tables to tap the drinking glasses with the cutlery. But surely this is natural in a musician, or at any rate part of a very old tradition. The first musician in the Bible, after all, was a hammer-and-anvil player (despite the façade at Orvieto, which portrays him striking bells suspended from a rack), and the music of the same instruments is supposed to have inspired the discovery of the relationships of intervals—by Pythagoras, another tapper of glasses filled to varying levels with water.

My recollections of *Svadebka* itself are happy, but the associated ones are painful: all of my friends of the time are dead, and I am the only and ever lonelier survivor. Stepan Mitusov comes to mind first: he was closer to me than anyone else at the time, and among other debts of gratitude I owe to him the encouragement of my *Svadebka* idea. The thought of Mitusov reminds me, in turn, of Rimsky-Korsakov. We were together at Rimsky's nearly every day at one time, Rimsky being as fond of him as I was myself, but did not accept him as a pupil—which gave me my first better opinion of myself: I had at least been accepted.

I do not know whether Mitusov ever heard *Svadebka*, or even whether the music was repatriated during his lifetime. (Has it been now?) And the world is so different now that the name Korsakov is less likely to remind me of my old teacher than of the dreaded syndrome of defective time-memory. 'Old men forget', of course, but they forget or remember selectively, like everyone else. These memories are a selection, then, but they are the only ones willing to be summoned today concerning a long-vanished episode in the making of my *Svadebka*.

Zürich, October 22, 1968

LETTERS

. . . in a wailful choir the small gnats mourn

KEATS

I

1260 North Wetherly Drive
Hollywood 69, California
January 5, 1962

Music Editor
Los Angeles Times

Sir: I have just received your reviewer's notice of the belated first Los Angeles performance of *The Rake's Progress* (*The Times*, Dec. 4, 1961). As I was unable to see this production, I have no opinion of it, though in all fairness I should confess that the fact that your reviewer found it of high quality is for me the worst possible recommendation.

I protest his misrepresentation of facts about my opera. The final ensemble, he says, 'borrows a page from *Don Giovanni*'. It does no such thing. He states that Tom Rakewell loses at a game of cards with Nick Shadow. This is also untrue. Tom wins the game, and he wins it in plain English, the language your reviewer so fervently advocates for all opera, even though he understands it no better than he writes it. Anyone who failed to follow that simple but crucial event in the plot could have understood little else about my opera.

Your reviewer calls my score 'eye music'. He writes, 'On the printed page it reveals all manner of intellectual devices.' This description proves that either his eye never fell upon the printed page or that he cannot read music. 'Intellectual' means nothing in your reviewer's sentence, but it does mark his inability to hear

202

harmony and melody; it is, of course, painfully obvious why the word is pejorative to him. 'Eye music', however, *is* a useful term, which he must have picked up from a musical acquaintance and misapplied. *The Rake's Progress* contains no example of eye music by any definition, and the opera's one short canon could hardly be more evident to the ear if it had been doubled by trumpets. I would challenge your reviewer to cite his examples, but I want no further contamination of him, even from the crossing of quills.

I repudiate your reviewer's errors of opinion no less than his errors of fact. 'The singers are required to negotiate all kinds of unvocal passages,' he says. This would have to be denied by the many singers who have scored notable successes in all the roles of the opera. To the professional musician, 'unvocal', 'unpianistic', 'unviolinistic', and the like, are so many refuge-words behind which the reviewer vainly seeks to hide his ignorance of the uses of vocal and instrumental art.

Still, your reviewer remarks that the Rake 'disported his fine tenor ably', which he could not have done if the music were 'unvocal'. Yet if 'disport' is what he did, he should have been censured rather than commended for it.

'The rhythms are tricky.' Well, yes, if your yardstick is the Overture to *Rienzi*. But as for the charge that 'never was an opera less theatrical or more undramatic', I can say that a few months ago in Stockholm it was one of the most dramatic theatrical experiences in my life, and as the performance I saw was the thirty-fifth sold-out one in four off-season months (in a city with one-eighth the population of Los Angeles), I do not think my reaction egocentric.

For many years now I have had to observe your reviewer stumbling through the musical world in quest of the absolute middle in mediocrity; serving as a mouthpiece for the opinion of the *pons asinorum*; consuming space about X or Y's 'interpretation' without having the slightest notion of what was being interpreted; dismissing masterpieces old and new simply because they are invisible in his mole's-eye view of music history; denying the composers of yesterday, then using them as clubs to cudgel the composers of today.

The time has come to protest. In the case of this ignorant, errant, and smug review of *The Rake's Progress* I had thought for a moment that some of my colleagues might do so, especially those who profess to admire my work (and who have helped themselves to pieces of it). But I was forgetting how careers are made. So, then, *I* protest, and not only what your reviewer wrote about my opera, but his incompetence to write meaningfully about music of any kind.

Yours, etc.

Igor Stravinsky

II

Hollywood
March 18, 1962

Music Editor
Los Angeles Times

Sir: Not surprisingly, the qualities which distinguish *The Times*'s appreciation of my new book are ignorance, prejudice, and error.

I will deal first with error. I have recently remarked your reviewer's inability to read, a conclusion I reached after he demonstrated that he was unable to follow the most important event in the last act of my opera. Now, to bear out my conclusion, he exhibits his inability to read correctly a passage in my book. He has mistakenly attributed my comment about the late Deaf ('he tends to use the first person') for a remark about the late Langweilich. A small difference, he will say, but it is as significant as the late Deaf's failure to distinguish between a twelve-tone scale and a twelve-tone method—which is not, as your reviewer claims, a slight misuse of terms but a basic misconception.

And prejudice. Specifically, your reviewer's prejudice against the vocabularies of educated people. I myself am quite naturally interested in words, if only because of necessity; I have had to become fluent in three languages other than my own, and to learn to make my way in three more. But my interest in words is not merely philological. I recognize that words are the very instruments of thought, and that a large vocabulary permits the making of distinctions. Your reviewer, as an aspirant writer, ought to understand this, and he should welcome being sent to the dictionary to learn. And not only to the dictionary: how could he, as a would-be music critic, have failed to learn 'esurient' from the title of the eighth phrase of Bach's or any other composer's *Magnificat*? How could he have read any popular history of painting without knowing 'wain', and how could he have done basket-weaving in kindergarten without learning 'osier'? And for that matter, how could he have turned his back on my later music without knowing that he was 'tergiversating?' These words which he objects to in my book are at least spelled and used correctly, however, and this much cannot be said of his own excursions into what he calls a 'sportive' vocabulary. He describes the late Deaf as a 'Stravinsky apostate', which is an impossible verbal construction, and his double-errored 'ola-prodida' (olla podrida?) can hardly be blamed on a printer.

And ignorance. Your reviewer confesses that he has never heard of some of the composers whom I nominate as qualified reviewers for a composers' magazine. Still, every one of them has been discussed in *Musical America*, an exoteric journal of which the local correspondent is none other than your reviewer. With that source of information so close at hand, it should not take much effort for him to keep abreast of musical activities. Such an effort would be worthier than the one on which he has spent so much energy recently.

Yours, etc.
IGOR STRAVINSKY

P.S.: I append some lines by Goethe. They were no doubt written with someone like your reviewer in mind, and they should help him to a better understanding of his problems. 'All great excellence in art, at first recognition, brings with it a certain pain arising from the strongly felt inferiority of the critic; only at a later period, when we take it into our culture, and appropriate as much of it as our capacities allow, do we learn to love and esteem it. Mediocrity, on the other hand, may often give unqualified pleasure; it does not disturb our self-satisfaction, but rather encourages us with the thought that we are as good as another.'

III

11 April 1968

Mr. Wolfgang Wagner
Bayreuther Festspiele
8580 Bayreuth, Germany

Dear Mr. Wagner:

I am sorry to be so late in acknowledging your letter, but I was in Arizona when it came, and have been exceptionally busy since my return. I am sorry, too, and ashamed, not to *have* any thoughts to contribute to your programme book for the *Meistersinger* centenary; I have not heard a performance in a very long time. If you think the adjoining remarks worth printing, I am glad to give them to you, but I will certainly not mind if you decide against including them.

I still recall my excitement and pleasure in hearing the *Meistersinger* for the first time. This performance, which I attended with Rimsky-Korsakov, turning the pages of the score for him, was given in the Maryinsky Theater by a German company, and I remember that the accuracy of the musical execution, which far surpassed our St. Petersburg standards, amazed and delighted me.

Because I was following the score, my memory of my impressions of the stage is less strong than my recollection of the effect of the music. I had known it since childhood, but from the piano reduction. The actual sound was a revelation whose force, all musical experience being 'live' then, a young composer today is unable to appreciate. I was a composer myself, after all (not merely a listener), and each opportunity to compare my imagination of an orchestra score with its realization in performance had to be used as a lesson and a chance to acquire some skill of my own. And skill is a large part of what the *Meistersinger* is about.

It has been such a long time since I last heard the *Meistersinger* that I am unable to say what it would mean to me now. But I think I would still listen to it as an active composer listening to an active composition, for at the age of a hundred the *Meistersinger* is a very lively monument.

IGOR STRAVINSKY

IV

Hollywood, California
1 April 1969

To The Editor
The *Composer*

Sir:

I have just read Mr. Geoffrey Bush's 'footnote' to my *Dialogues and A Diary*, in the Autumn number of the *Composer*. Mr. Bush says that a 'point of considerable musico-ethnological interest is involved', and he offers 'to try to put the record straight'.

In fact Mr. Bush's elaborations have little to do with musico-ethnology. What does concern him is my attribution to the late Noah Greenberg of a 'discovery', near Tiflis, of 'an active performing tradition of music ranging from 10th century conductus and organum to High Renaissance'. That my word was misleading, Mr. Bush's misconstructions prove. But surely Mr. Bush is being wilfully naïve in taking it to mean universally unknown, and in supposing that I had thought an Intourist could be in a position to uncover anything of so unsecretive a nature not already known at least *in* the USSR. (In fact I had heard of the existence of the tradition during my visit to the USSR in 1962.) Mr. Greenberg's discovery was purely his own, obviously, and that of the other musicians with whom he shared it on his return to New York.

Now Mr. Bush supplies a new link, explaining that Mr. Greenberg's discovery was the result of his encounter with Mr. Bush and Mr. John Gardner, two 'much less interesting curiosities' (Mr. Bush's phrase) than the music itself. Messrs. Bush and Gardner had merely invited Mr. Greenberg to 'tag along' and hear the music with them. I cannot think why Mr. Greenberg failed to mention Messrs. Bush and Gardner to me, but clearly no slight was intended.

Yet Mr. Bush's assumptions do not 'set the record straight'. One obstacle is that they are not exhaustively logical. He asserts that Greenberg 'cannot have discovered and transmitted to Stravinsky anything that the three of us had not already heard; for Stravinsky's remarks are an exact description of the music which had been played on tape and performed for us that morning . . .' Then what about the music I did *not* describe?

Nor do I understand why Mr. Bush is so nicely precise about matters of which he is not certain—saying that the claim of the 'discovery' was 'not necessarily advanced by Greenberg himself' (then by whom?)—but so casual about the New York Pro Musica Antiqua: the statement that 'Greenberg had with him a party of singers and instrumentalists' sounds more like a reference to Mr. Greenberg's namesake in the train of the Duke of Mantua.

What Mr. Greenberg *did* say, to the best of my recollection, was that the music performed by his New York group, and the resemblances noted in it to the music of the local tradition, had excited the interest of Georgian musicians. Then, as I understood it, after his concerts Mr. Greenberg and two or three members of his ensemble were taken to villages near Tiflis, where they performed for the villagers and the villagers for them.

But my recollection is rickety, and it is several years since Mr. Greenberg played his tapes for me. In fact I would be inclined to believe in Mr. Bush's doubts and call the story a daydream, except for one circumstance: I am positive that my wife and Mr. Greenberg compared notes about two villages near Tiflis in which she had lived and which Mr. Greenberg most certainly had visited.

Mr. Bush cavils at the 'anti-Soviet inferences drawn from the episode by Stravinsky' (they were drawn from a great many other episodes as well, of course), though he finds them natural for a 'White Russian' with a 'built-in prejudice against Soviet Communism'—as if it were possible to be unprejudiced about Soviet Communism, and as if the classification accounted for my emigration, for artistic reasons, long before the existence of a White Russia. 'As anyone at all familiar with the USSR knows,' he continues, 'it is Party policy to stimulate . . . manifestations of local culture'. I daresay I am 'at all' familiar with the

208

USSR, but apart from that, Mr. Bush's contention is by no means self-evident, as he seems to think; in fact, *pace* Mr. Bush, the USSR's policy of *suppressing* manifestations of religious culture (notoriously of late in the case of the Jews) would be, I think, far more generally conceded.

As it happened, only shortly before I heard the tapes, Mr. George Balanchine had visited his brother, the Georgian composer, in Tiflis, and Mr. Balanchine's expression of his views on his return undoubtedly influenced my own remarks. As a native Georgian, Mr. Balanchine is at least as prejudiced as I am, or as Mr. Bush is. Which is why his report, reflected by me, of the intense dislike of many Georgians for a Party policy many of them described to him as one of cultural containment, is as valid (insofar as opinions of the sort have any validity) as Mr. Bush's impressions of beneficent Soviet stimulation.

May I add that not long before his death, Mr. Greenberg sent some additional tapes to me, and that my pleasure in the music was as great at the later date as at the time of the first experience?

Respectfully yours,
IGOR STRAVINSKY

V

Hollywood, California
November 18, 1965

Music Editor
The New York Times

Sir: Mr. Harold Schonberg's tribute to Edgar Varèse (*Times*, November 14) employs some remarks of mine in a context they do not aptly serve.

He quotes me as saying that 'the best things in [Varèse's] music—the first seven measures from No. 16 in *Arcana*, the whole of *Deserts*—are among the better things in contemporary music.' Mr. Schonberg's comment on this is: 'Yes, it became very fashionable to give blanket endorsement to Varèse.' *That* is 'blanket endorsement?' . . . to choose seven measures out of

209

four hundred and fifty, one complete work out of a dozen, and then qualify the selections as 'among the better things?'

Mr. Schonberg further states that 'around 1950 [Varèse] found himself in the enjoyable position of having all of his works called masterpieces. Stravinsky's reaction is typical.' The typical reaction is quoted: 'Varèse's music will endure.' Around 1950? But I had heard no music by Varèse until almost a decade later. And in 1950 no one could have called all of his works masterpieces, as no more than a handful of them were known. Where, in which publications, is this chorus of flattering opinion to be found? I knew nothing of it, at any rate, and though I was aware of a respect for Varèse on the part of the younger generation, my own regard for him was not directed by any fashion. After all, the two recordings that offered the first fairly comprehensive introduction to his music originated not in Donaueschingen or even Downtown New York, but in the wilds of Los Angeles. My opinion of the music was formed thanks to those recording sessions, and it was formed first hand. And I expressed that opinion (in my *Memories and Commentaries* of 1960) not at all in a hedging manner as Mr. Schonberg says.

Mr. Schonberg further claims that 'blanket endorsements' such as mine 'did not help [Varèse] get performances'. Perhaps not, but then again perhaps they did. In fact, I know of an instance in which a work by Varèse was played together with one of my own precisely because of what I wrote; but the assertion is simply not probative. And the inference that the blanket endorsers might better have spent their energies promoting performances is likewise misdirected in my case. In fact, I gave a portion of the recording session for my *Renard* so that a recording of his *Offrandes* could be made, an act of no sacrifice or virtue on my part, to be sure, and certainly it is deplorable that Varèse did not have a recording period to himself; nevertheless, the music *was* performed by this means, and by it has become known.

For the rest, I found Mr. Schonberg's piece most eloquent, especially the quotations from Varèse. I only regret that *The Times* did not devote a leading article of the sort to Varèse while he was alive, but by way of reparation Mr. Schonberg might still encourage some visiting foreign orchestra to interrupt the forty-year neglect of *Amériques*; this way American orchestras can carry on with *Finlandia* and *España* undisturbed. Or would that be too fashionable?

I became acquainted with Varèse myself only toward the end of his life. A big, gruffly restless man, he had extraordinary power to vivify, and I will not soon forget him as he moved about his basement studio one night striking his beloved gongs, then rushed around the block to buy a pizza. I also remember him—it was the last time we were together—listening to the electronic interludes of *Deserts*, which he had just revised (the machine-guns were made to enter at new places, I think). He pleaded with the sound engineer to increase the already fuse- and brain-blowing volume, I recall, and he could hardly contain his eagerness to wiggle the dials himself. I am deeply saddened by his death.

Yours, etc.
IGOR STRAVINSKY

VI

Essex House
160 Central Park South
New York City, New York
May 1, 1970

To the Music Editor
The New York Times
229 West 43rd Street
New York, N.Y.

Sir: Due to illness I have only just seen Mr. Harold Schonberg's notice of the Juilliard *Rake's Progress* (*Times*, April 24). It is mysteriously confined to speculations. He says that Mr. Leinsdorf 'conducted with every indication of confidence.' Every indication? Can't he tell? And anyway, who cares about the state of Mr. Leinsdorf's confidence? The point is, what did he do with the music? '. . . The director had his singers operating at full strength'. Meaning what? No absentees? 'At full strength', he continues, 'in everything but the diction'. As if 'everything' explained anything. Nor can Mr. Schonberg decide whether the poor diction is my fault or the singers'. 'Has there ever been a production of the opera,' he asks, 'in which the words come through with any degree of clarity?'

(The answer, by the bye, is yes, but probably not in New York. The words came through clearly enough at Santa Fe, the Boston Opera, and Sadler's Wells. But, then, one wonders what proportion of the Russian words of *Boris*, the Czech words of the Janáček operas, *etc.*, 'come through' to Mr. Schonberg.)

Mr. Schonberg sticks no less closely to speculation with regard to the work itself. 'Stravinsky may have had the Mozart of *Così fan tutte* in mind when composing the opera'—again, can't he tell? if I did have, the remark might even be relevant—'but the vocal settings are peculiarly his own'—surprising?—'and they pose all kinds of problems'. This is too bad. But what *are* these problems? And why, unless the truth has been kept from me, do singers never complain?

Mr. Schonberg is quite certain about only one thing. It is that the opera bores him. But that is irrelevant. By itself it says nothing about the opera but only something about Mr. Schonberg, which is an altogether different subject. And this is why in *my* review of Mr. *Schonberg's* performance I must overlook his good-natured confession: 'It is my misfortune to be more bored with *The Rake's Progress* every time I hear it'. Otherwise I might have said that I consider it my good fortune to be more bored by Mr. Schonberg every time *I* read him.

Yours, etc.

IGOR STRAVINSKY

VII

Essex House
160 Central Park South
New York, N.Y. 10019
June 6, 1970

To the Editor 'DANCE MAILBAG'
The New York Times
229 West 43rd Street
New York, N.Y.

Sir: I have not yet seen 'Balanchine's new *Firebird*', but Mr. Barnes's review under that title (*Times*, May 30) misleads on the central point and demands comment on some others. 'The score used,' he says, 'is Stravinsky's own recension of 1949, which I almost secretly think inferior to the original'. Apart from the question of how one can 'almost secretly think' in *The New York Times* (is circulation down?), Mr. Barnes plainly does not know what was performed. The score used was a revision (1945, not 1949) of the *Firebird* Suite, a concert piece about half the length of the original *Firebird* ballet, and never intended as a recension or contraction of it. Mr. Barnes should be able to tell a half from a whole, moreover, as he is so certain that Fokine's original 'did undeniably have a choreographic integrity' that Balanchine's new version lacks; this though Mr. Barnes 'only saw revivals of the Fokine work, of course . . .' (Why 'of course?' Is Mr. Barnes too young to have seen it? He writes as if he were 102.) I had many reservations about the Fokine original myself, but I can neither confirm nor deny its 'choreographic integrity' not knowing what the phrase means (the first English sense of the noun rather than the first American?).

What seems very odd is that while Mr. Barnes on his own is not positively able to identify Mr. Robbins's share in the choreography, he finds it, at the same time, 'rather better' than Mr. Balanchine's share. (The production having been billed as a collaboration, why did Mr. Robbins's name not appear in the heading of the review?) 'Gossip' *did* identify the Robbins share as the Kastchei dance, Mr. Barnes admits, but, refusing to rely on hearsay, he will venture no more himself than 'This is almost certainly the same hand that created the mass mysteries of Robbins's version of *Les Noces*'. 'Mass mysteries'? Mr. Robbins should sue.

Finally, however, it is obvious that the real subject of the review is not the *Firebird* at all, but Mr. Barnes: ('And you know I found myself remembering . . .' 'I did not care for it at all . . .' 'I did not like that either . . .' 'I am of two minds . . .' *etc. etc.*). Not that, in principle, I object to the switch. Mr. Barnes is an interesting subject, after all, and he certainly deserves review. Only given the title and the occasion, something helpful concerning the *Firebird* might have been more suitable.

Yours sincerely,
IGOR STRAVINSKY

P.S. The wizard's name is 'Kastchei', not 'Kotschei'. The latter is not a possible variant either, nor, since it is repeated, a printer's error. Nor do I think my correction pedantic. 'Kastchei' is as well known in the Ballet world as, say, Merlin in the world of Arthurian Romance. (Marlon who?)

VIII

Hotel Royal
Evian-les-Bains
Haute-Savoie (France)
June 23, 1970

The Music Editor
Los Angeles Times
Los Angeles

Sir: Owing to travels, I have just received Mr. Bernheimer's notice, 'Stravinsky Switches Off Switched-On' (*Times*, May 29). It is largely confined to tattle; but before I come to that let me say that the description of myself as an 'irreverent octogenarian' perplexes me, not because it seems to omit something; nor because it is so obviously my reverences that matter, not my irreverences; but simply because, who is, why should anybody be, *reverent* about television?

Mr. Bernheimer omits any mention of context, making me out as a mere latecomer inveighing for no reason against the already well-abused CBS programme. But the lines of mine he quotes both illustrated and depended on an important distinction; and they were written before I 'switched off', which, needless to say, was before the end of the hour. Why, I wonder, did Mr. Bernheimer find my account of the event worth a column, especially since *The New York Times* published virtually the same opinion of it the next day? Why, instead, did he not mention my far more valuable comments, in the previous issue of the same magazine, on the Beethoven Piano Sonatas?

As for the tattle, he counters an imagined deprecation of Mr. Mehta, aspects of whose performance I praised, with the report that 'the maestro' (Mr. Mehta, that is) feels no 'temperamental affinity' with my later music. Well, I can only say that I am taking this stoically; and even with some sympathy, for Mr. Mehta is doubtless suffering from the generation gap, a conclusion I find practically inescapable as so many of his youngsters, among them his own former assistant, Mr. Thomas, who played my *Variations* fourteen times with the Boston Symphony this season, *do* feel an affinity with it.

Mr. Bernheimer further reports that if I 'do not approve of all of the efforts of [the maestro], there may be comfort for some in the realization that the feeling is mutual'. Apart from the preposterousness of the idea of anyone deriving any 'comfort' from that improbable 'realization', Mr. Bernheimer seems to be mistaking a reciprocation for an equation. Besides, he does Mr. Mehta an injury, making it appear that he is afflicted with delusions of grandeur—*i.e.*, in assuming that I am in the least concerned with 'all' of his efforts. But, in fact, since the 'Switched-On' fiasco I *have* become aware of one more of them, and for this I wanted to congratulate him. His new recording of *The Rite of Spring* errs in many ways (especially in *tempi*), but is always exciting, at least—in contrast, say, to the more mature (over-mature, in fact heavily mannered) new recording by Boulez.

Which brings me to Mr. Bernheimer's final bit of fomenting,

his reference to an interview (neither quoted nor named), in which M. Boulez is charged with impugning certain recent statements of my own (also unspecified but perhaps referring to an article in which I defended M. Boulez from the growing view of him as not so much a conductor as a solfège-ist). Apparently M. Boulez 'suggested' that my 'arch-disciple' had put words into my mouth—though whether or not Mr. Bernheimer has put the words I quote into M. Boulez's mouth I cannot tell.

Nor have I had any contact with M. Boulez myself since, shortly after visiting me in Hollywood three years ago, he talked about my latest compositions (in an interview) with unforgiveable condescension, then went on to play them at a prestigious concert in Edinburgh. This was not the first proof of disingenuousness I had had of that arch-careerist, but it will be the last in which I have any personal connection.

As to the ventriloquism, the only instance I know of that, in the sense of imposing an idea that was not mine, could never have become mine, and actually misrepresented me, was when M. Boulez talked me into deleting a measure from *Les Noces* (I was less than sober) that did not fit *his* formula for the passage; and did it, obligingly enough, for the television camera.

Concerning the contributions of my 'arch-disciple', on the other hand, may I say that it would be strange indeed if we had *not* put words into, or helped to get them out of, each other's mouths; after all, we have been working together for twenty-three years. What he is guilty of, however, is having introduced me to almost all of the new music I have heard in the past two decades (Boulez's included, for which I am ill-disposed to forgive him, my extravagant advocacy of it at one time having brought me nothing but criticism); and not only to the new music but to the new everything else—which is why 'disciple', arch or ordinary, is hardly apt. The plain truth is that anyone who admires my *Agon*, my *Variations*, my *Requiem Canticles*, owes some gratitude to the man who has sustained my creative life these last years.

When I moved from, and severed all connections with, Los Angeles, a year ago, I expected that my tiffs with the *Times* were at an end. Now, however, I am thinking of how agreeable it would be if I could look forward with a little security to a few more. I am girding for my ninetieth, in any case; but if I make it, and we collide once again, please don't call me an 'irreverent *non*egenarian'.

Yours, etc.

IGOR STRAVINSKY

IX

Hotel Royal
Evian-les-Bains
Haute-Savoie (France)
June 24, 1970

To the Editor
The Nation
333 Avenue of the Americas
New York, N.Y. 10014

Sir: Professor Karlinsky's review of some recent books concerning my music (*The Nation*, June 15) is so generous to me that I feel ungrateful taking issue, as I shall, with some points both of fact and of emphasis. 'Igor Glebov's brilliant *A Book About Stravinsky* was published in 1930', Professor Karlinsky writes. *My* copy was published in 1929; I have it with me, by coincidence, and I have been reading the rubrics with which I decorated it at the time; they, at least, call for a radically different kind of adjective. But Professor Karlinsky also commends another, more recent, Soviet publication, Vershinina's study of my early ballets, more highly than I would have, gratified as I was to find such a change of heart toward my music in my native land, as well as such vastly improved musicological standards.

Miss Vershinina's book includes an essay, 'What I Wanted to Express in "*The Rite of Spring*".' Professor Karlinsky says that 'It was written by the composer immediately after finishing the score and published in the journal *Muzyka* in 1913. In the Russian text of that essay there is a curious stylistic spillover from the ballet: Stravinsky uses the same archaic, shamanistic, bogeyman style he devised for the titles of various sections of the music'. This is even more curious than Professor Karlinsky suspects, for I did not write that essay. It was concocted by a French journalist, and the Russian version is a translation. I disavowed the essay not only at the time, moreover, but on several later occasions, which explains why it has never been reprinted outside the USSR. Nor are the titles of the ballet movements mine, except for a 'non-existent Russian word' which Professor Karlinsky objects to, but which, perhaps only because I coined it, I still like. The other titles were composed by my co-scenarist, Nicolas Roerich. Professor Karlinsky does not like my new English rendering of one of them, '*Igra Umykaniiya*'. Neither do I; and, looking at the manuscript of the full score recently, I noticed that I didn't like the Russian title either, in 1913, and cancelled it then in favour of the French, '*Jeu de Rapt*'. Professor Karlinsky also prefers the spelling '*Idutvedut*' to my '*eedoot-veedoot*'. And, clearly, '*id*', as in Freud, and 'ut', as in utter, *are* different sounds than 'eed' and 'oot', which is how I pronounce the Russian syllables. But, then, I do not understand any transliteration system, and have rarely been able to recognize the words of singers who are dependent on them.

Professor Karlinsky cites the absence of that spurious 'What I Wanted to Express' essay as the 'most glaring omission' from the new volume of facsimile sketches of *The Rite* (Boosey and Hawkes, 1969). But his own omission in reviewing the publication, the failure to mention its measure-by-measure description of the original choreography, is far more glaring. So much more valuable than any commentary, the score of the choreography (recovered in 1967) not only changes and deepens the interpretation of the music (especially in matters of phrasing), but makes possible the recreation of the ballet as it was conceived. *The Rite of Spring* has never been staged by an American company, and, impertinent as it may be for me to say so, what better excuse could be found than the chance to revive the Nijinsky original, for the first time since 1913? I would come back to see that myself.

Yours, etc.

IGOR STRAVINSKY

X

Essex House
New York, N.Y.
March 3, 1971

The Editor
Dance Mailbag
The New York Times
229 West 43rd Street
New York, N.Y.

Sir:

Mr. Barnes's '*This Firebird Is For Burning*' (*New York Times*, Feb. 21; London *Times*, Feb. 24, retitled '*The Ashes of a Firebird*') adds several cubits to the stature of his incompetence as a commentator on ballet.

'The world is full of bad productions of *The Firebird*', he writes, and I have seen enough of them here and there myself to feel confident in the justice of his world-wide report. But, he goes on, 'No one else—other than Fokine—has managed a viable *Firebird*'; and he dismisses my criticisms of the Fokine as 'ridiculous', the truth being that 'Fokine knew what he wanted, and Stravinsky provided perfect incidental music to his vision'. *If* it were that simple! In fact, the only charitable explanation for this claptrap I can provide is that Mr. Barnes has been seeing too many Ken Russell films. Real-life composers, this one anyway, cannot write incidental music to something so nebulous as someone else's visions. And apart from that, the music of *The Firebird* is by any measure very far from 'incidental'.

Mr. Barnes further rules that 'this was Fokine's ballet, not Stravinsky's, and Fokine knew best'. Here I should perhaps remind the reader that Mr. Barnes's point is limited to choreography, since comparatively few people have ever seen *The Firebird* and millions have heard it. But how can Mr. Barnes decide that Fokine knew better than I did, not knowing what I knew? And, anyway, knew *what* better? I was at least there. I worked with Fokine. And I had been brought up on ballet since early childhood, hence may have had as keen an appreciation of it as Mr. Barnes. And though this is boasting, I had a reputation with the dancers for a choreographic imagination. Finally, my letters, which are now being prepared for publication (and may this be the last addition of the sort), bear out my later criticisms in concrete terms. Not that any of this proves that Fokine did not know best, of course, but it certainly weakens Mr. Barnes's claims to know.

One wonders what is behind Mr. Barnes's all too evident malice aforethought? Why, for example, throw in the remark that 'Stravinsky was not even first choice as composer'—would it matter even if I had been *last* choice?—without saying that when the commission was given to Liadov, I was almost totally unknown, and in fact still a student? Why, too, does Mr. Barnes call me a 'querulous old man' when he has so plainly picked the 'querul' himself? Is it because of the growing complaints about his facile reviews and the way they oscillate between the 'rave' for one kind of mediocrity and the 'roast' for another kind? Or is it simply Reviewers' Disease, an irritation brought on by the species's sense of its own profusion, and the relative scarcity—merciful scarcity, as Mr. Barnes must think—of such products as

Yours sincerely,
IGOR STRAVINSKY

PART FOUR

On Conductors
and Conducting

ON CONDUCTORS
AND CONDUCTING[1]

The Imperial Kapellmeister gave the beat.
- QUANTZ, describing a performance
of an opera by J. J. Fux in 1723.

Conductors, like politicians, are rarely original people. (It is not for their conducting that Mahler and Strauss are remembered.) Another resemblance to politics is that the conducting field is one for career-making[2] and personality-exploitation rather than for the application of exact and standardized disciplines. In fact, a conductor may be less well equipped for his work than his players, but no one except the players need know it.[3]

The incidence of ego disease is naturally high to begin with, but under the sun of a pandering public it grows like a tropical weed. As a result, the conductor is accorded a position out of all proportion to his real value in the music, as distinguished from the music-business, community. He soon becomes a 'great' conductor, in fact, even a 'titan of the podium' and, as such, a tremendous obstacle to genuine music-making. 'Great' conduc-

[1] The tone and provocation of these remarks, in reply to a question about 'eminent conductors I have known', are to be traced to a recording of the Brahms First Symphony to which I had just been listening, but which I could not follow, the second beats in the 6/8 movement being so delayed that the time signature might have been $6\frac{1}{2}/8$. I imagined how the conductor would call the distortion emphasis, though it was only weakening exaggeration; and expressive freedom, though the natural rhythmic vitality was corrupted. My mood, therefore, was that of a composer irritated by the impossibility of being played without the editing and the uninteresting comments of his conductors.

[2] See the analysis of the orchestral conductor in Canetti's *Crowds and Power*.

[3] Though orchestra players are by no means reliable judges of conductors.

223

tors, like 'great' actors, soon become unable to play anything but themselves. And being unable to adjust themselves to the work, they do it the other way around, adjusting the work to *their* 'style', *their* mannerisms. The cult of the great conductor tends to substitute looking for listening, moreover, so that to conductor and audience alike (and to reviewers who habitually fall into the trap of describing a conductor's appearance rather than the way he makes music sound, and of mistaking the conductor's gestures for the music's meanings), the important part of the performance is the gesture.[1]

If you are incapable of listening, the conductor will show you what to feel. Thus Mr. Bernstein will act out a life of Napoleon in 'his' *Eroica*, wearing an expression of noble suffering on the retreat from Moscow (TV having circumvented the comparatively merciful limitation to the dorsal view), and one of ultimate triumph in the last movement, during which he even dances the Victory Ball. If you are unable to listen to the music, you can watch the corybantics, and if you *are* able, you had better not go to the concert.

Let me mention two other disadvantages resulting from the conductor cult. The first is that it stultifies the repertory. Each conductor must make his mark in the standard pieces, *La Mer*, *Le Sacre du printemps*, and so on. Thus you may have had Herr Professor von Schnell's versions only a few weeks ago, yet you must now endure the aberrations of Herr Doktor von Langsamer; no wonder that conductors, whose work is largely repetition, easily develop an occupational indifference to music. Second, the typical conductor is a delinquent, quickly rusticated from the creative musical ideas of his age; or perhaps *arriviste* is a better word, in the sense of no progress, for progress would oblige him to sell stocks that pay handsome dividends.

[1] I quote from a recent review by Mr. Schonberg: 'Here was the young man vigorously beating time when his hands were not occupied at the keyboard. His beautiful fingers cued everybody in, his beat was strong and sturdy, his eyes darted hither and thither. But when he was playing the piano, the orchestra did just as well without the cues of those beautiful hands, those expressive eyes, those rhythmic shoulders. The entrances in the last movement were just as precise, the ensemble just as co-ordinated, the shadings just as accomplished. People may get the idea a conductor is not really needed.'

I have admired the work of many conductors during my long career as a listener. Felix Weingartner, for instance, was a near idol of mine in my youth, and a Beethoven cycle I heard him direct in Berlin in 1900 was a very great event in my life. In later years, too, I attended his concerts at every opportunity. Another conductor I admired was Alexander von Zemlinsky. In fact, I remember a *Marriage of Figaro* led by him in Prague as one of the most satisfying operatic experiences of my life. I should also mention such exacting and reliable musicians as Fritz Busch, Roger Desormière, and Hans Rosbaud.

As for the better conductors of today, I was never much of a hand at testimonials, nor have I become an encomiast with age. I have the highest regard, nevertheless, for such skilled and conscientious craftsmen as Szell, who can give prophylactic performances of the classic repertory; Reiner (*l'amico* Fritz), who made the Chicago Symphony into the most precise and flexible orchestra in the world and who was a salutary antidote to the windmill school of conducting; Eugene Ormandy, who gave the Philadelphia Orchestra its chinchilla sheen, and whose performances of *Fledermaus* at the Met a few years ago were a great treat; Maazel, who has overcome the publicity handicap resulting from a debut at the age of one and a half and become the most able all-around conductor at large today (but who directed a *Don Giovanni* I heard not long ago at the Met exactly as if he were a drum major); and Scherchen, who in spite of eccentricities, or protective discolorations (the supersonic finale and the *adagio 'andante'*), could give crisp and clean band-masterly performances of Haydn and convincing performances of Bach, even though he was without a clue to Bach's style. (It is unfair to single him out for censure on this point, however, since all great conductors' performances of Bach are grotesquely anachronistic; Bach, of course, leaves no room for great conducting.)[1] As for New Look conductors, Ozawa is the only one I know anything about. In fact I have just listened to his

---

[1] As nobody wants to hear any new music more than once, the young conductor might best make his mark today in the music of the 'continuo' period, though not by resurrecting yet more minor *ottocento* Italians and deservedly forgotten baroque operas (in concert performances). The Bach cantatas are still a fallow field.

breakneck *Rite of Spring* (RCA)—as far, that is, as the *tutti* in *Spring Rounds,* which he ruins by turning the three timpani *appoggiature* into straight triplet upbeats, a ludicrously comic effect.

The better conductors will probably continue to be bred in the field of the elastic beat (opera), and we can probably continue to look for them in those same old Mittel-europa mills in which the apprentice learns the routines of a dozen masterworks while still in his teens. The opera repertory is more extensive than the symphonic, after all—compare Verdi with Brahms as material—and interest in opera is much greater than interest in any other musical domain at present.

Furtwängler, when I played my *Piano Concerto* under his direction in Leipzig and in Berlin, was at the height of his reputation (as 'the last of the great tradition', though old-timers contended that he was the first of the small). He conducted it wretchedly, even worse than Kussevitsky at the première, which surprised me because other musicians of his and still older generations had guided the orchestra without difficulty. A few years after the Berlin performance, I was in the Villa d'Este at Como one day when a telegram came from him requesting first-perform-ance rights to my *Capriccio.* I replied that the piece had already been played twenty times (this was in 1931), but that he was welcome to play it for the twenty-first. I blame his telegram, and my less than perfect sobriety, for a misdemeanor that has troubled my conscience—not too profoundly—ever since. Walk-ing between a pair of 'Greek' statues on one of the Hotel's garden paths that night and noticing that the marble figures were scrawled with tourists' signatures, I took a pen myself and printed WILHELM VON DER FURTWÄNGLER on the *gluteus maximus* of the most obviously ersatz Apollo. Furtwängler looked like Goethe, but, a Goethe with a chromosome misprint.

Nor do I greatly cherish my memories of Mengelberg. At the first rehearsal of the *Capriccio* he began to conduct in an impos-sible *tempo.* I said I was unable to play at that speed, but should have specified, for he could not tell whether I had meant that he had been too fast or too slow. Greatly flustered, he embarked on a self-justifying oration: 'Gentlemen, after fifty years as a conductor I think I may claim to be able to recognize the proper *tempo* of a piece of music. Monsieur Stravinsky, however, would like us to play like this: tick, tick, tick, tick'. And he cocked his forefinger in mockery of Mälzel's very useful invention.

But Mengelberg was always a speech-maker, an after-dinner Demosthenes of impressive volubility (at least). Once at a banquet in Amsterdam honouring Respighi, he proposed a toast but glancing in my direction somewhere toward the end of it and no doubt finding me staring at my watch, pronounced my name at the climactic moment instead of the composer of *The Pines of Rome.*

I met Otto Klemperer in the early 1920s, I think in Dresden. He was regarded not only as the most skilful of the younger conductors then, but as the most sympathetic to contemporary composers, a reputation he managed to uphold throughout the 1920s and even in his first American years. Klemperer's *tempi* were sometimes erratic; in the twenties they raced, as now they are inclined to mope—in fact the main tension of the *Fidelio* I heard him do in Zürich in October 1961 was in seeing how slow it is possible to conduct without actually stopping. His musical impulses, at the same time, were often amazingly right. He was the only conductor who knew how to build the measure-and-a-note upbeat in the *Allegro* of the 'Clock' Symphony. Klemperer, that great, gaunt, Polyphemus of a man, was also, and surprisingly, a profoundly droll character, though it was difficult at times to be certain that drollery was intended.

The performance of my *Piano Concerto* with Bruno Walter, in Paris in 1928, was a pleasure, the more so for being unanticipated. I had not expected this '*Romantiker*' from another era to be able to count my scrambled meters, or, knowing his habit of slowing down for the second subject of a symphony, expected him to keep my metronomic *tempi.* Yet he followed me as nimbly as anyone with whom I ever played the piece.

We saw each other next at a League of Composers concert in New York in 1935, and after that in Hollywood, where for twenty years we lived only a few blocks apart. Our tastes and tempers—his melting Viennese manner and my explosiveness—were very unlike, but we were drawn together in some way, perhaps if only because octogenarians come to regard each other as counterchecks in an elimination game.

Bruno Walter called on me a few weeks before his death, inviting me in the name of the Vienna Philharmonic to conduct in Salzburg. I had heard that he was ailing and proposed to come to him instead, but he would not have it that way. I found him, as always, animated, warm, almost laboriously gentle. He described a performance of *Pique Dame* that he had conducted in Leningrad in the 1920s. And he talked about Rudolph Steiner—not critically, as I would about that sort of thing, but Steiner belonged to Walter's background. In parting I told him that I regretted having had to wait so long for his *Fidelio* recording, and he said that he hoped I would hear it one day soon. But that day will not come. Shortly afterward he lay in his coffin, the 'he' still incarnate, as Steiner would have it. On the wall above was a framed invitation to Beethoven's funeral.

I cannot add to what I have said elsewhere about Pierre Monteux except to remark that of all the conductors I have known he offered the least in the way of calisthenic exhibitions for the entertainment of the audience, but gave the clearest signals—conducting is semaphoring, after all—to the orchestra.

My first experience of Kussevitsky as a conductor of my music was his execution—firing-squad sense—of my *Symphonies of Wind Instruments* in London in 1921. He came to see me in Biarritz after that, to mend relations and invite me to conduct my *Octuor* in one of his Paris concerts. Twenty years later he commissioned a work from me as a memorial to his wife, Natalie, but his performance of this *Ode*, as I called it, was another disaster. The trumpet player misread the key of the instrument required in the third movement, failed to transpose, and played the part a major-second flat. Worse still, two systems of score from the final page were copied as one, and played that way, so that my simple triadic piece concluded in a cacophony that a few years later would have won me some prestige with the *avant garde*. This sudden change in style not only failed to excite

228

Kussevitsky's suspicions, however, but he actually confided to me that he preferred 'the original version'.

Ernest Ansermet introduced himself to me in a street in Clarens one day in 1911 and invited me to his home for dinner. Although I had heard of him as a schoolmaster and musician, his appearance—the beard—startled me: he was like an apparition of the Charlatan in *Petrushka*.

Ansermet became the conductor of the Kursaal Orchestra in Montreux shortly after, and our next encounter was at the home of the *chanson* composer Henri Duparc, a morose old gentleman then living in retirement near Vevey. At about the same time, and I think in company with Ansermet, I also made the acquaintance of the Geneva composer Ernest Bloch, whom I saw again many years later in Portland, Oregon.

When Pierné and Monteux left the Russian Ballet in 1914, I induced Diaghilev to hire Ansermet to succeed them. As a conductor he was especially skilful in regulating orchestral balances, and besides, he understood the Franco-Russian new music. I was on close terms with him from that time until, without authorization, he cut one of the dances in *Apollo* and later eliminated a section of *Jeu de Cartes*. Some years after that he began to criticize my revised versions of *Petrushka*, the *Symphonies of Wind Instruments*, and other early pieces, forgetting that he had been the first to perform the 1919 revision of the *Firebird*. Still later he began a kind of campaign decrying my new music, publishing a heavy but not very weighty tome full of *a priori* arguments and up-to-date phrases (*'conscience logarithmique'*) but only proving, and sadly, that he could not hear or follow it. We quarrelled, of course, but made up again before his death. And now all that is forgotten, but not the merry hours shared together—the time, for instance, when we drank a whole bottle of Framboise after which he pretended to be a dog and even began barking like one under my piano in the Salle Pleyel. It was a very convincing performance.

Leopold Stokowski came to see me in Biarritz in 1922 to make a cash deposit for first American performance rights to my future works. He was as sleek as a Russian wolfhound then, and in fact it was not until his career as a film star playing opposite Mickey Mouse that he became ungroomed and *had* to dishevel his hair in exactly the right way. He must have had second thoughts about the business agreement, however, as I did not hear from him again until the time of *Perséphone*, which he also wished to introduce in America. I attended a Stokowski concert in Carnegie Hall in 1935 or 1937 and greeted the maestro backstage at intermission. Then in 1942 he came to see me in Hollywood before attempting to conduct my *Symphony in C* with the NBC orchestra.

Few conductors have done as much as Stokowski to gain a hearing for new music, and now, in his eighties, he has crowned his achievements by his painstaking preparation and performance of the Ives *Fourth Symphony*. Nor has any conductor been a better orchestra-builder, all the way from basic sticks and stones to chromium plate. Some of the tricks he taught still survive, too, as in the way cello sections stagger their bowing in the *Tristan* Prelude for a smooth and consistent *crescendo*. But I suppose that he is largely to blame for the popular image of conducting as a kind of legerdemain.

I knew little about Sir Thomas Beecham's musicianship and I never heard him perform any of my music. But I did know his generosity. He sent 2,500 Swiss francs to me at the beginning of the 1914 war, in the event I might be cut off from my income in Russia. The money came like manna, too, on the very day I had to pay my mother's passage back to Russia (on a Brindisi-to-Odessa boat, the only route still open). Beecham and Edwin Evans were my first friends among English musicians, and Beecham was, first and last, the most spirited. We saw each other from time to time in later years and, perhaps because we never shared a concert together, were always on good terms. I remember two particularly lively evenings in his company in the 1940s, one in Mexico, the other with Percy Grainger in New York.

I would like to mention two other English conductors as well, Edward Clark and Eugene Goossens and, if I can, to honour their memories. Clark was the first English musician directly associated with the Schoenberg school, and when his efforts on its behalf are finally known, his name will be engraved in English musical history. He was also a jolly person and a wonderful friend.

Goossens was a natural musician in a family of natural musicians, and he was a master of orchestral technique. I recall his performance of *Le Sacre*, in London in 1921, with pleasure (and Diaghilev's jealousy at a triumph that, even by reflection, was not his).

Dimitri Mitropoulos had conducted *Petrushka* and *Histoire du Soldat*, but as a missionary of Mahler and a specialist in the *Alpine Symphony* he could not have been very interested in my music. I was surprised, therefore, when he came to call on me in Hollywood one summer evening in 1945. He spoke French, mixed with Slavonic, and this together with his wobbly movements, quickly endeared him to me. We talked about the Orthodox Church and looked at my collection of icons. The next day I went to hear and watch him conduct and play Prokofiev's *Third Piano Concerto* in Hollywood Bowl, and was amazed by the virtuosity of his performance. But Mitropoulos was not only a freakishly gifted man, he was also gentle, humble, very generous, and very kind. I was deeply moved by his death. But I see that these remarks are turning into a necrology and that I am inclined to praise the dead and damn the not-quite. Leonard Bernstein came to see me in New York one day in 1945. His visit was to have lasted a few minutes, but it filled the entire day. The young Bernstein was readily likeable (he still is), and he obviously adored music (he still does). He was personally very attractive, too, with a most becoming pompadour, and not yet leonine or English-sheep-dog. Since then he has become so well known that guided missile experts study his career for basic technique. In fact, I would not be surprised to hear of his conducting several concerts at the same time, giving an opening downbeat in Carnegie Hall, then flying off to lead the first measures of another concert in Lincoln Center, while subordinates—for he has become a department store—rush in and bring the various pieces through to the end. But how dull New York would be without Leonard Bernstein. A few days after that first meeting I went to his performance of the *Symphony of Psalms*. WOW!

PART FIVE
Reviews

SPRING FEVER

A Review of Three Recent Recordings of 'The Rite of Spring'[1] (June 1970)

| | Cleveland Orchestra
Conductor: Boulez
CBS Records | Los Angeles Philharmonic
Conductor: Mehta
London Records | Columbia Symphony
Conductor: Stravinsky
Columbia Records
(1960, re-issued 1970) |
|---|---|---|---|
| Introduction | This is puzzling. M. 6 is marked 'accelerando' but Boulez makes a broad ritard. Worse still, he does not distinguish between the two tempi of the movement; and with no quickening at the 'Più mosso', there is of course no return, with the bassoon, to a tempo primo that was never departed from. As a result, the performance is very dull. Faults of balance—the over-miked bass-pizzicati at 10, for one—are innocuous in comparison, and mainly of the recording - artificiality type. | The 2nd note of the horn comes with, instead of before, the bassoon, a mistake that changes the whole character of the beginning. M. 6 is then ruined by a ritard. The English horn lingers lazily on the 3rd note in m. 2 of 2, and 3 m. later, the 'Più mosso' does not happen. The clarinet trills between 4 and 5 are too loud. Etc., etc. Nevertheless, the performance is more livening (and less wayward) than Boulez's, and warmer in sound, which is also, in part, a quality of the London label. | Not being aware of myself as an object, in the same way that I am aware of the other two conductors, I can only review myself in terms of the same deficiencies that I note in them. And in these terms, I am obliged to say that this performance, though far from definitive, is the best of the three. As a recording, alas, it is obsolete. |

[1] A review by Igor Stravinsky of three previous recordings appeared in *Dialogues and a Diary*, Faber, 1968.

Augurs of Spring	The *tempo* is good, apart from unsteadiness at **22**. The clarinets are too loud at 2 before **27**, and the first trumpet wrongly dominates the quartet of trumpets after **28**; but the trumpets are generally too loud, throughout the recording. At **31**, the contrabassoons and fourth horn *should* have been over-miked.	Mehta ignores the continuity of the pulsation (the old 16th equals the new 8th), taking an unrelated, and vitiatingly fast, one. **18** is ragged and at **20** the trombone and bassoons are radically out of tune with each other. At **1** m. before **22** the triplet reaches the 2nd beat ahead of the tubas; and in spite of the double bar and *fermata*, the m. before **22**, and **22** itself, overlap. The *tempo* at **32** is pushed.	I reduce the *whole* dynamic level after the first eighth. The triplet before **22** is unclear, and **22** itself wobbles. The end of the movement is rushed.
Ritual of Abduction	This is perniciously slow, not a '*Presto*' but an '*Allegro moderato*'. And, even so, the quarter-notes after **47** take too much time.	This is sluggish, but better than Boulez. The quarters are too long at **47**—overtime that in fact amounts to almost time-and-a-half.	The *tempo* from **47** to the end is unsteady.

	Cleveland Orchestra *Conductor: Boulez* *CBS Records*	*Los Angeles Philharmonic* *Conductor: Mehta* *London Records*	*Columbia Symphony* *Conductor: Stravinsky* *Columbia Records* (1960, re-issued 1970)
Spring Rounds	This is on the slow side but greatly to be preferred to my own very hurried reading. (The 16th-note *appoggiaturas* in m. 3 and 4 of **48** are *too* slow, however.) The first 2 m. at **55** sound as if they were conducted in 2, rather than in 4, hence the can-can effect. I dislike Boulez's '*ritenuto*' 1 m. before **57**.	The '*tranquillo*' is too slow at **48**, and again at **56**, which is at least consistent. But so is the dance proper too slow, as well as wrong in character —oversweet and lacking an edge. The '*poco ritenuto*' before **54**, moreover, is so '*molto*' that the wind players must have practiced special breathing exercises (no easy undertaking in Los Angeles). **54** itself is brisk and good.	The '*tranquillo*' is too fast, both times, but so is the whole movement. **54**, on the other hand, is too slow.
Ritual of the Rival Tribes	The first 2 m. are messy, but at 3 before **62** I prefer Boulez's phrasing (*i.e.*, after the 5th quarter only) to my own. The accent is missing on the 2nd quarter of the 3/4 m. after **62**, and the bass-drum at **64** produces one of the deadest and most depressing thuds I have ever heard.	This is very good, clearer than the Boulez at the beginning, and more exciting all the way. I like the chords at 4 and 2 m. before **59** the way Mehta plays them, *i.e.*, *forte* and in *tempo*. But the horns are weak at **65**, where they should come through like Roland at Roncesvalles.	**57** is too slow but clearer than the Boulez. I make *crescendi* at the chords before **59**, but prefer the Mehta. The *tempo*, unsteady at 3 before **61**, is in general too slow.

Procession of the Sage	The tam-tam is too loud at **68**, and the trumpet *ditto* at **70**, where I would prefer to hear the 4-scratches-to-the-beat of the *güero*.	**70** is an acoustical mess, and at **68** the tam-tam is too small (a cymbal?). The correct instrument can be heard at **175** in the *Sacrificial Dance*, where, furthermore, its dynamic presence is just right.	This is less a performance than an exhibit on the progress of recording technique in a decade. *No* part has enough separation here. And what will another decade bring? More *mastri*, certainly—thanks to the rapid (*sic*) transit in that business—whatever the chances of a new *Rite of Spring*.
The Sage	The leading voice—in the second contra-bassoon—is the weakest voice here, and the *tempo* is approximately twice too fast.	This is too fast.	My performance is no better than the other two.
Dance of the Earth	This may be the slowest *Prestissimo* ever clocked—and from Boulez!, never exactly a slow-poke. The cello part at **75** is clear, as a result, but the overall dullness is too great a price to pay for that. The one-bar phrases (3rd and 6th m. of **77**) should have been carved out by punctuation.	This is the best performance of the three.	The *tempo* is too slow, and the bass drum bumps along at the beginning without getting the *crescendo* started. The trumpet 7 m. after **75** is too loud for the over-all level.

	Cleveland Orchestra *Conductor: Boulez* *CBS Records*	*Los Angeles Philharmonic* *Conductor: Mehta* *London Records*	*Columbia Symphony* *Conductor: Stravinsky* *Columbia Records* (1960, re-issued 1970)
Introduction II	This is a shade too fast, but the string balance at **84** is perfect. Thereafter, the trumpets should be twins, dynamically speaking, instead of, as here, older and younger brothers.	The trumpet duo is nicely balanced but too loud. The section at **87** lacks accents, rhythmic articulation, tension.	This is too fast, not very well balanced (the flutes are too strong), out of tune, poorly phrased, and the *tutti* attacks are sloppy. In m. 5 of **86**, the cello and violas articulate the 4th beat 4 times, instead of 3.
Mystic Circles	The violas are too loud, and the *tempo* is too fast, being, in fact, the *tempo* of the '*Più mosso*' at **93**—which, however, is no faster. Consequently, the three-part shape of the dance, a fast movement surrounded by two equally slow ones, is destroyed.	This is not only too fast, but pushed. The conductor ignores the *fermata* before **101**, and allows the trumpets to win their race against the horns at **102** by a wide margin.	This is too fast and too loud. But unlike the Boulez, **93** is at least faster in proportion, and **97** is proportionately slower. At **102**, the wide horn intervals drag and the close trumpet intervals pull.

Glorification of the Chosen One	This is very good, in spite of the premature beginning of the "*Molto allargando*". Boulez surprisingly fails to correct the old mistake, in the m. before **118** where, obviously, the bass-drum should play with the violas and basses (as in the m. before **105**), *not* with the upper strings, oboes, and horns.	This sounds rushed all the way. The drums are too loud at **114**.	I am guilty of the same error as my younger competitors with regard to the bass-drum 1 m. before **118**.
Evocation of the Ancestors	This is perfect—exactly the way the music should be performed.	Mehta once again loses the continuity of the pulsation, which should be exactly the same as in the previous dance, and not, as here, adjusted to a slower *tempo*.	I dislike both the slower tempo at **123** and the *ritenuto* at the end, but was not aware of either when the recording was made.
Ritual Action of the Ancestors	This is good, too, but I am amazed that Boulez did not hear the clarinets playing 32nds, 1 m. before **141**, rather than 64ths.	This is good, except that the violas are too loud at **131**, and the clarinets are out of tune at **140**. The bass trumpet at **139** is better than in the other recordings.	The clarinets in the last measures are out of tune and not very accurately balanced. Yet the passage is better played here as a whole than in the other recordings.

	Cleveland Orchestra *Conductor: Boulez* *CBS Records*	*Los Angeles Philharmonic* *Conductor: Mehta* *London Records*	*Columbia Symphony* *Conductor: Stravinsky* *Columbia Records* *(1960, re-issued 1970)*
Sacrificial Dance	This is quirky and unsatisfactory. The beginning is a little slow, but clear, and incomparably better than Boulez's old recording. The long (unwritten) *accelerando* from **159** is deplorable, and at **174** the bass figure is more important than the timpani triplets, yet it is smothered by them here. The ending is a disaster. Boulez separates the upbeat from the downbeat, thus changing the rhythm and turning a not-very-good idea into a vulgar one.	The performance is rushed and lacks firmness, but it is more exciting than the Boulez.	The performance is ragged— the timpani are often late or absent (where is the F at **147**?)—but it has more strength than the others and is the only one even to attempt the differentiation of 8ths and 16ths. At **186**, however, the bass practically disappears, and the pages following are painfully ragged, the horns at **113** are too loud, etc.

Resumé Technically, the recording is better in every way than Boulez's earlier one. Musically, it is better in some ways, worse in others. It is generally slower (the middle-age spread?), and to advantage. But it is at the same time very mannered and strangely fails to generate any excitement.

The improvement on the performance I heard and saw Mehta do on French television a few years ago is almost unbelievable, and the Los Angeles orchestra sounds very good, too.

This is a pick-up orchestra which had virtually no rehearsal time, whereas the other two recordings were made with established orchestras after dozens of performances. Yet I think that this performance is better than either of the others, because the *tempos are* better on the whole and because there is more strength behind it. But can anyone wonder why I later tried to write conductor-proof (even mechanical) music, as in *Les Noces*?

WAGNER'S PROSE

Are Wagner's writings[1]—were they ever—helpful to an understanding of his musico-dramatic art? Can lovers of *Tristan und Isolde* glean any advantage from his clumsy apologetics? I doubt it (though I would not be surprised to hear an academic barrel-scraping 'yes' contradicting me). As I see them, the writings would be most useful simply as Exhibit A in a demonstration of the split between a man's genius and the accessory parts of his mind.

Wagner had little talent for theoretical exposition. He is better with cases, is in fact an acute, if injudicious, critic both of the theatre of his time and of other composers. But he seems to prefer those theoretical rambles. His criticism is remarkable above all, however, because it is governed by a consistent historical point of view. He appears to have been the first great composer to have begun from the outside, so to speak, with an analysis of music history, and to have determined his own place in its future from a historical perspective. His view of this role, moreover, seems to have occurred to him almost as early as the awakening of his musical talent; and thereafter it was to remain the 'drive', Bayreuth or 'bust', behind everything he wrote. History pointed straight home to the Fatherland, of course, and, as unerringly as a compass needle, from there to the Wagner front door. Besides that, it directed him away from 'absolute' music (though his own discussions of the term leave one with no clear idea of what he really meant by it) toward the 'unification of the arts' in a new form of 'dramatic expression'. Which may only be a long way of saying that he had the knowledge of his own gifts. And, finally, the accuracy of the historical

[1] *Wagner on Music and Drama.* A compendium of Richard Wagner's prose works, selected and arranged, and with an introduction by Albert Goldman and Evert Sprinchorn (E. P. Dutton and Co., Inc., New York, 1964).

diagnosis matters only because the prognosis was *Tristan* and the *Ring*.

The difficulty for the reader is with the manner in which the great conception plods along. Wagner does not so much argue as he coaxes and exhorts; nor has he any other method for relief. He labours mightily to be explicit, but achieves only labouriousness. 'Let me out with it in one phrase', he cries at one point, strangling from his own periphrastic disease, and for once the reader is in full sympathy. But it will not *come* out, except in a prodigious verbosity here rendered in the incredible dialect of Quakerisms, archaicisms, and syntactical Germanisms invented for him by his first translator, William Ashton Ellis. And although the literary merit in this tumble of unpruned talk must be nearly nil in the original, Ellis set out to find an 'equivalent style', and, alack, probably succeeded. Wagner's subordinate clauses can challenge all endurance records without tempting Ellis's fidelity. At first the reader backtracks, then after a few tapeworms of a hundred or so collectively unintelligible phrases, decides that skipping is the better method.

. . . the will is longing to become pure knowledge, but this is possible only in so far as it stays stock-still in its deepest inner chamber; 'tis as if it were awaiting tidings of redemption from there outside; content they it not, it sets itself in that state of clairvoyance; and here beyond the bounds of time and space, it knows itself the world's one and all.

It? They? Here? Where? Who? Legibility is still further impeded by insatiable addictions both to metaphor—as many 'stormy seas' being 'sailed o'er' in these pages as ever in Hakluyt —and to compound words, Mozart, for example, being the 'early-sped' and the 'song-glad' (slap-happy?). The grotesque style and the special pleading are obstacles few readers are likely to leap.

I have not read enough of Wagner's writings[1] to be in a position to appraise the editors' selection and ordering of the

---

[1] The quantity is enormous. My own output of printed words, in a life twenty years longer than his, would not equal the length of his autobiography alone, and that one tome took him only as far as *Die Meistersinger*.

texts. But more excerpts from the letters, particularly from those to Frau ('my child') Wesendonck and Judith ('the overflowing cup of my intoxication') Gauthier, could have been useful, if only for the reason that the composer's amorous style is at least a contrast. Some information would have been welcome at the head of each excerpt, too, concerning the occasion or occasions provoking it; but this deficiency is partly offset by an introduction relating the writings to Wagner's biography and practice, an excellent summary on the whole, and incandescence itself compared to what follows.

I cannot agree, however, that Wagner is a 'brilliant exponent of Beethoven'—except in music. In fact, Wagner's programme notes on the symphonies are all the worse precisely because the misrepresentation of music is by a great musician. He attempts to establish in words the 'real' subjects of the symphonies because a 'real subject', versus a merely musical one, is necessary to a 'real understanding'; and these attempts result in descriptions of scarcely printable fatuity. The composer of the *Pastoral* Symphony 'turned his steps toward life-glad men encamped on breezy meads . . . kissing, dancing, frolicking beside the tender gossip of the brook. . . .' And the composer of the Ninth Symphony achieved 'the redemption of Music from out her own peculiar element into the realm of *"universal art"* '. Wagner is always yearning to go beyond music, of course, and regularly serving notice that the 'art work of the future' will not indulge music for its own sake.

Nor can I concur with the editors' assertion that the 'basic argument' of *Jews in Music*, which they wisely place near the beginning of the book so that it colours the fake idealism to come, 'contains as much truth on the subject as anyone could have seen during the nineteenth century'. Nietzsche, for one, saw more, but never mind; the question is whether Wagner saw any at all; and I will labour the point because while everyone has heard of the pamphlet, I suspect that few have read it. I had not myself, in fact, and both its virulence and its contemporaneity greatly surprised me: Goebbels or Rosenberg might have written part of it. 'Judaism' is 'the evil conscience of our modern civilization', the great composer says, and the 'Jew' is 'the most heartless of all human beings'. The friend of Bakunin and the one-time radical from the barricades of 1848 then goes on to discriminate a 'commoner class of Jew'. But where is Wagner's 'truth on the subject'? In the logic which attributes a composer's failure in the 'formal productive faculty' to his Jewishness? Then what of the same failure in all the others? And where is the truth in the contention that 'imitation' and 'mimicry' are peculiarly Jewish characteristics in music? In fact Wagner's tirade on this point—'The Jew musician hurls together the diverse forms and styles of every age and every master'—reads remarkably like the critics of my own music until a few seasons ago. Even so, the substance of Wagner's attack is less shocking than the intolerably mean manner of it, above all in reproaching Mendelssohn for having modelled himself on 'our' Bach.[1] The unpleasant truth, which Thomas Mann himself could not whitewash, is that Wagner (not Nietzsche, not Hegel) was a prophet of the Third Reich. Again and again he appeals to those tiresome virtues of the uncorrupted 'folk'; to the 'direct expression of emotion' *vs.* 'intellectualized' (Jewish) 'speech'; to the 'inwardness' of the German soul in its 'war of conscience' against French, Italian, or other outwardnesses; to the necessity of purging the world of politics that it may again deserve a 'true poet' (guess who).

The other papers in the first section purport to analyse 'The Cultural Decadence of the Nineteenth Century'. But Wagner's arsenal contains only heavy artillery—howitzers, in fact—and many of his shells are even too big to load. The satire, which is all flat, brings Berlioz's *Evenings in the Orchestra* to mind, but by contrast and because it covers some of the same ground. Otherwise the French master's narrative skill is so vastly superior, and his human landscape so much richer in variety, that comparison is hardly possible.

Wagner is most effective dealing with opera, and the more concrete the better. 'The personnel of a first class orchestra consists, for no little part, of the only truly musically cultured members of an opera company,' he says, justly, and in a choice passage on Mozart and Weber in *The Origins of Modern Opera* he is the most penetrating observer of his time:

[1] Eric Werner's new book on the *Elijah* makes an interesting case for the influence of the music of the Hebrew Sacred Services on Mendelssohn's cadences.

Criticism, which at bottom always waits upon the public voice, has never dealt with *Euryanthe* in the measure that its uncommonly instructive content deserves. Yet, never has there been composed a work in which the inner contradictions of the whole genre have been more consistently worked out. These contradictions are: absolute, self-sufficing melody, and unflinchingly true dramatic expression. Here one or the other must necessarily be sacrificed—either melody or drama. Rossini sacrificed the drama; the noble Weber wished to reinstate it by force of his more judicious melody. He had to learn that this was an impossibility.

The chapter on Rossini is insufferably condescending; nevertheless, it reveals Wagner's ambivalent feelings toward Italian music, exposed in his own music in those Italianate melodic figures that curl through his scores from *Das Leibesverbot* to *Parsifal* (and on to *Verklarte Nacht*) without being entirely digested, which is to say Germanized. Concerning that new melodic quality in *Euryanthe*, incidentally, Wagner astutely remarks that 'one might almost say the melody was ready before a line of its poem'—which was in fact the case with parts of *Pelléas*, as we now know from the sketch score in the Meyer collection. Finally, before leaving the subject of opera, I should mention that at an early date Wagner condemns 'action' and that 'lust of the eye' which requires 'constant changes of scene', as if he were already preparing his audience for the statuary of *The Ring*.

The *Art Work of the Future*, judging by the compilation of excerpts given here, is in the main a muddle of Schopenhauer and phenomenology. The high point, moreover, a potentially fascinating inquiry into the relationships of spoken vowel sounds and sung tones, a musical '*alchémie du verbe*', is abandoned just as the reader's interest is caught. At the beginning of another section, 'Wagner's Development', the master seems for a light-hearted page or two about to do what Nietzsche shrewdly said he could not do: laugh at himself. Otherwise these autobiographical writings are notable in exposing Wagner's musical training as the skimpiest of any of the great composers, whereas his interests in everything else were the widest; but, then, music is 'the art which is easiest to learn', as he had said of certain

'Jews' who had perhaps learned more of it more easily than himself.

The remaining sections are: *The Art of Performance*, in which, among many still-pertinent comments, Wagner correctly puts the importance of tempo above all else; 'Bayreuth', which is Wagner on top, sounding off like a world minister of arts and sciences; and 'Politics', which is not about anything the reader will know by the word. In fact Wagner's later politics are at best whiggish, thanks to his royal patron, and at worst a parade of philo-German sentiments. He had already expressed the former point of view in that unconsciously comic scene in *Das Rheingold*, when Wotan refuses to pay the giants for building Valhalla. (The monster had promised them his sister-in-law.) Fasolt, the spokesman for the giants and a prototype labour-leader, warns Wotan that *'Was der bist, bist du nur durch Vertrage'* ('What you are, you are only by agreement'), which is a most unmythological intrusion of the idea that Godheads and monarchies are constitutional—as well as, in the context, a threat that Valhallas may be combustible.

The thrall of Wagner has abated for reasons as different as the shortage of Flagstads and the decline of the narcotic effects of the music, owing to the circulation of stronger drugs. (And it *was* an opiate, capable of giving Baudelaire, for instance, a big bhang.) This book will not rehabilitate the man. But Wagnerites deny that the man needs to be. For them, it is enough, as Nietzsche said, that 'some things have been added to the realm of art by Wagner alone'.

April, 1965

SCHOENBERG'S LETTERS

> By regarding the artistic innovator as abnormal, we
> accorded ourselves the luxury of believing that he did
> not concern us, and that he did not put in question, by
> the mere fact of his existence, an accepted social, moral,
> or intellectual order.
>
> LÉVI-STRAUSS, *Totemism*

If I had imagined the correspondence of most contemporary
composers to be crude and grubby, this prejudice was the fault
of my own epistolary labours. In fact the letters I myself have
been most likely to trouble over all my life were directed to
publishers, concert agents, conductors, and other industrialists.
The letter as a communication to friends is a medium the
contemporary composer lacks the leisure to develop; and he can
only very rarely undertake to say in that form what he has in
mind to say to the people to whom he would like to say it. If he
takes time on occasion to address himself to a disobliging
journalist, that, of course, is simply because it is momentarily
gratifying as well as very easy to do.

The most notable exception in our day is Richard Strauss,
who stands up to Hofmannsthal from time to time—a far
greater effort for him than the other way around—and gets the
better of him, I think, by sheer straightforwardness. (There, I
have done my bit for the 1964 Strauss millennium celebrations!)
But Strauss withdrew from the centre at an early age, thereafter
only living through a time, or, at worst, travelling through
a time in luxury class that Schoenberg lived and formed and
that now to some extent—for centripetal as he was, other
developments were and are possible—lives and finds its character
in him. And Schoenberg, in letter after letter, does undertake
to speak his mind, for which reason, considered as intellectual

248

autobiography, and because not meant as such and not dependent on recollection, they are probably as reliable as any in existence by a great composer.

In fact this seems to me one of a very few great books *by* a composer[1], and no one concerned with music, not merely contemporary music, can afford to be without it. But others should read it, too. An artist's engrossment in his struggles may fail to engross or edify a reader who does not feel the necessity of the art, but will not fail in this case for the reason that the lenses of Schoenberg's conscience were as powerful as those of any artist of the time, and not only in music. In fact he seems to have seen a length ahead in almost every question to which he gave his attention. One rubs one's eyes at the dates of the letters to Kandinsky, for example, with their references to Hitler—that they were written in 1923, not 1933. These alone, together with a Schubertian rent-begging letter to Gustav Mahler, are worth the price of possession. Nor should the non-specialist reader shy away from the musical discussions merely because what he may have tried to read *about* Schoenberg up to now seemed to have been written in intramural Fortran. The composer himself is clear and plain. His letters are stocked with insights, not with principles of analysis.

Unfortunately, the first chapters, the longest in most autobiographies, are missing. By the time of the first postmark, 1910, Schoenberg's name (at least) was already widely known and about two-fifths of his music had already been written. A random remark from one of the earlier letters, to the effect that the symphony orchestra is richer in treble than in bass instruments, shows him thinking polyphonically at a time when few, if any, others did. If only for observations such as that, one regrets the absence of more material from this period. Nor is the decade and a half after 1910 fully enough represented, I am obliged to add, and the arguments of those years provide some

---

[1] *Arnold Schoenberg: Letters.* Edited by Erwin Stein. Translated by Eithne Wilkins and Ernst Kaiser. (Faber, £3·15.) The translators should be congratulated, thanked, and re-employed to translate the *Harmonielehre*. My only criticism of the book would be to express the wish for a more complete collection, with fewer asterisks for fewer deletions.

of the best parts of the book. Here is a reply to a conductor who wished to blue-pencil a passage in an early work:

I am against removing tonsils although I know how one can somehow manage to go on living even without arms, legs, nose, eyes, tongue, ears, etc . . . A work doesn't have to be performed at all costs either, if it means losing parts of it that may even be ugly or faulty but which it was born with. . . Cutting isn't the way to improve a work. Brevity and succinctness are a matter of *exposition*. In this case the details are not conceived compactly; it is all long-winded. If I cut some such details, the other long-winded ones remain, and it remains a work of long-winded exposition. It will not take so long to play, but it will not really be shorter. A work that has been shortened by cutting may very well give the impression of being an excessively long work (because of the exposition) that is too short in various places (where it has been cut).

Injustices rankle him in the letters of this period but not yet the reader, as they do to some extent after another decade of that indignation which accompanies every page of the latter half of the book like a *basso continuo*. Now, in the early twenties, he even pretends to be resigned. 'I realize that I cannot be understood and am content to make do with respect', he says, though he was not, of course, nor ever could be.

The wit is not all bitter yet, either. To a newspaper which had asked for a list of five people he would save if he were a present-day Noah on the eve of another Flood, he replies by enclosing a self-addressed postcard, 'to let me know of anyone who decides to rescue *me* so that I can remain in his vicinity'. On another occasion he writes that 'I usually answer the question why I no longer compose as I did at the period of *Verklärte Nacht* by saying "I do, but I can't help it if people don't yet recognize the fact."' And in one of the most valuable statements in the book he informs a publisher that 'music never drags a meaning around with it, at least not in the form in which it [music] manifests itself, even though meaning is inherent in its nature.'

The tone changes *c.* 1925. A more facile new music had come to fashion by then, and it paid him little homage; and the by now

Old Master was losing patience with the slow corroding of the second-rate. The attacks on his first '12-tone' compositions exceeded even the harshest receptions of the early years, at which time, in any case, such things are easier to take. In consequence he begins to distinguish 'true-born' musicians from those who have merely 'become what they are'. He would hardly have subscribed to Sartre's 'genius is a way out that one invents'; would, in fact, have condemned it as a description of an altogether different activity, the cult of *kairos* and the Room at the Top.

He looks to left and right in anger now, though never, in that temper, back, for he had an exceptionally forgiving nature. And he can sound at times like the Leader of Righteousness. 'Laws of loyalty' are invoked and disciples warned against acknowledging other gods and keeping compromising company—myself included, I infer; at any rate the shoe of his satire on C-major endings fits five of my works at that time and about twenty since; but obviously Schoenberg thought of me as a mere exotic, at first, and at second as a *modiste*, or *maître* of *assemblages*.

Some of the letters during this phase are about as cordial as traffic citations. One of them, to the late Hanns Eisler, written at a time when Schoenberg was trying to keep his serial method under wraps, seems a shrill castigation to have been based on no more than a rumour. Contrast this with the letters, a few years earlier, to J. M. Hauer, who had arrived at a '12-tone theory' of his own, and with whom Schoenberg generously proposed an exchange of ideas and possible joint publication, like Darwin and Wallace.

But even in this time of public and personal trial the letters always exhibit that chief quality of the music, the passionate development of the argument. What they lack of the music, of the *Serenade*, the Quintet, the Septet, is the songfulness and the humour, scarcely surprising omissions when one considers that the aim of so many of them is to burn dry rot and expose dead standards—the standards, of course, of the very people who could have given him preferment. But this still leaves a book containing hardly any received ideas and none that Schoenberg allows to pass without an overhauling. And if all this merit does not seem to promise much entertainment, the damage of that impression, if I have given it, should be outweighed by the statement that the letters are as refreshingly unliterary as any I have read.

It is in the American years that they become painful. And occasionally pettish. More concerned with his Jewishness by each new act of Nazi aggression, he complains of neglect by Jews. They 'have never shown any interest in my music', he writes in 1938, 'and now, into the bargain, in Palestine they are out to develop, artificially, an authentically Jewish kind of music, which rejects what I have achieved'. Near the end, however, he expresses the wish to emigrate to Israel.

Nor did the great American ostrich pay him more attention than the small Viennese ostrich had done. 'It is my most intense desire to depart from Vienna as unnoticed as I have always been while I was here,' he tells a friend in 1925, and the Viennese love-hate burns on to the end, which, however, came too soon for Schoenberg to say 'I told you so' and is a little soon yet for the reader to do the same. But the improvidence of a young man in unpunished Vienna, and of an old and, moreover, famous one in the art-grant opulence of postwar America, are different humiliations.

Lack of money is lack of time. After sharing so much of his life with pupils, he now complains that teaching wearies him and leaves him no time for composing. He writes chits to a college president begging '$200 or even $150' with which to buy books for his students. The nadir is reached in the letter the seventy-year-old master addresses to the Guggenheim Foundation asking for financial assistance so that he can finish *Moses und Aron*. And though a few more measures of this opera would have been worth a whole catalogue of music the Guggenheim Foundation did sponsor, Schoenberg's request was denied.

The Schoenberg movement had ceased to exist, to all appearances, by 1939. Berg was dead, Webern was silenced—he had never been loud—and Schoenberg himself was writing either tonal music or nothing at all. 'I have not composed for the past two years,' he confides to a friend, and gives as the reason, 'unbearable depression'.

The last letters hint at the recrudescence, but no more. It

began during the war in Schoenberg's own renewed creativity, but gathered momentum only in the year of his death, by which time he had stopped priding himself on his unplayed music and was merely clinging to the achievement of not having given up the struggle.

A REALM OF TRUTH

Mr. Kerman is a high-minded guide.[1] I recommend him to high-minded readers, as well as to credit-minded students in need of a crib—if in these days of student power anyone still is. I also urge musicians to try the book, especially those who despise ancillas and tend to shirk harmonic algebra and the other relationships Mr. Kerman details. But general readers should try it, too. They will complain of key-naming and harmonic path-mapping. Yet Mr. Kerman never loses sight of the grand design of each quartet, and he can be followed at that elevation by sidestepping the thickets of technical exposition. Music is the subject of the book, in any case, not Beethoven's illustrations of the author's critical principles, and not 'functional' analysis or the other brands that prowl about nowadays like solutions in search of problems.

The discussion of the late quartets, to which I must confine my own remarks, is piecemealed under the headings 'Voice', 'Contrast', 'Fugue', 'Dissociation and Integration'. The diversity of stances is useful in dealing with Beethoven's own multifariousness, but unhelpful to those who would prefer to have the whole dossier on each quartet in one place, and who imagine that they are less concerned with group characteristics than individuating ones. The book is rich in insights, nevertheless, no matter how they are subsumed. Mr. Kerman has an acute grasp of the powers of Beethoven's tonality instrument; of, for example, the focal means with which he creates both anticipation—making distant destinations loom—and surprise. Nor is Mr. Kerman's study of the other aspects of the quartets, and of Beethoven in general, less perspicacious, valuable observations on such matters as the proprieties of the genres, and the rarity of relationships based on the augmented triad, being found on nearly every page.

---

[1] *The Beethoven Quartets*, by Joseph Kerman, Knopf, N.Y. 1967.

Earlier criticism is dealt with, but little of it seems to have been intelligent enough to cause irremediable mischief. (I would have made shorter shrift of it myself, and I do not see why Daniel Gregory Mason should matter so much, or at all.) I admire Mr. Kerman's . . . well, bravery—was stopped in my tracks in fact by his demonstration of how the 'prolix' first theme in the *Finale* of the Quartet in E Flat might have been trimmed. I admire his writing, too, if not such favoured locutions as 'contrasty', and 'doublet' (my mind insists on going to 'garment' first); but slips are so rare that when he does fall ('One almost thinks of the *Heiliger Dankgesang*': one cannot *almost* think of that), the reason can only be that he is so highly polished. His arguments are the crucial ones, and they are clearly and cogently propounded. They are arguments, after all, about the highest values in the art.

Restriction to the late quartets—and to some points in which I find myself most out of step with the consensus—is unfair to the three masterpieces composed for the Russian Ambassador in Vienna, Count Razumovsky. (It is unfair as well to *La Malinconia*, that trial balloon not only for later Beethoven but for the Wagner of the first act of *Die Walküre*; the interim quartets, however, are to my mind imperfectly sustained.) If the 'Razumovskys' had been the end of the line, we would be exhibiting them as the *ne plus ultra* of the literature, and no doubt putting a futuristic interpretation on such passages as the beginning of the Quartet in C Major, discovering in its breathbating, left-field harmonic movement the very fever of the future.

As it is the 'Razumovskys' hold their own, partly—but only partly—because they do not compete with the late batch, are in fact so different as to offer few comparisons. No music more abounds in high spirits (the operatic finale of the same quartet), and elegance (the tune with the skipping appoggiatura in the *Andante*). But these are hardly the first qualities to come to mind in connection with the late quartets; rather, by 'Razumovsky' standards, the anomalies and unevennesses, just as, with the view the other way around, the 'Razumovskys' inevitably remind the listener of the developments in depth and compression, in the conversion of the form to new expressive ends, in stylistic refinements, that lay ahead. But comparisons are odious. We cannot make love to the future, or listen to the 'Razumovsky' Adagios with the thought that the later quartets contain even 'better' music.

Razumovsky himself deserves a word. (More than that, in this nauseating election season: a twenty-one gun salute, say, and in time to obliterate yet another reverberation of paralysing platitudes from those unspeakable nominating morons, whose 'hoopla' in Miami, incidentally, included a 'rendition' of the *Moonlight Sonata* on fifty-gallon oil drums.) His duties representing the Russian Empire to the Austrian Empire, in the year of Austerlitz, must have been as demanding as those of Comrades Gromyko, Dobrynin, and others representing Soviet Imperialism to American Imperialism. Count Razumovsky not only commissioned these quartets, however, but acquired and kept the nimbleness of fingers and mind to be able to play one of the violins in them. I wonder how many ambassadors, political incumbents, spokesmen for the Ministries of Truth, or other high officials of the Great Powers today would even recognize them.

> Quartets are in demand everywhere; it really seems that
> our age is taking a step forward.
> BEETHOVEN, April, 1826

The string quartet was the most lucid conveyor of musical ideas ever fashioned, and the most singing—*i.e.*, human—of instrumental means; or, rather, if it was *not* that, natively and necessarily, Beethoven made it so. As for inborn powers, it could register a faster rate of harmonic change than the not yet fully chromatic orchestra of Beethoven's time, which was further impeded by a weight problem and balance problem. It is a more intimate medium, furthermore, partly by the same tokens; and a more pleasing one, long-term, as colour: to me at any rate, and in my case partly because I am least conscious of the colour element in it. Its sustaining powers are greater than those of wind-instrument ensembles, and its ranges of speeds, and of degrees of soft volumes, are wider. Compared with the piano, its advantages are in polyphonic delineation and in the greater variety of dynamic articulation and nuance.

At Positano, September 1937

With Lord Berners, October 1937

Hollywood, September 1946

E Flat Major

He heard nothing . . . but his eyes followed the bows
and from that he was able to judge the smallest fluctuations in tempo and rhythm.

J. Böhm, March, 1825

The E flat and the larger and more innovatory C sharp Minor
are the most unified, consistent, satisfying of the late quartets.
But apart from success, the parallels—'morphological' and
'architectural' similarities in the variation movements, mainly—
seem to me factitious. What the two quartets do share, incon-
trovertibly, is an influence on Wagner. 'Who comes after him
will not continue him, but must begin anew, for he who went
before left off only where art leaves off.' Thus Grillparzer, orat-
ing at Beethoven's funeral, and if the poet seems to have been
writing with Wagner in mind, so does Beethoven himself in the
Adagio molto espressivo variation in this Quartet in E flat. It is
clear that the music's message to Wagner, at any rate, was
'*Bonjour, "Tristan".*'

The *pizzicato* figure at the beginning of the *Scherzando* movement derives from the preceding movement (at m. 120 and,
with *arco* articulation, m. 95); which may not be 'hard' news,
exactly, but is an interesting connection all the same because
aurally obvious even with the interval inverted. A similar link,
no less apparent to the ear, is the recurrence of that feature of the
Scherzando, the accented second beat (and silent first and third
beats), in the last measures of the Finale. I prefer this Finale,
incidentally, to any other in the quartets, and *all* of it, the blust-
ery, orchestral second theme no less than the Coda, with its
graceful change of mood and meter. But, then, I am inclined to
resist Gypsy and Hungarian finales, even by Beethoven, and the
ending of the Quartet in C sharp Minor is a Magyar uprising.

A Minor

Beethoven describes himself in the epigraph to the third movement as 'one recovered' (*eines Genesenen*), but the continuing
trauma of the illness is more apparent in the music. 'Hysterical',
Mr. Kerman's word for the violin outburst with which the

Allegro begins, applies as well, I think, to the oscillations of mood throughout the quartet.

Whereas the first movement is slow in starting, and patchy and spasmodic much of the way, the second fails to stop in time; or seems to, probably because the subject matter is not grippingly interesting in the first place, and for a moment (m. 63–68) is actually dull. But the serenity of the Trio presages the movement by which—or by *part* of which: the hymn in white-key counterpoint if not the interspersions of minuet[1]—the quartet is remembered. Two slices of 'minuet' and three of hymn pile up like a five-decker Dagwood sandwich, except that the hymn decks and minuet decks fail to integrate, and even to react on each other. In consequence, the listener forgets the minuet and therefore that Beethoven ever did feel any 'new strength'.

The last movement is very odd: a march that might have been composed thirty years earlier and shelved; a bombastic recitative incorporating a version of the violin paroxysm from the first movement; a dance whose frenetic later adventures are unforeseen in its beginning as a *Valse noble et sentimentale*.

B Flat Major

This is the most radical of the quartets; most modern, too, in the local sense: the written-out violin *glissando* in the *Presto*, for example, would pass undetected as a contribution by Beethoven in a collage of last week's premières. But nearly everything about the quartet is controversial, I discover, including my assumption that the wide assortment of the pieces indicates a desire to enlarge the form and enrich the variety of the contents; which seems obvious if for no other reason than that an expanded form is again pursued in the next quartet, but realized through continuity rather than variety.

The substance of the first movement is rich, but the exposition vacillates. At moments such as the faltering at m. 192–197, and the premature return of the D flat episode in the recapitulation

---

[1] As the 3/8 is played on my recording, a performance otherwise notable for a great deal of Xenakis-like sliding about, presumably under the stress of emotion, and an inability to count from one to two steadily, and to produce two consecutively in-tune notes. Schnabel's dictum, 'Great music is better than it can be performed', is being taken too complacently.

—*I* am not ready to welcome it back at any rate—it does not altogether cohere. But to some extent the open stretch of *Allegro* at the beginning of the development section saves the movement: a mitigated disaster, then.

Reviewing the *Cavatina*, Mr. Kerman rightly takes to task a remark from an I-had-hoped-long-forgotten anthology of my own utterances. But I do not think—it is part of his argument—that the love and care which Beethoven put into the piece (never a dry eye later at the thought of it), and the evidence in it of emotional scar-tissue, are entitled to any allowance on the receiving end. Elsewhere Mr. Kerman concedes the impossibility of harnessing technical analyses to aesthetic results, and at the end of his study eloquently questions the efficacy of what in fact he has done so very well. But neither is there any ratio between the amount of labour and the value of the result; which is why the labour is strictly the artist's affair. Genius strikes where it will, in any case, even Beethoven's.

To my mind it did not strike in the *Cavatina*, apart from the '*beklemmt*' episode. (Which does not mean that I am right and Mr. Kerman wrong. But whether or not I am 'over-reacting' to Mr. Kerman, I am, as a composer myself, unavoidably doing so to Beethoven.) I do not find its melodic-harmonic substance especially distinguished, and the treatment attenuates it. The piece is handicapped in the first place, however, by offering a too extreme contrast to the preceding *Andante*. If the *Cavatina* is the most tormented movement in the late quartets, then the *Andante* must be one of the most insouciant (in the manner of the *Allegretto* of the Eighth Symphony, as Mr. Kerman notes of the ending, and I would add of m. 18–19 as well). But while the *Andante* seems to skim over the surface of the composer's 'personal emotions' as lightly as a hydrofoil—in comparison, that is, to the depth-plunge of the *Cavatina*—its musical emotion, whatever the cost to him and his later feelings about it, is the less shallow of the two movements.

The Great Fugue

And why didn't they encore the Fugue? That alone
should have been repeated! Cattle! Asses!

BEETHOVEN, March, 1826

The *Great Fugue* enlarges the meaning of Beethoven more than
any other work (which does not mean that I regard it as a
separate piece rather than as a quartet movement). It breaks all
of our measurements, too, human no less than musical, especially
the sudden, sustained, scarcely believable energy, as if from a
musical Platformate. The other quartets we can know, even to
faulting them, wanting what we love to be what *we* want it to be.
But the *Fugue* is not knowable in the same way. Prejudices as to
dimensions and elements must be overcome. When they have
been, if they can be, we discover that no chain of expectations
is built up in us, that the music defies familiarity by being new
and different every time.

Whether the substantive difficulties are attributable more to
isolation—the *Fugue* lacks ancestors and inheritors alike—or the
other way around, is an imponderable; and so is the question
of whether the possibility of the masterpiece is a consequence of
historical intersections, or whether the intersections are retro-
actively brought about by the event of the masterpiece. So far
as 'stylistic environments' are concerned, in any case, and works
of art as 'personifications of their time', parts of the *Fugue* might
have been incubated in a space satellite. As for the absence of
an influence of its own, this may be simply a case of no one being
able to 'join it', let alone 'beat it'. But if the music *had* entered the
consciousness of its time, Modern Music would have lost some of
its sting at a much earlier date, and where would we be now?
(Where are we?)

The *Fugue* still has a bad press, is still reputed to be abstruse,
intractable, dissonant, relentlessly loud; which proves how little
known it is. Nor has criticism, deprived of comparisons, its main
tool apart from the knife, won it new love; or, while picking it
apart, noticed the range in it, the annexation of territory reserved
for Debussy (from m. 581), for instance, and the playful delaying

260

of the cadence at the end of the G flat section.[1] But the critic must feel the ineluctability of new measurements, and is at best only guessing at something the artist knows.

The *Overtura*, Mr. Kerman says, 'hurls all the thematic versions at the listener's head like a handful of rocks.' The Davidic image seems to betray persecution feelings about the music, however, the more so since the versions marked *piano* and *pianissimo* are outstandingly non-lithic. (Hawkish similes are best suited to the first fugue subject, I think; in fact I was about to compare it to an ICBM, myself, as an example of musical escalation from the 'Mannheim Rocket' in the Sonata, opus 2.) If this is actually the case, the more remarkable Mr. Kerman's understanding of it, and of the main issue, which is the switch in focus from contrapuntal devices to thematic transformation.

The importance of design in this new perspective is apparent in the *Overtura*, a thematic index identifying the different versions of the subject as well as prognosticating and priming the larger components of the form. Each thematic version is endowed with distinctive secondary attributes (counting pitch and rhythm as primary): a trill and *appoggiatura*, for instance, in the version destined for the most complex treatment, and a slow tempo and soft dynamic in the version predicting an episode in the same speed and volume. These secondary characteristics constitute an auxiliary set of referents with which to identify thematic material in remote transformations, as well as to construct alternative views: silhouettes, for example, on the analogy that the full-face is revealed only in the pitches; and fragmentary contrapuntal refractions, as in the double mirror, rhythmically speaking, with which the A flat fugue begins.

The rhythmic aspect of the *Fugue* is the most radical, but the least isolable: the rhythmic units and patterns are so consistently identified with the thematic versions, in fact, that the barely numerate composer (he could not multiply) might have been using what is now called (by mathematical composers who cannot write Great Fugues) a parameter of rhythmic entities. The vocabulary itself is new, formed in part by an unprecedented

[1] Concerning the octaves immediately before, I wonder if the strategic effect of the same device in Bach's two-voice E minor Fugue had lodged in Beethoven's imagination at some earlier time.

use of syncopation, by a new degree of subdivision,[1] and by irregular durations. But here, above all in the A flat fugue which is the climax of this giant creation, Beethoven is exploring a region beyond the other late quartets. Who, being taken there today, can imagine that he would have reacted less dumbly himself, in 1826, than the 'cattle' and the 'asses'?

C sharp Minor

Thank God there is less lack of fancy than ever before.

BEETHOVEN, Summer, 1826

Everything in this masterpiece is perfect, inevitable, unalterable. It is beyond the impudence of praise, too (partly because of difficulties with the vocabulary in that service); if not quite beyond criticism, which can only be overstated, however, and is destined to disappear in context. Thus the *Presto* by itself could conceivably be considered repetitious, while the objection is obviously untrue of the movement in its place in the Quartet, where less would not be more and abridgement is unthinkable anyway. Thus, too, the final *Allegretto* variations, which fittingly succeed music of the most exalted feeling and ineffable radiance, could imaginably seem almost trivial 'in themselves', if they can be evaluated 'in themselves'. The *Presto* recalls the *Pastoral Symphony*, incidentally, in the character of the second theme and its accompaniment, the limited harmonic plan, the echoed hallooings, the silences like the pauses before the storm in the Symphony.

To say that each quartet is distinguished by a quality of sonority is probably to say nothing more than that the quartets themselves are different; yet the lustre of the instruments in these variations is unique. ('Singing masons building roofs of gold,' says the Archbishop in *Henry V*.) One's 'soul' actually seems to migrate during this music, in fact—to one's no small surprise, the earlier movements having formed and implanted this ill-defined zone by stealth. Nor is the ethereality shattered by the *pizzicati* in the 6/8 variation, even though this effect has now been associated with pirouetting hippopotamuses or other im-

---

[1] The tied-eighths-for-quarters notation 'conveys the grasping urgency of the theme', says Mr. Kerman, and so it does, at any rate to score-readers, but before doing that it conveys the imminence of rhythmic subdivision.

probable acrobatics by other denizens of the Disney animated zoo.

The most affecting music of all, to me, is the beginning of the *Andante moderato* variation. The mood is like no other ('impassive', one commentator called it, but he meant 'impenetrable'), and the intensity, if it were to endure a measure longer, would be intolerable.

F Major

It will be the last and it has given me much trouble . . .
BEETHOVEN, October, 1826

The weaknesses are obvious: the shortness of breath, the failure to push the argument, the stylistic jolt of the final movement with its musical snuff-box tune; but the strengths outweigh and outnumber them. The quartet is said to be short on innovations, too, but the repeated figure in the *Vivace* is the newest and most astonishing idea Beethoven ever had. The modulations in the end movements are new and fresh, too, but also abrupt, some of them, as if the composer's restlessness had been translated to a dislike of being confined in any tonality for long. In defense of musical snuff boxes, moreover, it is at least arguable that the now too-tinkly pretty effect of the *pizzicati* on the last page is really the fault of Tchaikovsky, who oversold it.

Beethoven described the slow movement in a preliminary stage as a '*süsser Ruhegesang oder Friedensgesang*'; but to me it is *Trauermusik*—not necessarily a contradiction. The second variation is a dirge, in any case, and the prescience of death in the elegiac fourth variation is unmistakeable.

These quartets are my highest articles of musical belief (which is a longer word for love, whatever else), as indispensable to the ways and meanings of art, as a musician of my era thinks of art and has tried to learn it, as temperature is to life. They are a triumph over temporality, too, possibly a longer-lasting one, as events are threatening to prove, than other triumphs in other arts, for at least they cannot be bombed, melted down, or bull-dozed by progress. This 'immortality' in the music appears to have been recognized even by Beethoven's contemporaries. 'He will live until the end of time', Grillparzer said, the words being read out in the Friedhof cemetery as the mortal part was lowered into the earth, taking with it the largest share anyone ever had of the power of musical creation. The poet then asked the departing mourners to 'Remember this hour in times to come when you feel the overpowering might of his creations like an onrushing storm.'

14/8/68

PART SIX
Columns

ON BEETHOVEN'S
PIANO SONATAS

The recommended general introduction to the subject still seems to be Eric Blom's thirty-year-old programme notes, *Beethoven's Piano Sonatas Discussed*.[1] Rudolph Réti's *Thematic Patterns in Sonatas of Beethoven*,[2] for comparison, is more 'scientific' and more narrowly musical. But it deals with only two of the piano Sonatas, is not for general readers, and in effect simply confirms that the *materia prima* was always and necessarily very similar, a fact not altogether unknown. So far as the actual listening experience is concerned, moreover, Réti's diagrams bring one about as close to 'the sound of music' as an aerial photograph of a lawn does to the scent of grass (or, for that matter, 'grass'). Nor is Blom any more successful in this regard, of course, except that he quotes the music fully clothed whereas Réti only exhibits skeletons.

But having settled for Blom, one rushes in with qualifications. For a start, his chapter on performance fails to take account of Beethoven's instruments, as if they were a mere musicological curiosity, and as if the reader were not interested to know that at the time of the earlier sonatas Beethoven's piano had a shallow keyboard on which rapid successive octaves were comparatively easy to play; and a relatively short reverberation time, thanks to which the bass register was more transparent than is generally the case with modern instruments; and that beginning with the '*Moonlight*' Sonata his pianos were equipped with a pedal which shifted the hammers from three strings to one, thereby effecting a change in tone and weight comparable to a change in registration on an organ or harpsichord. Piano-makers have

[1] Da Capo Press, N.Y., 1968, a reprint, including misprints (the wrong clef on page 29, for one), of the edition of 1938.
[2] Faber, London, 1961.

long since improved this '*Sopra una corda*' device out of existence, needless to say, and with it deprived the *Adagio* in the '*Hammerklavier*' Sonata (to name only one victim) of an entire dimension, for the alternation of two timbres and intensities indicates that the movement was conceived in dialogue form. No discussion of this is found in *Beethoven's Piano Sonatas Discussed*.

Blom's own tone is agreeably old-fashioned. When he muses that a 'note of apprehension' in the coda of an early sonata is 'just like him' (young Ludwig), the reader half expects the further reflection that 'they don't make them like that anymore'. The tone is also agreeably unmingled with the whirr of grinding axe or sharpening hatchet, except that in Blom's case perhaps these tools are unduly neglected. The larger one would be of no use to him, since he accepts the view that the greater boldness of invention in the sonatas, compared with the orchestral and chamber music of the same date, is due simply to the circumstance that the piano was the composer's domestic instrument. But the smaller implement could and should have been applied precisely to that undergrowth of banalities which Blom frequently and regrettably commends, to the extent of citing as 'penetrating criticism' an inane comparison of the emotion of the Sonata '*Pathétique*' and that of Verona's (and Shakespeare's) most cinematized young lovers.

It remains to be said that Blom is a more resourceful guide in the early sonatas than in the late ones, but that this is a lesser disadvantage than the other way around, as the majority of the sonatas *are* early; more than half of them antedate the Second Symphony, in fact, and more than two thirds are pre-*Eroica*. And Blom's presentation of these earlier works is at the same time simple and comprehensive, including, as it does, a survey of the elements of the form as Beethoven inherited it—of the principle of thematic duality, for instance (or 'duothematicism', as Réti calls it, for one of the items in which Réti 'surpasses' Blom is the progress of his jargon in the direction of our own). And, finally, Blom succeeds in his aim, which is to help the reader follow the growth of the form in Beethoven and to enable him to appreciate Beethoven's enlargements.

Reasonably good performances—those with just and controlled

tempi, precise articulation of rhythm and phrasing, balanced and proportioned voicing of the parts—are rare. Rare, too, are musician-type pianists; and pianists who are able to refrain from helping the meanings of the music by emphasizing the obvious; and pianists unaddicted to such stage business as the 'artful' delaying of the right hand and the deliberate (it can't *all* be untoward!) non-synchronizing of the treble and bass parts, as if taking the Bible literally about not letting the right hand know what the left hand doeth. My own addiction to these sonatas, and my dependence on recordings, has led me to wonder whether piano recitalists, locked in their own traditions and long isolated from ensemble musicians, might have begun to lack rhythm genetically and as a breed.

Backhaus's recording of the '*Appassionata*', for instance, must be rated a stunning success—if it was intended as a demonstration of the uses of unsteadiness. And the same pianist's negotiation of the A flat fugue (opus 110) is nothing short of a triumph —if his aim was to blur and obliterate the fast notes in the diminutions. (Did he believe that Beethoven was mistaken in introducing new figurations at this point? The *Meno allegro* is wholly disregarded, in any case, as if it had been put there not for any musical purpose, but simply as a concession to technically limited players.) Kempff, too, enjoys a success in—or, rather, at the expense of, as he uses it primarily to show how fast he can play—the *Rondo* of the '*Pathétique*'. And Barenboim, who phrases the last movement of the '*Waldstein*' intelligently, at the same time plays it so insufferably slowly that he also succeeds —in killing the piece. The above cases, moreover, are concerned with large and, one would have thought, obvious points. The slightly finer ones, to say nothing of the superfine, are correspondingly more voluminous. Thus, for one illustration, most players succeed in making the opening of the '*Hammerklavier*' sound not merely deliberated but *recherché*, which is not, I think, the most fitting way of dealing with a bolt from the blue.

I am prepared to believe, however, and on *no* further evidence, that even at their worst, pianists perform better at the keyboard than they do verbally, a prejudice I owe to a reading of the footnotes festooned to the sonatas by Artur Schnabel. Though never one to come very trippingly off the tongue, Schnabel outdoes himself here, as in, for example, the following bit of advice (?) on a quite unremarkable point of technique: 'As any truth can attain to permanent recognition only after a painful struggle with dissonant and opposing errors, in like manner, for acquiring certain mechanical accomplishments, the expedient is to be recommended, first of all—but, be it observed, with equal zeal—to exhaust all possible ways of how not to do it.' Well . . . yes. *Now* I get it.

Whether restrictions on verbal parking space can be blamed for my failure to provide an *apparatus criticus*, to say nothing of a thesis on the music's 'relevance' to the contemporary scene (unfortunately for the scene, it may have more), space alone is responsible for the confining of these remarks to the last four sonatas. With the exception of opus 31 No. 1, all of the sonatas are delectable to me. The mastery is absolute from the first, and the size of the gifts behind it is as evident as a mountain range in a light mist; hence the meaninglessness of the search for a 'turning' point or points from which prophets would have been able to say 'tomorrow the world'. Beethoven's powers were divinable (at least) from the beginning, and his hand was on the lever all the way.

In the piano sonatas, far more than in his other music, Beethoven discovers and sometimes maps out the different territories of several future composers, including himself. An instance of the latter is the connection, conscious or unconscious, between the left-hand half-notes in m. 51–62 of the *Presto* of the Sonata opus 10, No. 2, and m. 35–50 in the *Scherzo* of the Fourth Symphony. But the area designated for other composers covers almost the whole of the nineteenth century. Schubert and Mendelssohn, for example, are everywhere indicated. (I would quibble with Blom's assignment of the *Rondo* theme of opus 90 to the Mendelssohn rather than the Schubert heritage, except that the one point worth making about the movement is the overtaxing of the theme by the repetitions.) And in the case of Chopin, the sonatas do not merely indicate the path but very solidly pave it as well (*cf.* the first variation in opus 109). Some of Wagner's harmonic and melodic characteristics are blocked out, too, as early as the first movement of opus 31, No. 3—the third movement of which, as I have lately discovered, makes a fine funeral march, at half tempo. More surprising is the passage plainly earmarked for development by Tchaikovsky, from m. 11 in the *Maestoso* of opus 111. The territorial gifts to Brahms, on the other hand, are too numerous to enumerate. They include the first movement of the Sonata opus 28, this on the occasion of the younger composer's Second Symphony; the final *Presto* in the '*Appassionata*', this on the not-so-immaculate conception of his G Minor Quartet; and the beginning of the Sonata opus 109, this for the beginning of his Fourth Symphony—though the Beethoven contains a great deal more that Brahms did not 'get'.

The hammerer and thunderer not being Beethoven's most appealing aspects, to me, it follows that the more orchestral sonatas, the '*Waldstein*' and '*Appassionata*' among them, are not my first favourites. Nor do I concur with the highest estimates of opus 101, with its flat-footed march and too long final movement, or of '*Les Adieux*', in which the 'absence' is much more attractive than the 'return' (to the tune of 'Three Blind Mice'), the latter inherently possessing some of the more comic features of silent-film chase-music (the episode in G flat major). My favourite middle-period sonata is the slender one in F sharp. I admire, too, the second movement of opus 54; much is made of Haydn's influence, little of Bach's, yet the two-part counterpoint here is homage to Bach inferior only to that of the later fugues and later '*Diabelli*' Variations. Another small favourite is the G major Sonata which follows the F sharp. The *Barcarolle* is one of Beethoven's loveliest *Andante* movements, the *Vivace* is a delight, and the first movement is in Beethoven's best bucolic vein, a better example of it, in fact, than the *Scherzo* in the *Pastorale* Symphony, with which it begs comparison; but I should add that 'country-western' music, even of the Austrian kind, does not get a look in with me. And now, having given my own, what, may I ask, do *anyone*'s preferences matter? The sonatas together, after a century and a half, still exhibit the 'ageless spirit and undiminished breath of life' that Plutarch attributed to the works of the greatest age of the Greeks.

Opus 106

This mammoth Sonata resembles the later Quartet in the same key in its extraordinary fecundity, huge dimensions, and radical substance. Both works challenge our powers of absorption even now, in fact still await full appreciation from a future generation. In both, too, the radical music is largely confined to detachable final fugues; at least *I* prefer to come to the fugue in the sonata with fresh ears, finding it diffuse otherwise (my memory being a kind of dead-letter office now, receiving but not transmitting). And in both, once again, the ultimate coherence of the entity is considered problematical, with less point in the case of the sonata, despite the great difference in feeling of the first two movements from the last two, and of the last two from each other.

Much of the first movement could be included in my category of orchestral sonatas; but not the canons, at least not when played with a clean, prickly *staccato*, as they are by Ashkenazy. The *Scherzo* offers previews of the *Scherzo* from the Quartet in E flat, in the interruptions of the *Presto* movement and of the 2/4 movement, which is a Russian tune in the sonata. The predictive is balanced by the retrospective, too, the B flat minor canon at the octave quoting the '*Eroica*'.

Spaciousness, the main novelty of the *Adagio*, is the main hazard for composers-to-come. The movement is the richest harmonically in all of the sonatas, in so far as that element can be thought of separately, and the six-measure modulation to the second subject is the high point of the piece. As for the fugue, its prodigality is not only inexhaustible but exhausting; I will therefore content myself simply with the mention of one other resemblance to the fugue in the quartet, which is that the loud and dissonant episodes are relieved by soft and consonant ones. The three-layer linear style of the D major episode (in *pianissimo* quarter-notes) points toward the Fugue in the A flat Sonata.

Opus 109 and Opus 110

The three final sonatas represent a great ventilation in style— what a more Augustan writer would describe as a rediscovery of

With great-granddaughter, Svetlana, at
the Hotel Ritz, Paris, November 1968

Paris, June 1913

Eighty-sixth birthday

the classical spirit. Compression is more evident than expansion, and a more controlled emotion replaces the inconsolable feelings of the *Adagio* in opus 106.

The formalism of the middle movement, like that of the similar-in-function middle movement of opus 110, is anachronistic, hence the movement seems to be of a different period and on a different level than the rest of the sonata. The elimination of the middle movement in opus 111 was predictable; but, then, 'evolution' in the sonatas amounts to the elimination of a great deal of what was formerly thought to constitute a 'sonata', from the idea of contrasting themes and movements of set character down to many other rhetorical devices. Beethoven's path of discovery tended, at the end, to lead more and more to contrapuntal means, homophonic thematic developments giving way to thematic transformation in variation and fugue.

The necessity of the return of the hymn-subject of the variations—a reminder, and not the only one, of the *'Goldberg'* Variations—is the governing structural fact of the movement, and the long dominant (the entire final variation!) is its most striking architectural 'detail'. Suspense is generated by other means than the exploitation of the dominant, of course, and one of them is the meshing of metrical gears, 3/4 to 9/8 to 3/4, at the beginning of the variation—this being a rehearsal, as well, of the proportionalized meters of the variations in opus 111.

The third variation is a weak link, not so much because of its too obvious function of providing contrast, but because the theme is inaccessible to brisk, Hindemith-like treatment. The contrapuntal fifth variation, like the late-period fugues—as early, though, as the fugal exposition near the end of the last violin sonata—contains most of the sonata's share of 'modern' music.

Beethoven was apparently so fond of the opus 109 hymn theme that he could hardly bear to abandon it. It reappears in opus 110, in the form in which it breaks out in the 'Bach-Partita' variation (No. II) of opus 109, as the first theme, and the surprising number of restatements of it, strung together at different harmonic positions, is a feature of the movement. The *Allegro molto* movement, a masterpiece in and by itself, may seem somewhat too pat in the context, for the reason I have already given in connection with the middle movement of opus

273

109. But the truly baffling event in the Sonata is that of the ten repeated G chords leading from the second *Arioso* (the ancestor, incidentally, of the '*Beklemmt*' episode in the *Cavatina* of opus 130) to the inverted form of the fugue. They occur on the last third of each beat following two thirds' rest, but whereas the first two or three chords succeed in sustaining an off-the-beat feeling —and in this sense, looking back on them now, steal some of the silent thunder from Webern's Piano Variations—after that they become progressively, rapidly, and intolerably dull.

The fugue is the pinnacle of the Sonata, but the marvel of it is in the substance of the counterpoint and cannot be described. On second thought (or whatever number it may have been) Beethoven decided on a different direction from m. 15 of the C minor entrance of the subject. He rewrote the next 27 measures, and the cancelled and final versions can now be compared in the facsimile edition (Ichthys Verlag, Stuttgart), an exercise well worth the eyestrain. At the end of the fugue, incidentally, and thus of the Sonata, the dominant is delayed to very novel effect.

Opus 111

Whether the repeat in the first movement is miscalculated—as I think it is, though I admit that the anticipation of the Liszt Sonata in the theme may have influenced my judgment—it is difficult to listen to the beginning twice. When, after completing the sonata, Beethoven described the piano as an unsatisfactory instrument, it must have been with the extremes of range, the huge intervals and rumbling basses of this movement in mind.

Arietta, the title of the variation theme, was once suspected of concealing a joke, in the line of the '*non troppo serioso*' in the sixth '*Diabelli*' variation—a manifestation of Beethoven the wag, therefore, to be looked up under a more formal heading in Professor Nettl's *Beethoven Handbook*. And speaking of the '*Diabelli*' Variations, some of the direction of that work is discovered in the first variation of the sonata (*cf.* the 'adjacencies' in the bass part).

The rhythmic innovations are astonishing, above all in the boogie-woogie variation (No. III), but not more so than the new aspect of time itself (my sense of which I shall try to distinguish in a moment). The nexus between rhythm and 'time' is pulsation (Hamlet's 'My pulse as yours doth temperately keep time'); but whereas the metrical divisions of the variations change, 9/16 equalling 6/16 (*i.e.* the old dotted-eighth equals the new eighth) equalling 12/32 equalling 6/16, the pulsation is constant. Ratios such as these, and far more complex as well, had been used long before Beethoven, of course, but never to such effect—an effect of continuity and of overarching unity compared to which the contrasts and complementarities of the variations in opus 109 sound positively choppy.

But 'time itself' is inconceivable. To predicate something about a time element in a piece of music is to say something about the music as a whole, our awareness of the passage of time in music being a result—a consequence of the musical ideas and their treatment—rather than a cause. Yet it seems to me that the listener's subjective reckonings of time-passage, his apprehensions of its pressures, limits, inevitabilities, are more apparent and more urgent factors here than ever before in music. (Which may simply be another way of saying that the music is tighter.)

Our mode of time perception in the variations was developed through, and is inseparable from, the evolution of the tonal system, by which notes of music, like

> The Heavens themselves, the Planets, and this Centre
> Observe degree, priority and place . . .

It is an evolution from linearism to an ever more versatile relativism (words whose *lack* of explanation I try to explain in the next paragraph), reaching a point in Beethoven himself where powers of tonality (powers of music) are a power of and over time. Thus he can suspend our sense of time-passage (in the time-vacuum trill-variation); or reduce it to near standstill (in the slow-motion E flat variation, where, however, the enormous space between the two lines is a contributing effect); or postpone it through 'perpetual' turnings (the downward-drifting modulations) which, the unexpected becoming the expected, suddenly pivot to the home key.

Beethoven's measurements were not imposed on a void, of course, but the antecedent developments and processes are too tedious to be reviewed here; they involve some such argument as that, before Beethoven, large forms were really only accretions of smaller ones, which is why the time-scales of Handel's Biblical epics and Mozart's operas are elastic enough (if they are) to accommodate lengthy cuts and interpolations. But I lack the enterprise for such jobs. I am interested not in music history but in the *music* in music history, and certainly not in origins, developments, declines, or even in a 'sonata form', if such a thing existed abstractly.

Beethoven's own time-sense was a universality that for the better part of a century served as a kind of musical Greenwich. But what I really mean, of course, is the musical whole, which is why it hardly needs to be said that when clock trouble *was* eventually reported at the Beethoven Greenwich, it coincided with the challenge to the tonal system's pretensions to a universal musical grammar.

This is not to say that the time-sense in these translucent and transcendent variations has been either superseded or invalidated by the pulverization of time in our own age, an age when transience no longer seems to be a simple fact of life but something more like a goal. No goal, of course, could be farther from Beethoven, who sought to conquer transience by containing time dynamically, in his own shapes, as an engineer channels a natural force.

How will the boom in the centenary business affect the composer of the sonatas? The consumer might well ask the question as, herded by concert impresarios, festival directors, record manufacturers, he goes from death-of-Berlioz to birth-of-Beethoven celebration years. But the answer is: not at all. Novelties will be noisily taken down from their—in Beethoven's case, largely well-deserved—places on the shelf, but put back again, more quietly, next year. As for the *real* novelties, the permanent ones including these sonatas, 1970 will make no difference at all. They will be 'consumed' as much after as they were before, being part of our musical daily bread.

February 24, 1970

NOWHERE TO GO

The performing arts, indeed. Evenings at home, rather, what with the four-month blackout at the Met (had one a mind for Leoncavallo), a strike impending at the ballet, the drought in the theatre, a gift-tax bill threatening to shut down more than a score of grant-dependent symphony orchestras. At the present rate the next instalment of this column will have to be called 'Snowbound' and devoted to TV culture or, as a last resort, to 'literature'—a 'profile' of Jacqueline Susann or 'Penelope Ashe', perhaps, to choose at least a flourishing kind.

But in truth 'the arts', even the performing ones, *are* beset by a sense of futility. Not that a period of Periclean creativity was to be expected at a time when the leadership is a cloud of unknowing (in the wrong sense), and its life-style is at an all-time ebb (compare the combination of Louis Quatorze and Richelieu, in this wise, to Nixon and Billy Graham); and at a time, moreover, when the public conscience is so sick, the body politic so rotten, the motive so greedy, the individual morality (is there any other kind?) so corrupt, the self-respect so low. Yet art does not necessarily reflect the public mood.

Looking to my own art, I find causes enough—in fact too many to sift through—to account for a loss of combustion. To name only one, the concept of planned obsolescence seems to me oppressive, since it must remove at least some of the maker's incentive to give of his best. Nor does the gratuitous making of works of art differ in this respect from the profit-motive making of automobiles, an industry currently admitting to as many casualties as the population suffers psychiatrically: *i.e.* about one in ten.

Another cause is the feeling—first expressed in the contemporary sense, I think, by Ibsen's Hjalmar Ekdal—that everything worth doing has already been done. Thus an apparent indifference to the disbanding of a symphony orchestra might be due to a suspicion that the creation of great music for it belongs to the past, a view supported by such exterior omens as the shifts to other kinds and categories of musical entertainment, and by such interior ones as the now widespread conviction that orchestras will soon be playing only live electronic music anyway. But this is conjecture. And now lest my jeremiad become longer than my chronicle I will proceed to my somewhat-less-than-panoramic subject matter and tick off what, for lack of differentiating terms, must be called cultural events.

Except for Beckett's prize—which should at least make people look at ash-cans with a thought for who might be in them—none raised the spirits very much. To the majority of performing artists, the opening event of the season was the *Time* cover-story on homosexuality, which, however, greatly increased the bitterness and jealousy among all the countertenors, dancers, novelists, etc., who were *not* mentioned. The Juilliard opening followed soon after, but turned out to be only a change of venue. And next came *Towards-a-Poor-Theatre* Grotowski, the season's most expensive art-consumer product, for which I was unable to get tickets, although I would probably not have put up with the *chi-chi* and the bullying, imposed as an additional price of admission, if I had had them. Nor, by all accounts, would I, even inside, have been really 'in', not caring for, or finding sufficiency in, bear-pit drama, verbal unintelligibility, high-voltage acting, surgically perfect technique, the theatre of masochism (my own or other people's), and the theatre of noise —except for Shakespeare's 'noises off'.

Art makes the front page, as a rule, only when it is spectacularly sold, stolen, rediscovered, or—as in the case of the alleged acoustical improvement of Philharmonic Hall—repaired. By all the impressions I received, however, and they were later corroborated by a recording engineer, the improvement in balances is slight if perceptible at all. High trebles are still harsh and heavy—this was certainly true of the violins in the *Italian* Symphony—and basses are still weak, in the third movement the bassoons hardly being audible beneath the horns, while in Ligeti's *Atmospheres*, the main atmosphere of which was the drowning scene in *Wozzeck*, the lower strings sounded positively 'unmanned'. Nothing of the Hall's acoustical properties could be discovered from Scriabin's *Prometheus*, at the same concert, because of the distracting and irrelevant coloured lights that accompanied it. Blue was favoured (a confusion with Gershwin?), but both visually and musically the performance failed to come through with flying or even appropriately lurid colours. Incidentally, my elder son, visiting me soon afterward, reminded me that when he was a small child his mother used to frighten him from picking pimples on his face by saying that 'that was how poor Monsieur Scriabin died'.

My first annual performing-arts award would go to Mr. Jerome Robbins for *Dances at a Gathering*, and to his ten dancers whose equal I doubt could be matched, all-star, from all the other companies of the world. The work is beautifully conceived and executed—compared with Mr. Robbins, most choreographers seem merely to shuttle people about—and it makes intelligent use of music; in fact the choreographer's greatest feat is in having created so contemporary a ballet out of music whose moods we have become accustomed to think of as inseparable from a period. (The mood of the whole is abetted and sustained to some extent by lighting and darkening a sky in which a cloud becomes rosy or disappears almost subliminally.)

On the theatrical side, exits are exploited, walking is exploited, immobility is exploited (in the Nocturne in F, whose stormy middle part might well have made the dancers jumpy), and humour, a matter of postures, is exploited, but stopped in time and kept in bounds. On the ballet side, it is enough to say that the shape and progression of a ballet, which, given the musical programme, might be expected to creak from piece to piece, in fact subtly engage the viewer and leave him deeply affected. The competition being what it is, however, to hail *Dances at a Gathering* as the briefest—meaning most enjoyable—hour in the current theatre hardly even sounds like praise.

I await an *Oedipus Rex* and an *Histoire du soldat* at the Philharmonic later in the season, the *Soldat* to be simultaneously fiddled and conducted by Lorin Maazel. Neither piece, certainly not *Oedipus*, is likely to be heard during the Boulez tenure, which begins two years from now, and by which time the picture could change so radically that the musical needs, even of the New York Philharmonic, might conceivably overtake the commodity it thought it was buying. Meanwhile, in lieu of any current topic of musical interest, the pros and cons of the Boulez appointment exercise an amount of speculation hereabouts. The cons argue that the musical director of an orchestra ought to be in charge of more than a third of its time, expecially a director who, what with the BBC, Cleveland, Bayreuth, etc., might someday be in danger of turning into an International Business Machine. But the pros think that a third is enough, and they regret that their man has not yet taken over Boston, Philadelphia, Chicago and San Francisco as well.

Con criticism seems to come, in the main, from: (a) composers who realize that the pre-eminent exponent of contemporary music is unlikely to play *their* contemporary music; and (b) subscription audiences predisposed to find the new conductor deficient in sympathy with 'their' nineteenth-century repertory (Tchaikovsky and Brahms). But surely only a second-rate conductor, at any rate one greatly inferior to Boulez, could be very deeply *in* sympathy with that kind of repertory now; and as surely it is less important to have another Brahmsian at this time of day than a conductor sympathetic to the Triple A's (Arnold, Anton, Alban), long overdue for a hearing in New York (and for some expensively produced recordings). Boulez will become a better conductor of the classics in time; his *tempi*, hell-bent twenty-five years ago—an example of Pater's 'getting as many pulsations as possible into the given time'?—have settled down with age. (But he must not be obliged to play music that does not interest him, which, I take it, was the case with his recording of the *Water Music*; this is remarkable not because of the absence of double-dotting, ornamentation, rhythmic alteration—the DGG Archive performers of Bach, billed as specialists, are equally unaware of all three—but because the performance is a complete blank.)

Unofficially it is said that Boulez was chosen because of his 'fantastic ear'. But this seems an odd explanation, both because one tends to take for granted that a conductor has a good enough ear and because the totality of a performance does not depend on it. Besides, the truth of the matter is that the Boulez ear, a stickler with instruments, is much less keen with voices (*viz.* the off-pitch singing in the CBS *Wozzeck*), perhaps because Boulez was not reared in an opera culture and is still inexperienced in vocal casting (as he lately demonstrated by choosing a heroic tenor instead of a *baryton Martin* for Pelléas). But this will change. And as it is, Boulez is far and away the most intelligent conductor in orbit today. All musicians should applaud the Philharmonic, not least because in giving the nod to Boulez it was recognizing musical values over the values of magazine-cover mountebanks. In fact, it seems to me that the only loser is that part of Boulez himself which seems to use conducting as a cave in which to hide out from composing.

Returning to New York one night recently I thought I saw the legend 'Abandon hope, all ye who enter here . . .' over the entrance to the Lincoln Tunnel. And now I seem to see another Dantean warning in the maxicoat invasion, for there is some-thing sinister about these mostly dark sidewalk-length garments, as if a religious sect—Shakers? Puritans? neo-Savonarolans?— were starting a reformist crusade. But at times the coats also remind me—and this even though they are worn by tall, gracile girls—of the coachmen in *Petrushka*; while on 59th Street, thanks to the hansoms and the Raskolnikov beards, they help to compose ('visually synthesize', in the language of Brentano's 'act' psychology) a Russian scene.

The maxis are not yet common enough to close the gap between fashions and what people wear, but they are expected to proliferate in winter, and in this eventuality an interest is certain to be taken in them by the snow-removal department. And then, too, after many years, it will again be possible for Achilles to 'hide himself among women'.

In extreme contrast, of course—the pendulum at the other limit—are the micro-minis soliciting ('Want to have a party, mister?') on the sidewalks by Carnegie Hall (!)—the seamier aspects of the lower-Forties now extending as far north as my upper-Fifties hotel (itself not impregnable to bands of titubant revellers with inland accents and commercial badges in their lapels). The same aspects doubtless extend to more polar regions still, not including Central Park, however, whose sylvan asylums (bushes and ambushes, coshes and switchblades) are reserved for compulsory free love, and whose roads are designed for bottle-necking. But I could be mistaken about those micro-minis. Perhaps the girls were only trying to give away Metropolitan Opera tickets.

I will conclude with another 59th Street Russian scene, but this time a real one. As it happened, the first visitors to my new apartment were the Russian Orthodox Archbishop of San Francisco and Svetlana Alliluyeva. As the Archbishop wore only a black bathrobe, or cassock, with no touch of ecclesiastical finery, the hotel staff that escorted him to my rooms probably thought he was coming to give me last rites. Mrs. Alliluyeva, too, was plainly dressed and as unmade-up as a factory girl in an early Soviet movie. She is an attractive woman, with striking blue eyes and an agreeable Moscovite accent, which is to say more *cantabile* and less dry than my Petersburger one; but she was shy and said little, no doubt from long training in the uses of discretion, as well as from recent overexposure in the press.

She seemed pleased with my compliments on her book but expressed regret that I had read it in English rather than Russian. This led to a discussion about translation, in the course of which my wife quoted a line by Mandelstam in a new American rendering: '*Nezhizn . . . malina.* . . . He holds a raspberry in his mouth', which means, to Russian readers—satirically, of course—'This is no mere life but a paradise', and which is nonsense to English readers. Then she realized, too late, that the line was from the poem about Stalin for which the poet paid with his life. Did Svetlana recognize it as well?

She had followed my 1962 tour of the USSR from the inside, so she said, through her close friend the composer Alexis Tolstoy (son of the writer), whose acquaintance I had made in Leningrad. But I was wary of talking about the Soviet Union; after all, you do not discuss the construction of guillotines with someone who has just escaped from one. Still, she laughed at the story about the old refugee who was born in St. Petersburg, went to school in Petrograd, spent most of his life in Leningrad, and who, when asked where he would like to live now, answered, 'St. Petersburg'.

The daughter of Stalin! Imagine how lonely she must be! And imagine two such different refugees as the two of us—in spite of our common bond of having lived in and fled the same country and for some of the same reasons. Plato was right, surely. Children should be disinherited (from advantages no less than disadvantages), and ditched and forgotten at birth, just as turtles bury their eggs in the sand.

December 6, 1969

THE MAKER OF LIBRETTI

New York City: Of the performances, artistic and otherwise, witnessed by your cub reporter of late, only one is worthy of notice; and that, the conversation of a poet, took place within the circus of the reporter's private life. I shall come to it in a moment.

As the reader may recall, my last column nattered at some length on the perennially reliable theme that the arts are in a dire way; and it gave warning that in future I might be obliged to turn for material to the tube. In fact that experiment has now been tried, and radiation and damage to the psyche risked, though I am unable to give a balanced report of it because a reputedly better channel was not in working order at the time (unless I misunderstood and those psychedelic flickers were part of a programme on kinetic art). What I *can* say is that a mere two evenings of steady viewing were enough to leave me numb from newzak, saddle-sore (no less from message Westerns than the other kind), torn between the cigarette commercials and the anti-cigarette commercials, and anxiety-ridden over the outcome of dramas evidently written by, if not exactly for, the under-nines. Hope of a sort came when I accidentally tuned in on the nuptials of Tiny Tim, not because the latency barriers had held (the groom not having eloped at the last minute with the best man), but because of the imaginative quality of the publicity stunt itself; examples of this class are so rare that the only others I can think of at the moment are those of young Mr. Brody pretending to give away money—this received exceptional coverage—and that of the Beatle who 'vanished' and then noised it about that he was dead.

In sooth, one more day searching for television's very secret cultural life and I might have destroyed hotel property, and in consequence been sent to some *à la mode* institution such as

284

Esalen, which promises—and this may well be the ultimate mortification—'an entirely new awareness of being alive'.

Are the 'Environmental Sciences' purely theoretical? The question arises with regularity hereabouts, beginning with the onset of pile-driving on 58th Street in the morning, and re-iterated through each of thirty or so daily siren-escorted emergencies. It arose again one night recently from a less routine cause, a smell of kitchen-stove gas (methane? propane?) so it seemed, that enveloped the city as if this old-fashioned method of suicide had been revived on a mass, Masada-like scale. The next day's *Times* reported that switchboards had been 'jammed' (as if *that* were unusual), and that a special task force from the 'Air Resources Department' had been out collecting samples in plastic bags (one pictured net-wielding lepidopterist types chasing about the slushy streets and frozen park). But no analysis was forthcoming, and the identity and source of the pollutant, if known, were never revealed. The gas of hypothesis replacing the atmospheric one, it was rumoured that mercaptans had drifted over from a factory in New Jersey; and, alternatively, that a freak chemical reaction, such as sometimes occurs with congeners in alcoholic drinks, had taken place in the New Jersey air itself, due to compounding with certain exceedingly un-savoury odours lately uncovered by the Department of Criminal Investigation in Newark. But the most widely circulated theory, undoubtedly suggested by last year's nerve-gas scare, was that a canister of some new secret weapon, en route to dumping at sea, had sprung a leak. And this was certainly the most plausible explanation for the *lack* of a leak in the censorship.

The miasma, whatever it may have been, was dispelled dur-ing the night, but people who had had a whiff of it complained of the jitters afterward, not from the 'gas', of course, but from the shock that an incident such as this can occur in the centre of our largest city and yet remain a complete mystery.

Atmospheres of scientific certainty can be suffocating, too, for which reason we sometimes feel grateful for an occasional harmless small error or a prediction upset. (One such was the slow seismic reaction following the impact of the upper stage of *Intrepid* on the Moon; to judge by their verbal reactions, this seemed to have shaken selenologists almost as much as it did the seismic needle itself.) The same does not hold true in the medical sciences, of course, yet while unpredicted medical reactions, and errors small and large, are seldom if ever gratifying, it cannot be said that they are on that account any less evident. More reliable than prediction, in any case, if not the most reliable method of medical science still in use, is the ancient technique of trial and rather a lot of error. In fact, I am currently threatened with a demonstration of its merits myself, having weathered the vogue in 'atypical' diseases just in time to be caught up in the allergy vogue. In short, I am said to react allergically to the hotel rug, not including the threat of electrocution. (I do not believe in this diagnosis myself inasmuch as the symptoms are wayward and they disappear entirely when I listen to music, but that is beside the point.) Moreover it is now proposed to isolate the complaint—rather than, which seems simpler, replace the rug with linoleum—by trying the effects on me of 150 or so different kinds of food. Thus I would eat only radishes the first week, only turnips the second, and so on until, at the end, if I survived and paid the bill, I would be triumphantly told never to drink bourbon—which, of course, I did not drink before.

If poets are rare, an all but extinct species, it follows that a great one, who is at the same time a great moralist, is a rarity indeed. Hence at least the public uniqueness of my old friend Wystan Auden, who has visited me more than once of late. Hence, too, my assumption that the reader, if only because of the social facts of this introduction, is naturally as interested in Mr. Auden as I am myself; and that it will not greatly matter to him that I have been unable to make the poet say anything momentous, or even something that one would want to put in a locket and carry away. What the *reader* must assume, on the other hand, or take on my word, is that Mr. Auden's talk is not merely rich but diamantiferous. The loss of sparkle is the price of any attempt to indite it, which I do not say as an attempt to excuse the particular shortcomings of my own retelling.

Yet perhaps not quite all of the glitter depends on precisely *how* he says it, some minute amount just possibly being due, for example, to scenic factors. These are not exotic; in fact, except for fetching, pasha-like felt slippers, themselves remarkable only by contrast with the boots and overshoes favoured by other people in this season, they are not exotic at all. What one *is* aware of, and above all, are the invisible clocks. The poet's day is so strictly scheduled, his punctuality so tyrannical, that he will depart of an evening at some exactly predetermined hour— 9.15, say, and it is seldom later than that—even if this deadline should find him in mid-thesis and only half-way through the consommé. Moreover, he is a man of such firm virtue and fixed habits (if *I* had them I would look like the Dong with the Luminous Nose) that he will forbear even to glance toward the gin-containing fridge before sundown—at which time, however, one imagines him, binoculars up, rather anxiously scanning the western sky. And speaking of gin, both of us, at that first, pre-Christmas, reunion party, let our hair down somewhat (the more he, for reasons of supply), except that in his case the consequences were noticeable only by a certain difficulty in marksmanship as he attempted to reoccupy the sleeves of his overcoat, and a certain tactile dependency on the corridor walls, of a kind employed (one imagines) by spelunkers in very dark caves or by Secret Service agents searching for hidden compartments and trapdoors.

To judge by his conversation, as well as by some recent poems, Wystan is deeply troubled by the generation gap. Whereas the twenty-five-year age difference between the two of us hardly counted (he said), the distance between himself and the very young was unbridgeable. 'And the reason is that you and I are makers of objects; a poem is an object just as a table is an object, and one that, like a table, must be able to stand up'. He also said that we shared a sense of the continuity of the past, and he contrasted our own state of affairs in this regard with that of the young 'for whom, as for anyone else mad enough to suppose that it is possible to write or paint or compose independently of the past', he portended an unhappy denouement. 'One finds things in a certain way, and one goes on from there', he said, and with that *he* went on to outline his creed of 'work, *carnevale*, and prayer', which is a framework not merely of his intellectual beliefs, I should add, but of the way of life of a profoundly good man. I hardly need to say that it also constitutes a rather formidable obstacle between himself and the super-young.

Seeing the two purple tomes of *Blake and Tradition* on one of my tables, he remarked that he had not read them because 'I can't "take" the Prophetic Books'. Then finding a copy of his own *City Without Walls*, in the same pile, he set about correcting misprints: capitalizing the pronoun for the Deity in 'Song of Unconditional Surrender'; correcting a German spelling in the 'Elegy'; deleting a gratuitous introductory 'b' on 'oggle'. 'The proof-reader, poor dear, obviously had never heard of the word, and what else *was* there but "boggle"?'

He switched to German at one point, wanting to say something personal and probably finding it easier that way. *What* he wanted to say was how much I had meant in his life, beginning as far back as his sixteenth year when he first played my *Huit Pièces faciles*. I was moved by his remarks, of course, though they made me feel posthumous, and no less so by the unspoken thought behind them, though that came out, too, when he noted, near the end of the evening, that 'to record an obituary for someone and then have him die a month later—which is what happened to me in the case of T. S. Eliot—makes you feel as if you were in some way responsible'.

My wife translated his German into Russian—English accents are difficult for me not only in English—and my Russian back to German, which gave the scene an East – West aura and my wife the aura of the double-agent aware that both parties are only pretending not to speak each other's languages. A similar thought may have occurred to Wystan, for he began to talk about the Soviet poets, saying he had recently introduced an anthology of their work for Penguin and that he now considered Brodsky to be the best of them. Brodsky was to have been invited with Akhmadulina to a poetry conference in London last summer, he told us, but the Soviet official who had been approached to extend the invitation dampened the idea by advising us that 'they will probably be ill at that time'.

Wystan somehow got on to Goethe, perhaps only because we had been speaking German, but possibly because a thought had crossed his nimble mind about the drawing in of his own *Wanderjahre*; he said, at any rate, that he might soon cease to be a part-time or any-time New Yorker. Then, however, it became clear that the connection was a remark of mine about my dread of being recognized in public. 'Goethe,' he said, not altogether aptly, 'was the first intellectual pin-up, the first culture figure at whom people came to stare in the modern, movie-star sense; and in consequence he may also have been the most conceited writer before Vladimir Nabokov.' On the question, still debated in Weimar in my own youth, of whether Goethe 'did or didn't' with Frau von Stein, Wystan sided with the 'didn'ts'. The Stein woman was 'Hell', he said, and he gallantly defended Goethe's wife.

Part of our second evening together was spent looking at my manuscript sketches of *The Rake's Progress*—in which, incidentally, he seemed especially interested in my habit of translating syllables to note values before any real notes were composed. When we put the *Rake* aside, he gave me his and Chester Kallman's new libretto after *Love's Labour's Lost*. But about this unique achievement—Boito did not have to contend with Shakespeare's *language*, after all—I will say no more than that I became very envious reading the following exchange, so like the catechism in the *Rake*: 'What is the end of study, let me know/To know what else we should not know'—and wanted to compose the music myself. In fact, I *did* compose the song 'When daisies pied', with which *L.'s L.'s L.* (the opera) begins, and which the authors could do worse than to borrow.

Mr. Auden's recent thoughts on opera, *Words and Notes* (Festungsverlag Salzburg, 1968), include a number of distinctions between the requirements of libretti and those of spoken drama, all well worth carrying about in that locket, at any rate by aspirants to the librettist's art. Even more valuable, however, is a distinction, expressed in terms of grammatical function, concerning the nature of music itself. Thus he says that in contrast to the actors in a naturalistic stage drama, 'the singers in an opera address themselves primarily to the audience'. Whether they *do* anymore, on the *surface* level, is of course debatable, but 'address' is meant in the largest sense, the sense in which 'All musical statements are intransitive, in the First Person, singular or plural, and in the Present Indicative'. Music, in other words, is for everyone and no one, and it is always in the Present Tense. And Mr. Auden establishes his grammatical classification by comparing music to poetry, which does not have these limits, and should not, in his opinion, seek them. The attempt of the *Symbolistes* 'to make poetry as intransitive as music', could get no farther, he says, than a 'narcissistic reflexive'.

But music's intransitiveness is also proven by the circumstance that 'We may sing a tune without words, or a song where the notes are associated with words, but when we *feel* like singing, the notes will always seem the more important element'. (My italics.) And does the qualification, 'when we *feel* like singing', not say, as I would say, that the words even of the Ninth Symphony can be reduced to nonsense without affecting the meaning of the music?

The most beautiful of Mr. Auden's operas will be brought to the stage at the Juilliard School this spring, an event that will in turn be brought to the attention of readers of this column, providing *Harper's* and God extend the necessary contracts.

N.Y./Feb. 1/70

THE FILTER AND THE FLOOD

Will I ever become accustomed to New York? Will I, to begin with, ever *see* very much of it? Not, so it appears, in my own automobile, what with the difficulties of retrieving it from the garage, the hazards of manoeuvering it between the demolition and reconstruction projects of which my neighbourhood seems largely to consist, and the impossibility of parking it. In fact, we take the encumbrance out now only for *its* sake, not ours, as one walks one's dog.

Still, it was time, by the calendar, to come up for air, dangerous as that can be in New York. And where else but the Park, grimy and litter-blown though it was? And though the vernal influence was noticeable as yet only in the promiscuousness of the pigeons, the avidity of the start-and-stop squirrels, and the newness of the graffiti: FREE THE PANTHERS . . . MAO FOR MAYOR. But people were out: a young man with Dundreary sideburns; two elderly ladies talking about how glad they were not to be young any more; a distinguished-looking, old-worldly gentleman, full of airs, Pretender, perhaps, to a Balkan throne, but perhaps just bonkers; a college-age girl with bulging brief-case—dynamite-planter? bomb-hoaxer?: the apprehensions normally reserved for the potential purse-snatcher and incipient strangler were concentrated this spring on the undergraduate anarch from Barnard or Bryn Mawr who, it was feared, might blow up the cinema or the bank. But brief-cases were less in evidence than transistors (the need to keep in touch with disasters actual and immanent?), and these at least drowned out the bickering of the sparrows in the not-so-consecrated bird 'sanctuary' and the quarrelling of automobile horns beyond. As for amorous consummations—the Park is a major facility—it must have been too cold still, otherwise the erotic stimulus of an open space such as the Mall (according to

291

new studies on the effects of overcrowding) would have proved irresistible. But it was cold for me, too, and extra prudence was required then because of the gravediggers' strike. In fact, that night I had Spring Fever, 103° to be exact.

The accustoming process, to return to that, seems to be a matter of the length and intensity of conditioning in the city's natural incivility, irascibility, hostility. But conditioning takes time. It can take several days before one realizes that one's taxi driver has responded to a 'good morning' or a 'thank you' with a murderous look and dead silence because he suspects that these obscurantist archaisms are forms of affront. But not *all* New Yorkers are like that. As recently as one night last week the screams of a woman in the street aroused the curiosity of the neighbours opposite to the extent of poking their heads out of their windows (though not, of course, to any actual attempt to intercept the crime). Needless to say, I am beginning to be concerned about the degree of indifference I will have acquired myself by the time the next such incident occurs, and the one after that.

The most brilliant music criticism in the *New York Times* so far this year appeared in the Financial Section (2/1/70), perhaps as a warning to musically-minded stockbrokers hoping to change professions. '*Were Great Composers Paupers?*' Mr. Schonberg asked, and he went on to examine twenty-three cases from Bach all the way down to and including your columnist, who is described— incorrectly, I regret to say—as 'undoubtedly a millionaire'. And the worst of it is that undoubtedly I *would* have been if the U.S. and USSR had signed the Berne Copyright Convention. In that event my *Firebird* royalties alone, augmented by damages from the automobile companies now plagiarizing the title, would have made up the seven-figure sum—instead of the three figures and some loose change the music actually earns for me here. Since I do not enjoy the advantages that would be mine if Mr. Schonberg's assumptions were true, however, it hardly seems fair to expose me to the disadvantages, above all the moral taint attaching to plutocrats and the renewed attentions of tax collectors, donation-seekers, would-be borrowers. It sounds like poor-mouthing, but my medical expenses alone are so high that the budget border (between the red and the black) has had to be watched of late about like the Dewline, in fact so closely that one consideration weighing in our decision to move to a hotel was the saving on Kleenex.

By way of accounting for your columnist's millions, Mr. Schonberg explains that 'Stravinsky puts a high price on his services'. (A disapproving nuance in this?) Well, yes, I do, and did all my life, the highest I knew how, a price I alone could pay. But in Mr. Schonberg's sense (cash-register), my price was never high enough. It would be interesting, for comparison, to know how much Herr Stockhausen banks after each of *his* appearances as composer (guru, referee). What is his *cachet*, for example, for each performance of the six lines of verbal instruction that compose his latest occupation for symphony orchestra? (Greatly as I admire economy of means, incidentally, this tendency could put us all out of business, a *dernier cri* in more than the usual sense.) And, royalties for unwritten music apparently being the same as they are for written music, how much does he split with the orchestra players after each re-broadcast of the tape? (Isn't it contradictory, by the way, to record what was not intended to sound the same way twice?) I do not know the answers, of course, but today's sound-track entertainers certainly seem to be in a stronger financial position than the note-writers of my day, partly because the number of stunts of this sort that can be brought off in a year is limited only by the capacity of audiences to be bamboozled (*i.e., un*limited).

Perhaps I was lucky, after all, *not* to have made that million. Would a composing Croesus have felt the (interior) need to write an *Agon* at 75 and a *Requiem Canticles* at 85?—have felt it, that is, as urgently as *I* did?

A recording of the *Canticles* has finally been released, by the way, but nearly four years after it was made, for which reason, standards of live performances having long since overtaken it, I am inclined to say better never than this late. Yet it is by no means the worst performance in the album. That distinction belongs to *Abraham and Isaac*, the recording of which deserves a special niche in oblivion. The overdubbing of the vocal part— which, to begin with, ruled out the possibility of rapport and hence of music—is hardly even approximately synchronized; thus a syncopated passage between the voice and the bassoon comes out not as single notes in succession but both parts together, in two-part harmony. This mutilation offends me, of course, and it offends me all the more when I think of the publicized ephemera on which money *is* spent; for the inadequacy of the recording is entirely the fault of the inadequacy of the money. But don't let this keep you from buying the record. Stay away from it for the same reason that you no longer buy certain California grapes: namely that the workers deserve better.

Publicity often seems to be about all that is left of the arts. (And not only of the arts; even the solar eclipse was over-produced.) Hence the spectacle, *also* almost the only one left, of the prisoners of publicity relentlessly driven to ever more desperate devices, as the condemned, in the Fifth Canto, are blown eternally in the unceasing winds. Recently one of music's super-damned (in this sense) was actually reduced to 'cleaning up' the score of . . . *Cavalleria Rusticana*, obvious as it must have been even to him that the accumulated dirt of bygone 'interpreters' was also the protective make-up that had kept the ghastly piece going this long.

The relics associated with these unfortunates—the bits of paper and string from the packaging, so to speak—are devoutly trafficked in, nevertheless, and sometimes even deposited in Iron Mountain-type reliquaries (the opening of which, after the holocaust, may help to lighten some of the more terrible charges against us simply by attesting to our utter triviality). Meanwhile the objects are becoming more personal. Where once it was the death mask of the poet or the bronze cast of the pianist's hands, replicas of much less pertinent parts of the body are now in demand. Feet, for example. Once in Sydney, Australia, I myself stood foolishly in a pool of plaster-of-Paris while the Mayor read a citation and photographers recorded the *bêtise*. (Where is that footprint now, I wonder? In a podiatrist's waiting-room? Next to some extinct monster's tracks in a museum?) But that was years ago. The preferred mould of today's musicians (Pop), according to 'Chicago Plaster Casters', is of a more flexible part of the anatomy, except that in view of the susceptibility to distension one fails to see how the impression can be considered 'definitive'. (Sidewalk inlay for a future, more permissive Grauman's Chinese Theatre?)

I have been reading the new volume of Aldous Huxley's letters, with much interest in the years when I was closest to him myself. But in some respects the author of the letters seems to me different from my memory of the man. Humour, for example, and of several kinds, comprised a larger element of his make-up than the letters convey; but this side of him may simply have been foreign to his concept of the epistolary character and content. The letters also show him as more academic-minded than I had supposed; but then, too, my supposition must have been formed by his own reprobations of the academic establishment for its failure to grant scientific standing, if not respectability, to ESP, LSD, and the rest. Another difference is the puritan streak, so pronounced in the letters, whereas in relation to the man himself the word is somehow off target. Aldous tended to translate or reduce all moral categories to 'intelligent' or 'unintelligent' behaviour. Of course he conceded the existence of other levels. But not being tempted or bothered by them himself, as he was always so Absolutely Sensible and always so Perfectly Sane (in fact he lacked that certain *in*sanity ingredient of the artist), he would regard an addiction to alcohol, for instance, not as a vice but as a lapse of the intellect.

One of the letters to his son, a sermonette on purposelessness and lack of organization—the failure to keep a card-index, the desultory reading of magazine articles, etc.—is especially revealing in these regards. The letter is a masterpiece in its way, except that in the instructiveness, the somewhat stuffy, Chesterfieldian moral tone, the remoteness of the expression of the paternal feeling, its way is somewhat closer to the eighteenth century than to our own. It is also, of course, kind, wise, just, and—by its own lights—understanding. But of the *filial* feeling, of the position of the son who must have felt even more unworthy because of it than the son of such a man would naturally feel anyway, it shows no understanding whatever. And this is another reason why, in spite of a subject matter that is almost always far ahead of its time, the author himself—his Style in the largest sense—seems to belong to an earlier age.

Some of his defects—the credulity about 'authorities', the tendency to exaggerate (*cf.* the letter to Frieda Lawrence on the decay of England in the later years of World War II)—are even more apparent in the letters than in the essays (not that some of the *letters* aren't essays, even full-blown ones). But so are the far more important and more abundant virtues. The critical remarks about Valéry, Broch, and T. E. Lawrence, for example, are more acute and more candid than anything of the kind in his other books. And people, ordinary as well as extraordinary, are in general more fully and sympathetically observed here than they are in the fiction. More shrewdly, too. Thus in 1947, when our own acquaintance was still only a very passing one, he notes that 'Stravinsky has something of the elephant's memory for real or fancied slights'. (The book gives 1947 as the date of our first meeting, incidentally, but it actually occurred some twenty years earlier, in London, and had been renewed in any case during our first years in California. I might add that the meagreness of the correspondence to his California friends is to be blamed on the advent of Alexander Graham Bell: Aldous actually liked to chat on the telephone.)

Speaking for myself, the letters have given me more pleasure than any of the later novels and essays. But, then, I find I am more interested in the growth of the writer's ideas than in his conclusions about them—which may be another way of saying that I was less interested in the ideas in the first place than in the man.

'The Filter and the Flood' does not refer to pollution, as you feared, but to the recent, much publicized debate in Paris in whose aftermath the terms have become as popular as 'The Hedgehog and the Fox', with which in fact they share a certain analogous sense. In short, a handy new generality, slicing the world into a slightly different kind of two, though already marked for the scrapheap of withered catchwords as new emphases and alignments dull the point of the distinction or resolve the 'schism' into two aspects of a larger reality. As with all such parlour games and God-like games of division, the fun is in naming the prototypes. Thus Apollinaire is *the* proponent of the Flood, as Flaubert (and any practitioner of a single and traditional *métier*) is of the Filter. It follows, too, that the moral imperative of the filterers is precision of language; or, in other words, that language *is* the filter in the flood.

Flood philosophy can be put even more briefly as it is the dominant party at present, the party of multi-media, mixed media, new media—the search for new experience—and the party that seeks to destroy all frontiers, not merely between music and noise, poetry and prose, art and non-art, but between *life* and art. Flood criticism of the Filter is obvious: that in the present state of affairs the well-made sonnet may no longer be quite enough—to which the filterer's reply is that as hardly anyone can do anything well enough in *any* domain anymore, who can presume to amalgamate them all?

Flood philosophy suffered a set-back recently from which it may never recover, a television 'special' called 'Switched-On Symphony'. Based on the doubly disingenuous premise that 'Symphony' and 'Rock' a.) can be, and b.) should be, integrated, it demonstrated the exact opposite. Perhaps the two can, in some remote way, shed some dim light on each other; but essentially they are unrelated, and it is pernicious to pretend otherwise. Certainly they can be *played* side by side, but this amounts to no more than a variety show which in practice always seems to result in a lot of condescension and the worst of both worlds; or of several, except that while 'Switched-On Symphony' advertised a dozen flavours of ice-cream, it served and deserved only raspberries. No one denies the decline of 'classical' music, in its creation, its means, its function, and—clearly the point of 'Switched-On Symphony'—its sales. But that is hardly a reason to dilute it, even if it seems to be the reason of the new entrepreneur who, having no *métier* of his own, would like you to believe it is time to throw them all in (*i.e.*, out) together. *P.S.*: The one success of 'Switched-On Symphony' was Zubin Mehta's screen test as Zarathustra. He should be contracted at once by whichever airline (Icarus?) uses that same '2001' tune for its commercial.

With which I must stop, for words fail me.

March 28/70

APPENDIX

Vera Stravinsky to a Cousin in Moscow

I

1260 North Wetherly Drive
Hollywood 46, California
December 10, 1962

Vladimir Ivanovitch Petrov[1]
8 Pokrovsky Boulevard
Moscow

Dear Valodya,

As to your request for an account of Igor's home life, I will begin with a description of the house itself, except that, as it has only one bedroom and is very small—the low ceilings might have been designed especially for Igor's height—it is really only a bungalow. When we moved here, twenty-one years ago, the valleys of Hollywood and Beverly Hills were in panoramic view from the front terrace, but we can see no further than our neighbours now, thanks to smog, high-risers, and shrubbery. Twenty years ago, too, we still sometimes felt some of the wildness of the West, even here in Hollywood. Rattlesnakes were still found in the vicinity, especially before the large jungle of the near-by Doheny estate was divided into hundreds of small properties and then terraced into what are known locally as the Jewish rice paddies. Once, I remember, an opossum charged through an open door and into Igor's studio. And one hot night in August 1949, during a drought, a wildcat sprang to our roof from the hill behind the house, where we kept

---

[1] Son of Mrs. Stravinsky's mother's sister Olga (*née* Malmgren). Mr. Petrov is now professor of radiology at the University of Moscow.

298

chickens during the war,[1] clawing an awning. Adventures such as these are not only unlikely any more but hardly credible. The invasions we expect nowadays are either from autograph-hunters or the cadastral surveyors Igor forever fears to find distraining at the door.

Visitors say that it is a happy house. Certainly it is bright and cozy, with light-coloured walls and ceilings, upholstery, pillows, rugs, and always a plentiful array of flowers. Even the floppy rubber plants in the dining- and living-rooms are pleasant, though hunched by the ceiling. The furniture is recent, American, ordinary; we have no French dynastic chairs offering you their *'sentiments les plus distingués'*. The house is brightened, too, by many windows and mirrors—like Igor's mind. But it is so crammed and crowded now that we have had to part with one of our three pianos, leaving one in the library so that visitors (and possible souvenir-collectors) will not have an excuse to go to Igor's studio and 'try the piano' there.

Every room in the house is a library, for we have more than ten thousand books. They are classified by language, author, and subject, and of the latter, art books form the largest category, with poetry and *romans policiers* competing for second place. The Shakespeare section is extensive, and so is the collection of old Baedekers, but a catalogue of all the shelves would reflect Igor's widespread and changing curiosities as much as his abiding philosophies. But though varied and unpredictable as he can be, he is also a steady reader, inclined to pursue an author or subject to a rut. You may be interested to hear that since his Russian trip he has been reading Pushkin again, and dipping into Blok, Anna Akhmatova, and younger Russian poets. He also tends to converse in Russian now, more than at any time in the past twenty years, and he talks of orchestrating Mussorgski's *Sunless*.

The house bulges with art. What the visitor sees first are posters on the backs of the dining-room doors advertising

---

[1] The neighbours complained, of course, for the rooster crowed at 3 a.m. I can remember finding it in the dark one night and locking it in our bedroom closet. Then in the morning it flew out of the closet like an airplane, and Igor chased it with a broom. It had a marvellous comb and crest, like the cap of a French *révolutionnaire*.

Oedipus and *Perséphone* at the Warsaw Opera. The innumerable objects on tables and shelves include an antique atlas; glass obelisks from a bygone Murano, and glass *presse-papiers*, which I collect (marbrie weights, piedouche weights, and torsades and swirls); clumps of coral (one because it resembles Bourdelle's Beethoven), and bits of lapis lazuli and other semi-precious stones; a Joseph Cornell box of New York's Museum of Natural History; several New Mexican 'Santos'; a head of Igor in bronze by Dr. Max Edel, his physician and friend of twenty years; Russian cups, spoons, samovars, pyrogravure boxes; Igor's family silverware, which includes huge tureens and ladles, all bearing the crown-shaped Kholodovsky coat-of-arms; Inca and Copt textiles, for Igor's interest especially in Coptic art is long-standing; many squat and ugly pre-Columbian statuettes, the finest pieces having been smashed during a *terramoto* years ago: as you probably know, California is susceptible to terrestrial heart attacks. We own some Early American antiques, too, including a pair of eighteenth-century wooden ducks from Long Island, and a collection of entomological specimens taken from tropical boats that call at Monterey—horrid things, even when stuffed, mounted, and stored in glass cases, but they fascinate Igor.

The walls expose paintings, icons (Russian and Balkan), old maps, old cartoons (one of Rossini lighting a giant firecracker), new cartoons (a deliberately unreadable diploma drawn by Sol Steinberg for Igor and still his only academic credential), photographs of friends and of people Igor admires such as Lincoln and Pope John. One of the walls is pencil-marked with the heights of friends, the shortest of them, Beata Bolm, wife of the dancer, and the tallest Aldous Huxley and the poet Charles Olson. Except for a Turner pastel, a 'Monsù Desiderio' on a hexagonal marble slab, and tiny ink drawings supposedly by Watteau and Tiepolo but probably fakes, all of our paintings are contemporary. Nearly everything we have, moreover, was the gift of the artist, a description that includes ten Picassos, among them the well-known full-face line portrait of Igor, several Giacomettis, many Bermans, a Bakst, a considerable number of Larionovs and Goncharovas, charming pieces by Jacques Villon, Tanguy, Klee (including a drawing given to

Igor by Alma Mahler, who had it from Rilke), Henry Moore, Miró, Masson, Dufy, Tchelichev, Chagall, Vieira da Silva, Bérard, Léger. In fact, the only pictures we have ever purchased are by young painters we wished to encourage, but for a more complete catalogue I would have to mention my own paintings, of which more than a score can be counted about the house.

Igor's day is carefully routined. It begins with a headache, which in most cases is dispelled or forgotten in the shower. After that he used to stand on his head for about fifteen minutes, like a Hatha yogi, but he gave up the habit a few years ago. His bathroom, incidentally, looks like the prescription department in a pharmacy, what with all the blue-and-white porcelain apothecary jars. There are trays of syringes, also, and a mammalian display of hot-water bottles, while the vials of medicines, counteragents for every ailment, all neatly labelled in Russian by Igor himself, can be counted to the hundreds (and that, as the Americans say, is an underexaggeration). A branch office drug store is in business on his night table, too, and the powders, the supponerals, the unguents and ointments, the drops, the herbs and other *materia medica* are so mixed up with the sacred medals that his doctor fears he may swallow a Saint Christopher some night instead of a sleeping pill. Igor acquired his taste for medicines at the precocious age of five. It seems that his parents kept a cupboard of such remedies as aconite, belladonna, henbane, calomel, valerian, veronal, feverfew, centaury seeds, senna leaves, and that he soon learned to climb up to it and to 'tranquillize' and otherwise unhinge himself.

The apparent totality of Igor's belief in medical materialism is the most curious dodge in his character. Pretending to believe that every ill, serious or slight, must have a chemical solvent, he will actually clock the action of an aspirin, as if to test the claims of the advertisements. It follows that he is also concerned with the health of people near him. Puff your cheeks, in fact, and he will give you a carminative; or cough, merely from momentary dryness of the throat, and out will come one of his silver pillboxes (favourite objects of virtù) and from it a grain of antiplague or other placebo (as I suppose them to be) which he will press on you to swallow. As for Igor's own coughs, *they* are forelaid long in advance with one of his coloured treacles. No matter how well he feels, too, Igor will check his temperature at least once daily, for a half-degree rise of the thermometer may forecast a flu to him, and thus warned he can batten down with his medicines and conquer it weeks ahead. It should come as no surprise, then, that he rarely allows Nature to take its course, at least not until he has given it a nudge. Every meal is dispatched with two tablets of 'concentrated saliva', a Japanese peptic confection said to stimulate digestion.

Speaking for myself, I find it odd that a man of such wide medical experience has never developed a suspicion of doctors, yet he is always ready to rub out the whole of his own considerable medical knowledge and transfer his faith *in toto* to the newest and most transient practitioner. One penalty of these peremptory transfers is that he sometimes finds himself on chastening diets—boiled groats and turnip juice, say—younger diagnosticians being appalled at his intake of alcohol. He will observe these regimens with Mohammedan strictness, too, until after a few days when he may *really* be in danger of becoming ill, a new, whisky-approving physician will be called to the rescue. In 1951, Dr. Maurice Gilbert, a friend of Igor's in Geneva, concocted a special formula for him of one pill to stimulate and one to calm, and for years Igor swallowed this Swiss neutrality thirty minutes before each concert, with ideal effect. Need I tell you that I am not *frileuse* myself, that I abhor medicines, that I am not very patient with invalids, and that I would be the world's worst nurse?

Igor's breakfast, which is later than mine, coincides with the arrival of the post, and by that time I try to be out of the house. Years ago in Paris we used to play a game of choosing apt substitute vocations for our friends, and 'postman' was always mentioned for Igor, next after 'pharmacist'. (Other choices were carpenter, frame-maker, bookbinder, paper-hanger: Igor likes to work with his hands.) In fact, he is so keen about receiving and sending mail that the Sabbath is a hard day for him, lightened, with luck, by a Special Delivery. In his desire to hasten a letter on its way, moreover, any visitor is impressed into the postal service. The President of the United States, if he were to come to lunch, would leave with two or three letters in his hand and Igor's request to 'drop them in the corner mailbox'.

The humours of the day are determined by the contents of the post, which, with packages of books, music, letters, is generally large enough to fill a laundry basket. The bulk of the letters are from autograph hunters of the sort, 'Dear Sir, I already have signed photos from Socrates, Stockhausen, and Schweitzer. Would you mind sending . . .' These are destined for a special outsized dining-room wastebasket, as Igor will allow himself to be victimized by the autograph racket only when it seems the easiest way to get rid of a nuisance. I may add, too, that he has managed to keep the public-institution attitude at bay more successfully than any other eminent octogenarian. But he is *not* fond of the patriarch role, and much as he loves children he will not allow those in the neighbourhood to call him 'Gramps'— which some of them did once when he appeared at the doorstep at Hallowe'en with some candy.

If Igor feels compelled to answer letters immediately, he demands the same alacrity in his correspondents, sometimes calculating the minimum time in which an answer *could* be expected, and if it has not come by then, sending a copy of his original. His rooms must contain as many filing cabinets as the State Department of Liechtenstein. And no wonder. In addition to a mountain of correspondence going back sixty years, he has amassed a whole library of programmes and articles concerning his music since 1906. The articles are all heavily underscored and their margins are filled with rubrics vehemently unflattering to the intelligence of critics.

The trauma of the mail leaves him only one or two hours for composition before lunch, but another three hours are set aside in the late afternoon, and as many as three more at night. I can tell you nothing about the biochemistry of his composing processes, of course, and little enough about the habits governing those hours. I do know that his body temperature rises when he works, as Beethoven's did, and that, like Beethoven, he always opens the windows afterward. And I believe him when he claims to prefer the act of composing to the end product, listening. He is composing a cantata in Hebrew at the moment, and he says that the musico-syllabic qualities of the language, as he understands them, have charged his musical enzymes; they must be highly charged, I would say, judging by the ardour with which he has worked of late. He starts each day by playing over the work of the day before, and while he complains of the meagreness of the daily yield, each new opus continues to appear with the regularity that has marked his production all his life, the genie never failing him, and his genius showing no sign of weariness. From what I have said of his impatience to post letters, you will not be surprised to hear that as soon as a dozen measures have been completed he will write them in score and send them to the publisher. He rarely rewrites in any depth, but will recopy an entire page of orchestra score rather than leave the smear of an erasure.

Igor cannot bear any odour while he is composing, which is why his studio is the most distant room from the kitchen. Pungent smells interfere with his hearing, he claims, and a friend once explained the phenomenon to him as an interference of the functions of the amygdaloid nucleus with the computer functions of the cerebral hemispheres. He composes at a tacky-sounding and often out-of-tune upright piano dampened with felt. Nevertheless, and though the studio is soundproofed and its double doors always tightly closed, little noises as if from mice on the keyboard can be heard in the next room. A plywood drawing board is attached to the music rack of the piano, and quarto-size strips of thick white paper are clipped to it. These are used for the pencil-sketch manuscript. Smaller sheets of paper are pinned to the board around this central manuscript, like sputniks. They are the navigation charts of serial orders, the transposition tables, the calculations of permutations: 'here the twelfth note becomes the second note'. To the side of the piano stands a kind of surgeon's operating table, except that the cutlery consists of electric pencil-sharpeners (they sound unpleasantly like lawn mowers), styluses, with which Igor draws his staves and of which he is the patented inventor, an electric metronome, coloured pencils, gums, stopwatches.

Among the regular, established interruptions in Igor's day are the weekly visits to doctors, and the almost weekly late-afternoon visits by attorneys with whom he is sometimes closeted for hours at a time plotting ways of reducing the 'fisc' (Igor's word for income tax); the current way is a 'mineralogical development project', which is a euphemism for some desultory fossicking in a gold mine called 'Verigor'. Among the late afternoon visitors is Robert Craft, whom Igor calls 'Bobsky', and, dropping a 'ch' from Gogol, 'Bobinsky', a version first put into circulation by our friend the culture generalissimo, Nicolas Nabokov. Bobinsky comes to help Igor with musical affairs, as well as to contribute copious if not exactly coruscating conversation on other matters; but in the last few years he has become as indispensable to Igor as his memory (which, in fact, he is). Sometimes he stops to dine with us, incidentally (though perhaps not entirely incidentally, for he is something of a chow hound). I like to cook and sometimes I prepare the meals myself. Ordinarily they are prepared by Evgenia Petrovna, whose last name, Mrs. Gate, is used according to whether we are being Russians or Americans. The cooking is regularly French but periodically Russian: caviar *blini*, *piroshki*, *kulebiaka*, *borscht*, *stroganov*, *kasha*, *kissel*.

To the casual observer, Igor's comportment at table might seem somewhat odd, but the outstanding eccentricities, as doubtless they would be called, are common to Russians. Thus he appears to relish dinner-time discussions of liver, bladder, and bowel troubles; but so did Tolstoy (see the Countess Sophia Tolstoy's *Journal*), and as the same unseemly inclination is manifest in so many Russians of my acquaintance, I wonder if it might not be classified as a cultural trait. (One encounters it in the French, too, however, as in this description by the Goncourts of a dinner with Flaubert, Zola, Turgenev, Daudet: 'We began with a long discussion on the special aptitudes of writers suffering from constipation and diarrhoea.') Dr. Glover (*The Significance of the Mouth in Psychoanalysis*) would classify Igor as a 'sucker' rather than a 'biter', which would explain his preference, among eating utensils, for deep spoons, as well as his apparent dislike of the occidental system of impaling and lifting. (He quickly became very adroit with chopsticks in Japan.) He abhors oleaginous substances and will trim every hint of skin and fat, peeling a frankfurter and paring a piece of *prosciutto* so finely that the result is a carving. This meticulousness is not idiomatically 'Russian', to be sure, nor is the impressive capacity for liquids, though I have noted the same tendency to slosh alcoholic beverages about the mouth (to flush the remoter taste buds?) in other Russians, as well as the rich fricatives accompanying the intake of *potages*, rich enough in his case to increase an *avant-garde* writer's store of siphonic onomatopeoia—though the ultimate stage, in which the bowl is hoisted in the manner of a wassailing Viking draining his meads, seems more Scandinavian than Slavic. Russian, too, may be the habit of beret-wearing during meals, as if from doctrinal duress like that of a pious Jew, but on the other hand all of this could be attributed to nothing more than *génie oblige*.

Igor escapes from his work by playing solitaire; by listening to recordings; by catching and caressing Celeste, our puss*partout* cat; by watching television (he is fond of some of the commercials and has even composed one of his own, a shaving-cream jingle referring to Occam's razor). He strolls several times a day in our patio, but rarely walks in Beverly Hills any more, partly because of the danger of being run over by the Rolls-Royces of movie composers, partly because to walk at all has become difficult for him since his three 'cerebrovascular accidents' (as thromboses are described here; but, then, in California a janitor is a 'maintenance engineer', and gangs of juvenile delinquents are 'unsponsored youth groups'). He enjoys chatting with the gardeners, too, both of them, Vassili Varzhinsky and Dmitri Stepanitch, old-fashioned gentlemen-refugees who might be character actors 'on location' in a play by Chekhov or Ostrovsky. In fact, a film talent-scout, and a cigar-chomping agent who had been casing our house for weeks, once approached Dmitri Stepanitch, who has a Kaiser beard, to play that monarch in a war picture; but like all of our Russian retainers except our first physician here, Prince Galitzin, Dmitri Stepanitch did not speak any English—which may have been just as well, for Dmitri Stepanitch is a great ham, and his performance as the Kaiser would have been much too heavily scented. I might add that at times he creates small flurries in the kitchen by his attentions to the American girls who occasionally help Mrs. Gate. They complain of his gallant hand-kissing, not because of the embarrassment, however, but because of the tickle.

Afternoon tea, served between siesta time and composing time, is another relaxation. Igor likes *infusions* or *tisanes*, *tilleul-menthe* or *camomile*, but he will also lace these very mild brews with a tumbler of some more potent potation. His managerial cortex is very powerful and alcohol does not interfere with his work. In the Swiss years he drank white Neuchâtel while composing, and in the French years red Bordeaux. In America it has been scotch, Jack Daniels, Jim Beam, or even a bumper of beer. Every morning, the empty bottles of these temporary problem-solvents stand by the kitchen door, yet Igor never seems to show any ill effects. Doctors have sometimes gasped in disbelief after pressing his liver, however, and showing him the size, like the fish that got away.

We have almost no social life here now, but this was not always the case. In the '*Tagebuch*' for *Dr. Faustus*, Thomas Mann suggests that war-time Hollywood was a more stimulating and cosmopolitan city than Paris or Munich had ever been, and improbable as that sounds to a European visiting the subtopia today, it may almost have been true. The ferment of composers, writers, scientists, artists, actors, philosophers, and genuine phonies *did* exist then, and we sometimes attended their lectures, exhibitions, concerts, and assorted other performances. To compare *that* Hollywood with the Hollywood of today, consider that the premiere of one version of Brecht's *Galileo*, with the collaboration of Eisler, Charles Laughton, and Brecht himself, took place on La Cienaga Boulevard, where I once had my own art gallery, 'La Boutique', and think of how inconceivably remote are the prospects of such an event now. Igor was greatly impressed by that *Galileo*, incidentally, and shortly after it he protested the deportation of Eisler, saying he could see no possibility of harm from the man, whereas the exile of the artist, or of any artist, was a loss. But during the political fears of the late Forties, of course, culture decamped like Cambyses' army— culture as we knew it, that is, for Hollywood continues to boom, unmindful of the phase I have attempted to distinguish.

But now I am rambling, not ranging, and I must stop. Remember me to Caterina and, if you chance to see her, to Anna Akhmatova. We send our love.

VERA

II

1218 North Wetherly Drive
Hollywood, California 90069
February 25, 1965

Vladimir Ivanovitch Petrov
8 Pokrovsky Boulevard
Moscow

Dear Valodya,

We have changed houses! The climb up the hillside from the street had become an almost insuperable obstacle for Igor and the lack of space was an increasing inconvenience for me. The move is not great, the new house being on the same street and only a two-minute walk away. Still, Igor was unhappy about leaving his old studio, and though the new one is better equipped (whether or not with muses I cannot say), he regretted the transfer and was reluctant even to re-enter the old house, which we still own and which is still reigned over by Mrs. Gate. Igor is deeply attached to objects, but not until this move did I realize how much security he derives from them. And as strongly as he possessed them, of course, so now they turn on and possess him. For a time, before he learned the relocation of them in the new house, which he did like a cat, a fuzziness was noticeable in the corners and edges of his ego. During that transitional period, too, the night-light in his room had to be increased from his little blue *veilleuse* to a surgery-strength lamp.

The new property is more than twice as large as the old and it extends through the block to the next street, on which we have a guest-house. It has many more trees, too, palms, pines, magnolias in front, avocados and oranges in the back—as well as contributions from the neighbours' scabious and ever-shedding eucalyptuses. We also have a swimming-pool. Igor was never much at aquatics, and in fact he has a superstitious fear of water (said to be prevalent among Russians), staying below deck when at sea, like Goncharov on the *Frigat Palat*. But *I* like to swim, if thus you can call my splashless turtle stroke, especially when the Santa Ana wind, which is our solano or mistral, dries our sinuses and the air for a hundred electric miles around.

The house has two storeys—three, counting the basement, which we have made into a music room, furnishing it with a piano, record-playing equipment, many shelves of music and music books. At the well of the basement staircase is a wine cellar, and at the landing, conveniently situated for emergencies from either floor, is a W.C., one of five in the house. Salons, dining-rooms, libraries are on the ground floor, and so, of course, is the kitchen, which, with pushbutton dishwashing, garbage disposal, gravity heat, is a triumph of automation. The chief ornament of the living-room is a black marble fireplace, on whose mantelpiece Igor keeps silver bowls of white asters and wax gloxinias, but the only furnishing there from the old house is a triple-fold *paravant* papered with an enlarged photograph of Igor looking over the railing of a bridge at the Villa Manin.

The most effective improvements on our old house are upstairs, where Igor now has four connecting rooms as well as a labyrinth of closets and alcoves, the Fort Knox of his filing systems. He can go from a central-bathroom-base-of-all-operations to his bedroom, office or studio without interception by other inhabitants and without leaving his lair. In the arrangement of furniture and bibelots, incidentally, his new studio is a near replica of the old, except that it and all of his rooms are more spacious.

I fancy that by this point you must be thinking of my description as the typical dream of the *petite bourgeoisie*. But we ourselves do not feel thus classified by our amenities. Nor do we mind being regarded by our Minutemen neighbours as 'communists'—as we were after our Russian visit—and by our politically progressive European friends as 'imperialists', by the mere fact of our residence in the farthest-'right' neighbourhood of the left-hand part of America.

We were familiar with the house during the tenancy of the former owner, a remarkable lady and a friend of Igor's in ballet days, who paid for Diaghilev's funeral and interment when no one closer to the great impresario came forward. A very colourful woman herself—aspects of her fame have been established through the keyholes of more than one *roman à clef* (*Le Bal du Comte d'Orgel* among them)—she claimed a genealogy from the time of the First Crusade, and, on the dispensation of an

Avignon Pope, enjoyed an ancestral license to eat meat on Fridays. She had been prodigally rich, too, but her more tangible fortunes had dwindled in the course of a long lifetime shared with costly and impermanent paramours. She was obliged to dispose of her homes in London, Paris, Venice, Stra (Palladio's Villa Malcontenta, no less, which went to a former *cicisbeo*), until this was her only and also her last property, though it dwindled, too, by parcelling and desuetude. Toward the end, in fact, it had become a kind of flea market. Practically all of the contents were for sale, and even the ash trays had price tags on them. Needless to say, the house had to be entirely refurbished.

You ask about Igor's health. He is stooped and frail now, and he walks slowly, and rarely without a cane. For distances greater than a few hundred feet he uses a wheel-chair, which even a year ago he would disdain except in air terminals. This was a hard climacteric to him, as he was always an impatiently fast walker who only a few years ago used to trail me behind him like a Chinese wife; but he seems to have accepted it now. The greatest impediment to locomotion is not age, however, but a hernia, the result of an accident eight years ago, that, owing to partial paralysis on his right side, rendered him insensible to strain while lifting a suitcase; sometimes he feels as if the right half of his body had been separated from the left, he says, while his right hand feels as if it were encased in a glove. Other parts of the dwelling are out of kilter, too, and there are other malfunctions, but the impaired walking bothers him more than anything else, and the threat of immobility, of the wheel-chair as the only method of progress, is the most terrible of all his forebodings.

Apart from walking, Igor does not look his years. His reddish hair is still unmixed with grey—on the top of the head, though it must be admitted that not many hairs of *any* complexion can be found in that location—and his eyes and ears are as attentive and retentive as ever. The face has gained in flesh and lost in angularity, but is less striated than those of most other people of his age. That head, incidentally, is still the most striking I have ever seen. It is so small, for one thing, and so unlike the behemoth highbrow genius (in the best sense) dear to nineteenth-century phrenology. In fact the frontal lobes are almost delinquently low and concave, the glabella and jaw are unheroically recessive, and the nether lip is too thick—a cranial picture that, so far as this description goes, seems to resemble the simian prototypes Igor refers to (and pronounces) as 'aps'. Yet it is a face of almost unbelievable power and sensitiveness.

The change in temperament in the last year or so is very marked. The carapace over the feelings appears to be harder than ever, but for the very reason, one suspects, that the contents have mellowed. Corresponding to this change is a loosening of the characteristic economy, in time, talk, money—in fact almost everything except music, where, on the contrary, the specificity is greater. He is forgetful, too, and quick to reverse himself, and unduly suspicious—all ordinary signs of age. What is extraordinary is a new gentleness. In fact, the word *gentil* appears so regularly in his vocabulary now, but was so rare in the past, that I accustom myself to it with difficulty.

Rages and temper tantrums are rarer, too, any more, and even the small eruptions quickly turn to embers. Contrast this with the bad old days when an explosion a week was the rule, some of them protracted detonations involving furniture overturning and crockery smashing *à la* Baba the Turk, though they could be noiseless, too, as occasion suited, for Igor was able to fill a room with his black mood simply by passing through it, like a cuttlefish spreading its ink. *That* Stravinsky wrote the *Rite of Spring*, one thought, retreating in awe until the mood had subsided (the debris settling or the dusky fluids dissipating). In truth, too, as you can see, I am a bit nostalgic and would welcome a small, symptomatic cyclone from time to time, the gods being too easily mollified now and the breezes too bland—nothing, in fact, but the Trades.

Reading Jules Renard's *Journal* the other day I came across this passage which might have been written with Igor in mind:

What remains is to pick up the pen, to rule the paper, patiently to fill it up. The strong do not hesitate. They settle down, they sweat, they go on to the end. They exhaust the ink, they use up the paper. There are only oxen. The biggest ones are geniuses—the ones who toil eighteen hours a day without tiring.

Sometimes the sound of Igor's piano can be heard from his *sanctum sanctorum* late at night, even while a party may be in progress or decline downstairs, a party at which he has imbibed as much as anyone else, though he alone is clear-headed and able to work an hour after. Last night, while I watched television, he typed a dozen letters; but he is *never* totally inactive, and even when ill in bed he will study a score or read or write. I have no way of estimating the amount of work he wrests from his time, but I doubt that many composers of his years (are there 'many'?) have surpassed him.

The unkindest way to behave with Igor is as if he were a being apart. Still, few people are themselves with him, which may be desirable in some cases, but not when the visitor, entering the presence, performs three bows and three stumbles, and departs gold-framing each word for a future conversation piece. The only possible compliment to offer such a man is the (undisplayed) knowledge of his music. Yet many people proceed instead to humiliate him with flattery; no wonder he enjoys himself so much in the company of children, of animals, and of people who have never heard of him. Still, he has not suffered from mental isolation or an insusceptibility to what philosophers call 'other minds'. Quite the contrary, Igor is amazingly aware of and almost psychically able to read the contents of 'other minds', and in fact some people even complain of his remarkable acquisitive powers, and of his habit of repeating their ideas back to them, after having made them his. But I say that this shows he has a maieutic and an improving mind himself.

I have also wondered about how oppressive to Igor must be the weight of posterity. In fact it has hung around his neck for so long now that for three-quarters of his life he must have felt as burdened with it as a belled cat. Imagine what it must be like to know that your letters are destined to be collected and sold, and that your most offhand remarks are certain to reappear, distorted and adapted to the purposes of other people's woolly memoirs. Igor tries to avenge himself on this fate in advance by, so to speak, entering into correspondence with it, framing in red ink the idiocies about himself in books and articles, as if by so doing he could rub posterity's nose in the dirt. But, to tell the truth, I think that bad reviews are important to Igor's security. When you consider, after all, that he has hardly ever had a good one, and then look at the people who are raved about all the time. . . .

I have wondered recently if he is ever troubled by the defection of the so-called main currents from his leadership, but concluded that he is still too full of his own creations to give much thought to such shifts; besides, he has always felt cramped by the more overt of his imitators: it may actually be a relief to him to be alone. And what if he were to tell himself a few necessary lies? Who does not do that, and not only in old age but most of the time?

Now, at eighty-three, Igor receives about $10,000 for half a concert and part of a rehearsal. I have noticed that few people listen with very much attention to the *music* in these concerts and that, in fact, few seem even to have come for that purpose. What they want is the numinous presence, and while $10,000 may be a lot of money, so is Igor a lot of numen.

With love,
VERA

CONCLUSION

Indexes

COMPOSITIONS BY STRAVINSKY

317

PEOPLE AND PLACES

Huxley, Aldous, 66, 137, 295–6, 300

Ibsen, Henrik, 277
Isherwood, Christopher, 137
Italian Symphony (Mendelssohn), 278
Ives, Charles, 28, 53, 83, 131, 230

James, Henry, 80
Janáček, Leos, 79, 212
Janssen, Werner, 51
Jefferson, Thomas, 122
Johnson, Philip, 20
Johnson, Samuel, 55
Jones, LeRoi (I mamu Amiri Baraka), 139
Joyce, James, 69

Kafka, Franz, 130
Kagel, Mauricio, 30, 94
Kallman, Chester, 55, 289
Kandinsky, Wassily, 249
Karajan, Herbert von, 131
Kassner, Rudolph, 68
Keats, John, 29, 202
Kempff, Wilhelm, 269
Kerman, Joseph, 254–5, 257, 259–61
Kirstein, Lincoln, 46, 52
Klee, Paul, 56, 300
Klemperer, Otto, 227
Kodály, Zoltán, 80
Kondrashin, Kyril, 106
Kussevitsky, Serge, 226, 228–9

Laderman, Ezra, 150–1
La Fontaine, Jean de, 46–7

La Mer (Debussy), 224
Larionov, Michel, 300
Larkin, Philip, 139
The Last Savage (Menotti), 78–9
Laughton, Charles, 307
Lawrence, Frieda, 296
Lawrence, T. E., 296
Lear, Edward, 68–9
Leary, Timothy, 103
Léger, Fernand, 301
Lehár, Franz, 27
Leinsdorf, Erich, 211
Leningrad (formerly St. Petersburg), 164, 171, 206, 228, 282–3
Lenormand, Henri René, 177
Leoncavallo, Ruggiero, 79, 104, 169, 277
Leopardi, Giacomo, 110
Lessing, Theodore, 25n.
Lévi-Strauss, Claude, 91, 248
Lewis, Wyndham, 68–9
Leysin (Switzerland), 42
Liadov, Anatol, 220
Ligorio, Pirro, 70
Liebermann, Rolf, 150
Lippman, Walter, 30
Liszt, Franz, 21, 182–4
London (England), 23, 36, 58, 67, 94, 228, 296
Los Angeles (California), 49, 61, 66, 83, 116–17, 141, 144, 146, 155, 157, 164, 203, 210, 214, 216, 234
Love's Labour's Lost (Shakespeare, Auden-Kallman, Nicolas Nabokov), 289
Lowell, Amy, 42n.
Lowell, Robert, 133